D0316614

Water Features

A Guide to their
Design and Construction

H46 071 233 7

Water Features

A Guide to their Design and Construction

Peter J. May

THE CROWOOD PRESS

First published in hardback as *Designing and Creating Water Gardens* in 2004 by
The Crowood Press Ltd
Ramsbury, Marlborough
Wiltshire SN8 2HR

www.crowood.com

© Peter J. May 2004
Paperback edition 2011

All rights reserved. No part of this publication may be reproduced or transmitted in any form or by any means, electronic or mechanical, including photocopy, recording, or any information storage and retrieval system, without permission in writing from the publishers.

British Library Cataloguing-in-Publication Data
A catalogue record for this book is available from the British Library.

ISBN 978 1 84797 274 3

Dedication
Dedicated to Belinda, Josie and Tommy who have never had a water garden of their own ... yet.

Front cover images: (main image) 'The Royal Balinese Retreat Garden', built by Anglo Aquarium Plant at the Hampton Court Flower Show 2002 and designed by Amanda Broughton; (top) garden by Dougie Knight at the Chelsea Flower Show, 1997; (centre) Chenies Aquatics pond 'Golden Pond' at the Hampton Court Flower Show 2002 by Brian Toms. Back cover images: (left) pond with fountain, designed and built by Dean Iles at his home near Bristol under the author's guidance; (right) Brian Aughton and Theresa Potter's 'English Country Garden', Tatton Flower Show 2002.

Photograph previous page: At the Hampton Court Flower Show in 2003 the paving and walling suppliers, Marshall's, display an 'Outdoor' Living Room' created by the Xternal Dimensions team. Although the water feature has been shrunk to a 'safe', inconsequential bubbling fountain of water, it is still an important axis to the garden design.

Typeset by D & N Publishing
Baydon, Marlborough, Wiltshire.

Printed and bound in Singapore by Craft Print International Ltd

Contents

Preface and Acknowledgements

A past client of mine, who just happened to be the picture editor for the *Observer* newspaper, said that I ought to photograph everything I did, even the really boring bits like digging holes and making block walls: 'Your whole life is one great photo opportunity,' she said.

Well, that was towards the latter end of my landscaping days, and it was a sad fact that many of my own projects had been completed with no record of what was done, let alone *how* it was done. I just had not seen the usefulness of what we were doing for anyone other than ourselves or the client we were working for. I would never have foreseen that I would end up writing about landscaping and water gardens. At the time they were being built they had seemed so unphotogenic, just ugly landscapes of mud and sludge. When we started a new project, I would feel so sorry for the client for wrecking what was often a perfectly tidy and serviceable garden and converting it into a quagmire, I would never ask for any advance on the quoted costs. Instead I would wait until some semblance of order returned to the scene before I felt had the right to ask for any money. But even at the end of the project, the completed water garden would not seem worth photographing. It would have no glamour and nothing appealing, not enough even for my portfolio to persuade people that a water garden was what they might want. In the real world, a real water garden takes months to evolve its own ecosystem, and it is only as that begins to affect the rest of the garden that it blends in. It hardly ever happened that I went back to view a project after it had acquired its pre-ordained character; the pressure of work simply kept me away. And some of the times that I did, I found that the ponds had been left to run into dereliction either because the original owners had gone away, or they had not bothered to nurture the pool through its 'juvenile' stages.

So in these pages you will find that I have taken a lot of examples of water gardens from the garden or national flower shows. There is hardly ever a garden at any of these shows, no matter what style, that does not feature water in it somewhere. Although some ideas at the shows are quite often right out of order and totally impractical, the ones included here are (usually) examples that are well within the realms of possibility as water gardens. First and foremost they are sustainable (or at least maintainable if they are just water features), particularly if you observe the principles set out in these pages. Secondly, they are inspirational: as they appear in the shows, with their mature planting and crystal-clear water, they give you a snapshot of a water garden in a florid climax. It would take months, if not years, to orchestrate the same scene in real life, and it would take me a lifetime to collect the diversity of images that can be found at any one flower show.

Some of the images, particularly the 'step-by-steps', have been taken from small projects I have decided to do for myself or for old-established clients. Others come from projects by colleagues of mine who have adopted my techniques, although not necessarily entirely. So between all of these I have managed to assemble a complete introduction to water gardens and water features, also the materials to build them, the techniques with which to get it right, and with water gardens in particular, the ingredients you must have so they can become self-sufficient little worlds in their own right.

I would like to thank all the designers, landscapers and builders of all the gardens featured in these pages, since I have created this book partly off their backs. I hope that the credit I can give them by using them as examples for the techniques I am trying to convey, will serve to advocate their workmanship.

A special thanks must go to Anglo Aquarium Plant Ltd, and to David and Ros Everett, whose advice can always be depended upon, and whose beautiful gardens at the Hampton Court Flower Shows are an invaluable source for photography and topical trends.

For some of the step-by-steps I would especially like to thank Rob Treble and the crew of Treble Landscapes. Also Rob Hembrow (who has worked for me off and on for more years than I care to remember) and Douglas Knight, all of whose work features regularly throughout the book. Also thanks to Evergreen Landscapes and Nick Harding, the most skilled 'slew' driver in the known universe.

Thanks are also in order to many of my past clients, especially John and Nicola Bennetts, and Mr and Mrs McHattie, who recorded in photographs their raised preformed pool project from start to finish. Thanks also to Mr and Mrs Wilson, Mr and Mrs Ken Cookes, and Mr and Mrs Batton.

I am indebted to the present owners of Blagdon Water Gardens, Roger and Gordon Smith, for allowing me to photograph on their site, and also the past owners and creators of the business, the Chivers family. Without them and their referrals, I may never have become quite so involved in creating water gardens.

Thanks must also go to my wife Belinda, and credit to her for her photo at the Alhambra.

Nymphaea *'Gonnère' looks very special with its multitude of petals.*

CHAPTER 1

Inspiration

So why do we want to dig a huge hole in the garden and put water in it? Does this notion come from our historical background, or is it from contemporary influences? Either way we must have an idea of the style of garden we want, and although we might not be able to describe precisely what that style is, we could probably say whether it was formal or informal. Then if we went on to describe it as Italian, or Moorish, French or Japanese, 'modern' or 'natural', this would evoke a whole host of preconceptions. However, it could be just an expression of current fashions, of the luxurious lifestyle we have adopted, or of the way we think in the present philosophical climate – but in some way it has style, either relating to today or the past. Style is ephemeral and hard to capture in the present, but in retrospect, or from other cultures, it always seems an integral part of that time, or of the character of that culture; and philosophy, religion, social structure, politics and even science play an enormous part in the creation of that style. So even today, we, as 'children' of our own time and culture, cannot help but be affected by current trends – and this, funnily enough, affects the way in which we include water in the garden.

There is not a style of gardening past or present that has not used the element of water to its advantage in garden design; indeed, I would venture to say that a garden is not a proper garden without water featuring in it in some dramatic way. A brief

OPPOSITE: *The formal 'Dutch Canal' at Westbury Court, perhaps the most tranquil of formal water gardens.*

TOP RIGHT: *A modern formal 'Secret Garden' by Tim Newbury at the 1995 Chelsea Flower Show.*

RIGHT: *An artist's modern garden design at the Westonbirt Garden Festival 2003: 'The Diamond Light of the Sun and Moon and ...' by John Thompson.*

The strictly formal, clean lines of a pool constructed in the 1930s at the Bristol Botanical Gardens.

BELOW: *'The Carpet Garden' designed by Michael Miller for the Prince of Wales at the 2001 Chelsea Flower Show was inspired by Persian carpets at the Prince's house, Highgrove. In ancient Persia the owner of a garden would have a symbolic representation of it woven into a carpet, so that in winter when the plants lost their leaves or died back, the power imbued in the owner of the garden for creating it would be encapsulated in the carpet. Hence the stories that were handed down to us when we were children, of the mythical magical power that some of these carpets possessed.*

look at the historical development of European garden style might inspire us even further, and it will certainly show us how significantly water figures in the gardens that man builds around himself.

GARDEN STYLE THROUGH HISTORY

Take any major historical civilization, any major human development such as the Renaissance, the Industrial Revolution, or even the present-day concerns for the environment and conservation, and examine their effect on the art of garden design at the time – and what do you see as the major focal point in the centre of the resulting gardens? *Water.*

The city states that sprang up over 5,000 years ago in the Near East around the Tigris and the Euphrates rivers, and also, of course, around the Nile in Egypt, probably gave rise to the art and practice of horticulture as we know it, for growing food and for social amenity value. Water was naturally important in these baking hot areas for the irrigation of crops, but here the ruling classes, which were synonymous with the high priests of the current religions, had the luxury of water channelled directly into the confines of their own palace grounds for the purposes of stocking fish and plants in pools, or the watering of trees.

The Persian Empire: Paradise on Earth

By the ninth century BC, with the rise of the Persian Empire, the concept of the garden had evolved into that of 'paradise' on earth. In the dry stony landscape that is now Iraq, small enclaves of civilization sprang up that were totally reliant upon a meagre water supply that very often had to be channelled several kilometres from the base of a mountain. To these people a water-rich oasis would equate to Heaven on earth, a place where wondrous fruiting plants and sensuously scented flowers flourished, fed by the life-giving force of water. So the privileged in the land would have the main water supply distributed through their property by irrigation channels, and only the excess would be channelled out to the rest of the community. Their enclosure would be planted out with fruiting trees and fragrant arbours, through which would roam a huge array of animal life, for the pleasure of ownership and for sport. It is significant that the old Persian word for 'enclosed space' is 'Paradaeza', from which derives the modern word 'paradise' and the concept of the perfection of God's creation on earth.

By the Sassinid period of the Persian Empire in the third century AD, the garden had taken on a wholly symbolic form. The perfection of God's creation could only be represented symbolically, and as far as gardening was concerned, the irrigation channels remained, dividing the garden into four quarters, meeting at right angles in the centre: this represented the universe that was divided into four parts. A tree, and then later a fountain in the centre

The Court of Fountains in the gardens of the Generalife and the Alhambra Palace in Granada, Spain. The apogee of the Moorish style in the thirteenth and fourteenth centuries, it still influences the terms we use in reference to our own gardens. These courtyards, for instance, were referred to as patios – and haven't you seen that little water feature somewhere before?

represented the Tree of Life. This concept was to seep into Judeo and Christian consciousness, giving us our naive images of the Garden of Eden. The idea in Genesis, or Milton's concept of Eden in *Paradise Lost*, nearly a millennium later, is a mirror image of this model. But most importantly for us, here were the basic principles ordained for the layout of the formal garden. It is from these times that the concepts of patio and courtyard garden and the 'room outside' evolved.

These principles would be further refined and developed to a true magnificence in the cultures generated by the Islamic faiths; these reached their climax in the Moorish gardens of Spain, and most effectively in the gardens of the Generalife at the Alhambra in Granada, and the Indian Muslim

A Koran-inspired garden entitled 'The Mughal Garden' by Fortescue Lockwood Design Ltd for his Highness the Maharaja of Jodhpur at the 1997 Chelsea Flower Show. The four water rills are said to represent the four ingredients of life: milk, wine, water and honey.

garden and mausoleum of the Taj Mahal. The holy book of Islam, the Koran, is the word of God direct from source, in which these same principles of garden layout are reinforced.

The Grecian Grotto

Meanwhile, during the fourth century BC in the equally refined Greek civilization, we find another very self-conscious type of philosophical man, reflecting on his place in the universe. He felt superior to nature, and made models of the gods in his own image as he developed the art of sculpture. The Greeks did very little to develop the art of gardening, although certain grottoes and holy places may have been tended as natural gardens, accessible only to an élite or a cult of the resident god or oracle. The concept of the grotto would continue through Roman times, re-emerging constantly right through to the present time.

The Greeks did think a lot, however. The Greek philosopher Epicurus (341–270 BC) was one thoughtful Greek who did build himself a garden, where he could indulge in a practical expression of his view that serenity could be achieved by living a modest life avoiding strong emotion. A hybrid of this view would resurface in England in the early to mid-1700s, as a philosophical precursor to the landscapes of Capability Brown.

The Roman Empire: The 'Golden Age'

The Romans believed there was a 'Golden Age' of peace, harmony and tranquillity before their civilization. But cultures that grew up after the demise of the empire that the Romans built across the Western world regarded the calm three or four hundred years that it flourished as a 'Golden Age' in itself. It was that empire, with its control and dignity, which was perceived as an ideal civilization, and an ultimate goal for following aspiring cultures. Because of this, waves of the 'classical' style harking back to antiquity recurred constantly, starting with – or continued by – the Italians during the Renaissance period.

As far as water gardens and gardening were concerned, the Romans left a double stylistic legacy, over and above the science and technology to move and contain water – important places and people had reliable and efficient water supplies that had been developed almost to the standards that we would expect today. There is no doubt that there were proper water gardens, possibly with influence from Persia in garden layout. There is also the legacy of the architectural layout of the sort of house a noble might live in. It would generally consist of a peristyle or loggia surrounding an open courtyard in which a formal pool would be a natural focal point; but it would also be an access point for the water supply to the household. This was incredibly important, and the household water supply was often considered to be the dwelling place for the most important household gods. Here, votive offerings would be thrown in on a regular basis, perhaps small coins for a day's good luck. The habit persists even today: look in any public fountain or ornamental well, and you will see the bottom littered with coins.

For the Romans, water was also for getting in, and for socializing around. At the writer Pliny's rustic retreat, a formal pool was contained within an arbour of marble, around which would be recumbent dinner guests. The main food courses were served on the edge of the pool, whilst the side dishes floated on the water. So the idea of the garden as being a room and social area was continued and developed in Roman times.

The poets and writers of Rome, particularly Ovid and Virgil, provided the other legacy of inspiration: this was for the informal or natural landscape. Their ideal was to get away from the frenetic world of city life and 'unwind' in the contemplation of the rustic agrarian landscape around their villas. Later, the landscapes were taken up as ideals and included in the paintings of some late Renaissance painters such as Nicholas Poussin and Claude Lorraine. These in turn became the inspiration for the English landscape schools of the eighteenth century. Of course, water was always part of the scene, and often half obscured in order to draw the inquisitive observer down to get a better view.

The Garden in the Western World

It was nearly a millennium after the Romans that the garden re-emerged in the West as an area for pleasure. There had been a further cultural input from the Near East by the Crusader interaction with the Moors, but the spiritual flavour of what the returning knights had learnt about their 'pleasure gardens' was lost in favour of the 'pleasure-seeking' side of the concept, where gardens were seen as a place in which to carouse or to show off your wealth or social standing.

There was a time in Italy during the fourteenth century when the monastic garden, with its 'fountain of salvation', was regarded as a sanctuary from the outside world. This changed to something that was a metaphor for the outside world, with the rediscovery of the ancient poets and various concepts handed down from as far back as Plato.

At Chatsworth House in Derbyshire a relatively new fountain or water sculpture rekindles the tradition of animated and moving water features. The Revelation Fountain by Angela Conner looks like a giant pomegranate that splits into segments to reveal a large golden globe at the centre.

The world was seen in a new light. Nature was a mirror in which the order of a perfect and divine reality was reflected. This could be arranged according to your whim, for the pleasure of your senses or spirit, within certain parameters of architectural proportion. Since garden designers were all architects, and because gardens reflected the architecture of the house, the same rules as for architecture were applied to garden design.

These rules and proportions had been laid down by the Roman architect Vitruvius at the time of Augustus, and where further extrapolated by Leon Battista Alberti in his ten books on architecture *De re aedificatoria* (1452). Here, the garden was an extension of the architectural plan of the house, perfectly balanced and laid out on a central line square to the façade of the house. Water, the loose element, was used to add a new dimension and life to the garden (plants were secondary). It was contained and controlled in such a way that it exemplified a theme further developed by the French: that Man was considered to have absolute power

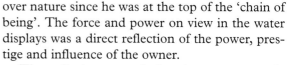

Another popular feature in gardens, and particularly grottoes, were 'joke' fountains that drenched the unsuspecting onlooker or passer-by. This one is at Chatsworth House, host to one such surviving pre-eighteenth-century garden feature.

over nature since he was at the top of the 'chain of being'. The force and power on view in the water displays was a direct reflection of the power, prestige and influence of the owner.

These displays were designed to attract people and their comment. The great gardens created by competitive wealthy individuals became centres for socializing whilst enjoying the arts of music and theatre – but very often the artistry of the water features were attraction enough. Hydraulic engineers were as important as gardeners in creating fountains and cascades, even to powering automata with water that re-enacted scenes from mythology or made mechanical birds twitter in trees, very often in awesome grottoes.

The Renaissance moved to a more unsettled period in the development of the European intellect, but in garden style we move through the amazing world of the Mannerist gardens, almost totally dependent upon water for their effect. The formal strictures of the earlier classical period of the Renaissance gave way to more intellectual freedom, and as this freedom flourished throughout the whole continent, each culture or country that was affected by it added its own emphasis to various elements. However, in the seventeenth century the French developed the classical style even further, evolving it into their own 'French Style', the French aristocracy considering it to be the very embodiment of how they saw themselves. Without sparing any effort or expense, they refined the style to the extreme in the hope that the vision of national character would be seen as the pinnacle of stylistic achievement.

The Great Cascade at Chatsworth was finished in 1696; it was designed by Grillet, a pupil of the French garden designer Le Nôtre, the architect of Versailles. The effect the Grande Tour would have had on a young aristocrat, such as the first Duke of Devonshire, would have been to encourage him to create a feature like this as part of a larger scheme, of which very little nowadays remains.

Italian gardens had been based mainly upon hill-sides, where their noisy water effects cascaded through gardens on different levels. French gardens, on the other hand, were formal layouts on a single plane that ideally stretched to the horizon. Certain elements of this style, such as the canals, fountains and statuary, were copied and developed all over Europe, including England (despite its national pride and distaste of the French). Meanwhile in Italy there emerged the ambiguous concepts of the Baroque garden, where the gardens were still dependent on water, usually employed as an element of surprise.

THE DEVELOPMENT OF GARDENING IN ENGLAND

By the beginning of the eighteenth century the English, decidedly uncomfortable with the suppressive French approach, were going back to nature, to appreciate it in all its natural glory. In England there

was a new class of extremely wealthy merchants and entrepreneurs that looked to a new brand of philosophers, poets and visionaries (such as Alexander Pope) to express a new mode of thought. Garden builders borrowed themes and ideas from Italian gardens and artists, to come up with the 'natural landscapes' that would eventually be developed and epitomized by William Kent, Launcelot 'Capability' Brown and Humphrey Repton, and the 'Picturesque' of Gilpin and others. Initially antique images in the form of statues or temples and tombs were still there – but the setting was a natural landscape in which there was always water. The style of ornamentation evolved to become romantic ruins, rustic hovels and derelict hermitages, but there were always large stretches of water to reflect and amplify the romance and beauty.

Launcelot 'Capability' Brown (1715–83) was the one person to 'buck the trend' by refusing to embellish his garden creations with little more than the odd temple; though he might be described as a

Stourhead Garden, the creation of Henry Hoare II over thirty years from 1743. Perhaps inspired by the art of Poussin and Lorraine, it was originally inspired by Virgil's Aeniad *and Aeneas's search for Arcadia after the sack of Troy by the ancient Greeks. The temple represents a classical ideal, and a story from a previous golden age. As time passed, the garden acquired several layers of fashionable garden features of different styles, but the water remains the focus around which they lie, and blends them together in a fantastical tour from one to the other.*

Launcelot Brown was responsible for more gardens in the pastoral English landscape style than any other designer. Here at Bowood House in Wiltshire a small village was cleared away to create the desired uncluttered pastoral view. One house was left to imbue the scene with the correct rustic charm.

BELOW: *Weston Park in Staffordshire shows us that, by the beginning of the nineteenth century, it was once more acceptable to have a formal area, at least around the house. Water as usual takes its central role.*

'trend' in his own right in his own time, and the fact that he was so much in demand – and did indeed achieve so much – was proof of that. For him, water was always an essential requirement in a rolling landscape that ideally came right up to the house, essentially cleared of all marks of degrading humanity apart from a few sheep, deer or cattle. This was truly harking back to the Roman poets.

It is interesting to note that in the latter half of the eighteenth century, whilst the Picturesque landscape was in its heyday, there was a certain amount of interest given to the overpowering style of the Japanese and Chinese. In 1772, William Chambers' *Dissertation on Oriental Gardening* had a profound influence in Europe, resulting in a sprinkling of temples, pagodas and pavilions throughout many of the major 'natural' landscapes of grand English houses, generally placed in and around a significant stretch of water. However, there was a reaction to this policy of completely abandoning all elements of formality, and with the likes of Humphrey Repton, the successor to Brown, formal parterres were reintroduced next to the house, to help blend the formal architecture of the main building into the landscape of the site.

The greatest influence on English gardening in the nineteenth century came not only from the East, but from the whole world, as the finds of new and wondrous plant material came flooding into gardens from plant hunters abroad. Here was a period of gardening in which the landed classes sought to have a little bit of everything, to such an extent that the water garden was almost eclipsed.

The Return of the Water Garden

For the return of the water garden in a stylish and properly landscaped garden it took another architect, Sir Edwin Lutyens, working hand in hand with the great plantswoman Gertrude Jekyll, to bring it back to centre stage. Well designed formal gardens, with channelled and formal water gardens, were built to match the architecture of the house, and then softened by skilled informal planting. This was a trend that continued through to the modernist designs between the world wars.

The influence of Japanese gardens continued off and on, but it also came to us from a hybrid of Japanese and Spanish influences that had evolved in the United States. As gardening became more accessible to all of us in our small homes, so the garden became less of an area to look at, but rather one to live in and use like any other room in the house. 'Low maintenance' is a consistent demand from people who would rather not be tied to garden chores, and so the influences from abroad were welcome. But despite this, and the plethora of new products for the garden, the water garden has stayed an essential ingredient of the garden scene. Sometimes the concept has shrunk to a mere spurt from a wall fountain, or a fountain out of the ground in very small gardens – but this magnifies its importance as a focal point: it becomes the object that draws you into the garden, and the axis around which you will move.

Hestercombe gardens in Somerset have a formal garden by the Lutyens, Jekyll team; although strong, new and vibrant at the time, the layout harks back to a concept used at least 500 years before.

Japanese gardens, along with all the plants from Japan, had phases of being popular, especially for those who could dedicate a particular area of a much larger garden exclusively for that style. One of the best examples in the country is the Japanese garden in Holland Park, London, an amenity created for the general public.

Designed by Christine Pritchard for the 1997 Chelsea Flower Show, this 'Cotswold Garden' was intended for a modern rural garden using natural materials, although it seems to contain some very old-fashioned elements. Some commentators feel that the Cotswolds were very much the home of a tradition of garden design that was a continuation of the Gertrude Jekyll approach. Names such as Penelope Hobhouse and Rosemary Verey spring to mind.

Lucy Huntington's garden at the Chelsea Flower Show, 'A Space to Breathe, a Low Allergen Garden', in 1994 may have seemed innovative in certain respects at the time, but now it looks very much part of a long tradition going back to the thirteenth-century Alhambra gardens.

With the concept of the garden as 'an outdoor room', and because it is a much more visible expression of our likes and dislikes than any of our interior styling, the fashion gurus are there at our doorstep telling us how to arrange it, and ready with the new bits and pieces and paraphernalia that will make our garden look more in line with current trends than those of our neighbours.

Gardens as an Art Form

If we consider the creation of gardens as an art form, as such it is naturally affected by the fashions and tastes of the time. When we do see something we consider to be totally new and original, it has quite often been inspired by some profound thoughts in a field completely divorced from the art of gardens itself. Today, as much as before, what seems like a real spark of originality comes from a 'crossover' – a short circuit between styles or cultures. It can be a mixture of unfamiliar materials used in standard roles in the garden, or new technologies that are in themselves a reflection of the society the owner lives in.

For instance, the first could be the use of washers or glass from factories as a mulch, or chain pots and wooden fountains, or raised pools made from drainage pipe. In the second we could have laser technology and electronic music filling our garden made of concrete, steel and plastic, but water is always there to add life, sound, movement and reflection, and also to act as some representative element from the natural world.

If you want to know what the new trends in garden design will be, then you must see what is happening at the shows. But it is interesting to note that recently the most significant developments in garden design have come from the same group that had so much influence on garden design in the past: the architects. The likes of Christopher Bradley-Hole and Michael Balston have created garden designs that, whether you love or hate them, reflect a mood of the times: they resonate *style*. It is the hard landscaping, and the moulding of the site that marks their designs. The only things that are lacking are the plants, which for many of us gardeners is a major minus.

Drainage pipes used to make a raised pool in this 'Pet Friendly Garden' by Robert Frier at the 2002 Tatton Park Flower Show.

Another resounding image of an ideal in this 'Contemporary Man's Garden' by Andy Sturgeon, in which he bravely uses modern materials to create a modern feel to our concepts of the garden. Although it is totally impractical, it makes us re-examine our preconceptions.

WATER IN THE GARDEN?

In modern gardens we find that demonstrations of power, philosophy and symbolism take second place to the extra stimulation that water adds both to the garden and to our senses by its presence. With water you can add sound, movement, new colours and new perspectives in reflections: these make even the tiniest garden seem bigger. Even in the hubbub of a city, the smallest water garden or water feature provides a focal point in the garden so that you are less conscious of the outside world.

Whether your garden is already established, or you are looking for a key element in a completely fresh design, the new water garden is going to add further possibilities for choice of plants: the damp-loving marginals, in the water but around the shallow edge, the deep-water aquatics and lilies, and the oxygenating and floating plants.

ABOVE LEFT AND LEFT: *Images that stay in the mind even though you may not relate to them on an emotional level, perhaps because they seem so totally divorced from the original concept of the garden, do in actuality hang on to some of their fundamental facets. But without the water there, one could easily be excused for asking whether it really is a garden or not. Michael Balston's (above left) 'Reflective Garden' Chelsea Flower Show 1999 and Christopher Bradley-Hole (left) 'The Living Sculpture Garden'.*

Blending the margins into a boggy area adds even further possibilities.

And for those of you who are not committed to the world of plants and gardens, with a water garden you are creating a new dimension of interest in the garden that is not just about plants, but is a habitat for animals. Furthermore, as well as creating a world for fish or even ducks, there is the dynamic world of pond life itself, and the turmoil and drama below the water surface is always fascinating, particularly in summer. This is closely allied to the idea of bringing nature and wildlife to your back door, which seems to be an innate desire of suburban man. Being close to nature is stimulating, and gives us some relief from urban stress; but more importantly, creating a water garden makes a valuable contribution to environmental resources, and will be of enormous benefit to wildlife in your area. And if all this is new to you, then finding out what will be sharing your water garden will be a wonderful journey of discovery.

Anglo Aquarium Plant Ltd at the Hampton Court Flower Show in 2003. Every year they create a garden that really demonstrates the huge range of extra plants you can indulge in when you add a pool to your garden.

'A Garden for Otium' designed by Andrew Loudon for Tatton Park Flower Show 2003; this is a place for quiet relaxation and contemplation.

A pool dedicated to wildlife like this one brings the real world of nature right to your back door.

CHAPTER 2

Considerations

BEFORE YOU START

Before you begin your water feature, there are various things you should bear in mind that might affect its design, where you site it, and the materials you use: these include children, wildlife, pets, even vandals.

Children and water attract each other like pins to a magnet, so for your own peace of mind, if you have children – and those between eighteen months to three years are at particular risk – you will have to fence in your water feature, grid it, or even abandon all thoughts of having one for a few years. The alternatives are to have either a small fountain feature, or a completely failsafe design as regards play – for example, a shallow waterway as a play area, emptying into a hidden reservoir and conduits.

Many of you will be creating a water garden specifically as a wildlife habitat – others are not so keen, and prefer to have their wildlife contained within the television. For those in the latter category, be aware that invasions are inevitable, particularly as the weather becomes milder, when all the bugs and beetles associated with ponds will be busy

mating and spawning. If you find this abhorrent, then build the pool well away from the house.

A large proportion of the population of cats and dogs thinks that the construction of a water garden is for their sole benefit, and pet owners should take this into account when they come to choosing materials, and in particular, working out the design of their pool. For instance, if you own a golden retriever that loves taking a bath in hot weather, then buy as tough a liner as you can afford.

OPPOSITE: *The wonderful 'Garden Gang' created 'Don Quixote's Backyard' for the Hampton Court Flower Show in 2000. However, the hand-painted tiled edging might only survive in a frost-free area, and the underwater tiles would have to be laid onto a secure rendered face. This would be a case for the concrete pool specialist, or for putting the blockwork on the inside of the liner.*

RIGHT: *The garden dedicated to the memory of Jill Dando in Weston-super-Mare built by the BBC TV Ground Force team has a super safety-conscious pool as a centrepiece. Not only are there miniature railings around the pool, but a safety grill just below the surface of the water prevents anybody falling right in, even if they wanted to!*

Hundreds of baby frogs emerging all together from a quiet pond in early July.

Where vandalism could be a problem, you might have to think again if your initial intention was to build your pool adjacent to the main route to and (more importantly) from the local pub. Similarly, if you were thinking of building it in your back garden and you have neighbours with destructive and malevolent offspring, you might need to re-site it, well out of their range. An alternative strategy is to persuade the local vandals to help you make it, in which case they will henceforth regard it with parental pride and 'mind' it for you for ever after.

The most important decisions regarding this water garden or feature, be it large or small, should be made before you begin practical construction. Furthermore, many of them cannot be taken in isolation, but must be considered in relation to each other. Your reasons for wanting a water garden in the first place take priority; then come the practical considerations outlined above; and after that the geographical and environmental factors in your garden will help you make any other decisions. However, the factor that most governs the size of your water garden, much of its design, and the materials you use, is the budget you must work within. So first let us consider what you really want, and what will be appropriate for the garden, and then we will see how this affects the costs.

WATER GARDEN DESIGN

You probably already have some sense of the style of water garden you would prefer, and this will certainly play a part in all your subsequent decisions and the various immutable factors that govern the water garden you create. For instance, if you want a formal or a raised pool, then this is going to cost a lot more in time, effort and materials in the 'hard' landscaping phase of operation.

Informal or natural features look best away from the house, unless it is a very large piece of water that wraps moat-like around its walls; it therefore needs to be *big*. Such a design brings the house right into the landscape, where it provides the best views. This requires strong planting, particularly on modern buildings, and is very effective when used in conjunction with wood as walkways and decking.

Traditional or contemporary formality is best close to the house, or in a formal enclosed area. The initial impact is enhanced with sculpture or fountains, plus careful, stylized planting.

These ideas are really only those derived from our heritage and the past. To see how the modern practitioners try to develop new concepts, keep an eye on the garden shows of Chelsea and Hampton Court. Not all their ideas are expensive. However, beware of the lack of practicalities in some of the designs when it comes to long-term maintenance and healthy water.

Maintaining the Water Garden

The question of maintenance is very much in peoples' minds when they are considering a water garden, or even just a water feature. If you are forsaking your lawn for what you think is a 'preferred low-maintenance option of a water garden', then you would be right as long as everything is running smoothly. But if there have been short cuts in the planning, and inadequate pool management – for instance, a plague of blanket weed in high summer – then things may take on a different hue.

In general, the water garden needs less maintenance than a perennial herbaceous border (without even the traditional staking). But for those of you for whom the water garden becomes something

Mark Gregory managed to create an effective formal pool at the 2003 Chelsea Flower Show with a water garden arranged around a personal office building, using formal decking and a rampant herbaceous planting that softened the formal lines. The glass stepping-stones, although a talking point, may have proved impractical in certain weather. Note the chain that guides the water from the gutter into the copper receptacle. Although essentially a practical idea, here it was used as an eye-catching water feature.

Innovative and perhaps bizarre designs at the flower shows can be exciting stimulants to inspiration, but taken as a complete package they are not always practical in the long term. Here Roger Bradley and James Carey use a combination of modern materials with a traditional planting to achieve a dramatic and confrontational effect that can only be taken piecemeal.

of an obsession, there is the Aquatics Industry, with a whole host of cures for any problem or upset. So it is largely your choice as to how much work you put into it.

Choosing a Site

There is a right and a wrong place for a pool, and a lot of other places in between; but if you start from the best possible site, then you have the best chance of succeeding with this project.

The ideal site is sheltered from prevailing and cold winds by evergreen shrubs or screens, though in England it must also have at least six hours' sunshine during the day. It should be accessible for installation and maintenance, but should not be too close to a neighbour's wall or boundary. If it is to be in near proximity to buildings, be aware of the strange eddies and funnel effects that these can create, especially if you are considering a fountain feature or a gentle waterfall.

ABOVE AND LEFT: *The site might not seem very inspiring to begin with, but by the time you have finished your water garden, it can seem quite magical. One of the author's creations for a client in Somerset.*

It must be away from trees, particularly if prevailing winds are likely to carry poisonous leaves into the water: those of willow, elder, poplars, laburnums, yew and oak are highly toxic, as is the pollen of some of these. All leaves as they decay in the pool will cause an excessive load on the pool environmental system. Wind-borne pollution from aeroplanes, and two-stroke and diesel engines can also be a problem.

Avoid the boggy, waterlogged areas of a high water table, unless you are building up out of the ground with footings in the soil. There are ways around the problems of these sites, but if this is your 'first time' water garden, then it would be as well to keep it simple. Although boggy areas might seem the most suitable place for a pool, if you are using a liner there is always the risk of the ground water table pushing this up from underneath. And if you were to use this ground water and expose the area as a catchment, there would always be the danger of pollution in 'run-off', or of nitrates and phosphates leaching from the surrounding land.

Pools that are 'out of sight, out of mind' are potentially dangerous if there are children around, and they are very often left to become unkempt, however well-meaning the owners. Besides, since we spend so much of the year looking at our gardens from inside our houses, it is a good idea to have a view of the water garden, or at least a part of it, from the home. You could even have it rigged up with lights for effective and atmospheric scenes at night.

If there are to be lights, waterfalls or fountains, you will need to consider the distances involved for connecting to the electricity supply, since this can be a major expense. You will need a site for the junction box at the poolside outside, and another one at the house end, inside or out.

Consider accessibility to a water supply for filling up and topping up. Automatic top-up devices are not always a good idea, since there comes a time at some point in the future when they fail – generally when you are away on holiday.

Avoid drainage pipes, mains cable and bedrock. Any of these obstacles can generally be overcome or compromised singly, but if you are going to come up against more than one, then plan the feature in an area with fewer potential problems.

PRACTICAL CONSIDERATIONS

The Level of the Water

There are two basic ground rules to consider at the start: first, it is better to cut into undisturbed ground than to build on loose earth, unless there is a structure solid enough to support the volume of water in the pond, supported by footings built from solid, undisturbed subsoil or bedrock. Second, on undulating ground the pond or pool will look more 'comfortable' at a lower level. This is definitely the case if you are after an 'un-engineered', 'natural' look, without much of the contrivance we see in many water gardens.

But there are times when you may not want this: for instance, you may want to see the pool from the house, even if the garden slopes away from it. This is when it is imperative to ascertain the final level of the water in order to ensure that the contour of the bank, as it slopes away, does not obscure most of the pool surface. In a situation like this, the far side of the pool may need to be raised in order that the near edge is visible. A supporting skeletal framework is needed at least on the far side in order to maintain the view of the whole pool, or indeed any of it.

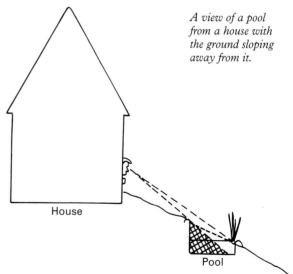

A view of a pool from a house with the ground sloping away from it.

House

Pool

Pool set into the ground that falls away from the house. The hatched area not only represents the area hidden from view but also a large proportion of extra spoil to be excavated.

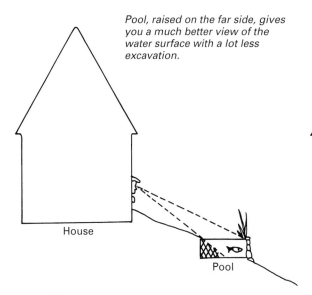

Pool, raised on the far side, gives you a much better view of the water surface with a lot less excavation.

House

Pool

View of a pool from a house with the ground rising away. (A) shows how much soil would have to be excavated if it was raised to house ground level, plus the restricted view of the water.
(B) shows how much soil (plus A) would need to be excavated if the pool was set in the house ground level. However, the whole surface of the pond can be seen.

Pool wall (A)
Water level (A)
View of pool (A)
Water level (B)
House
Pool
View of pool (B)

A view of a pool raised on the far side, as seen from a house with the ground sloping away from it.

The volume of soil to be excavated from a bank that slopes down to a house, and the comparative view of the water.

This is particularly effective if the garden is dropping away to reveal a view that can be reflected in, or joined to, your view of the pool; and even more so, if the view is of a larger body of water, such as a lake or the sea.

With the slope running down to the house, ensure there is enough depth of soil to dig into: a minimum of 45cm (18in), if the pool is going in at house ground level. You will probably find that by cutting into the slope you can gain support for the rear of the pool, but that the front needs some supporting framework as well as the bank. If you decide that the pool will have to be raised, then this will compromise your view into it from the house.

Pool Shape and Dimensions

Informal shapes should be as simple as possible to allow the natural convection currents in the water a smooth flow. If you are using a liner to line the pond, convolutions, clever angles and large indentations can create unsightly folds that use up more liner than is visible. You can otherwise affect the

shape with shoreline ornamentation and decoration such as jetties, decking, large marginal planting areas, or beaches.

In design, the shape of the pool should look its best from your main view of it. In an informal garden this will probably mean having the longest dimension running horizontally from left to right, thus giving a greater impression of size. With a formal pool you may be wanting to play with perspective, or to lead the viewer's eye in a certain direction, in which case the length should fly away from the viewer.

If you are undecided about the size, use a main feature of the house (if it is near to the house and relates to it in the scene) – the largest windows, a door, or its whole façade – and build the pool using the same proportions. In terms of length by breadth, you could use the classical proportions provided by the 'Golden Triangle', created from the dimensions of the '7, 3, 5' triangle; unless you are looking for the dramatic 'canal into the sunset effect' like Louis XIV's Versailles, or the Dutch style of William and Mary in England at the turn of the seventeenth century.

Depth and Volume

Unless you plan to keep koi carp, a depth of more than 75cm (30in) is unnecessary, and 45–60cm (18–24in) is adequate. Koi carp would prefer one metre of water, and two metres gives them enough room to get frisky.

The absolute minimum surface area for a pool with fish, and for it to be a balanced, self-sufficient world in its own right, is just under 3sq m (30sq ft). With a minimum depth of 45cm (18in), that makes a minimum volume of just over 1,280ltr (280gal). Many pools however, and particularly rigid pools, are smaller than this, and fish seem to live quite happily in them, as do many other things – although their owners should expect to have to clean them out on a regular basis, or get used to them looking alternately sick and then unkempt.

The volume of your pool in gallons or litres should be worked out roughly, even at this stage, for the sake of a few budgetary calculations. If you are going to have a waterfall, fountain or filter, then you will need a pump, and the volume of your pool will be an essential guide as to the amount of water the pump would be required to circulate, and also what size filtration unit would be necessary. The formula for the gallonage is:

gallons = length × breadth × depth × 6.25

(all in feet)

litres = length × breadth × depth × 1,000

(all in metres)

The Pond Profile

The traditional design of a water garden has shelves at different depths around the inside edge of the pool to support water plants. Some preformed pools incorporate two levels, one for deep-water marginals, and one for marginals that like only their roots submerged. There are relatively few of the deep-water types, and most of these can grow out to deeper water from shallower margins anyway. So if you are fitting a flexible liner, to keep it simple, your shelves need only be 23cm (9in) below the proposed level of the water surface, and can run around the whole of the inside edge of the pool if you are undecided where they ought to be. They can be cut out

of the underlying soil, or built up with concrete blocks before the liner is fitted, depending on how loose the soil is. Note that they can use up a significant amount of extra liner material if they make a large, curved intrusion into the pool. The shelves want to be a regular final width of 22–25cm (9–10in) when the pool is complete – large enough to support the large size of planting baskets.

If you are considering a shallow beach effect, keep this in proportion and keep it to the minimum to make your design effective. Very shallow areas around the edge of the pool enable the water to heat up quite quickly in those areas, and quite soon they become slimy with algae and the pebbles get tangled together with blanket weed. Good water circulation will discourage this.

Jacquie Gordon's 'Mr McGregor's Garden' at the Chelsea Flower Show 1999.

Raised Pools

What's so special about a raised pool? In the process of building a raised pool you are creating an instant focal point in an otherwise dull, flat, and usually formal area. Not only that, it also has the potential for a seating area, or to be incorporated into raised beds. Children and wheelchairs are less inclined to wander into it, and the infirm and disabled have a better view of the contents. Built to the correct height and if it is accessible from all sides, the wheelchair user has no problems maintaining it for themselves throughout the year.

For many koi carp enthusiasts, the added expense of building up and out of the ground is more than compensated for by the ease of maintenance, particularly when it comes to maintaining the obligatory filter system.

Streams and Waterfalls

A pool with a backdrop of a rock bank with a stream or waterfall tumbling down it makes a perfect scene. In fact, the rock bank does not have to be completely rock and stone: it can merely be suggested. It can actually be lawn or ground cover with only rock showing around the cleft of the stream, and where there is a waterfall drop. In more modern scenarios the rill and the 'mirror waterfall' from a letterbox or chute seem to dominate.

Modern or not, a stream or waterfall should not be disproportionately large in relation to the pool. When you switch on the submersible water pump in the pool to start a stream running, that stream needs at least 10mm (approximately ½in) extra water depth added to its surface to get the water flowing effectively. Not only this, there is a backlog of water

A waterfall in 'A Modern Structured Garden' by Nicholas J. Boult at Tatton Park Flower Show 2002.

that seems to get hidden in the system, and added together, this can mean a considerable loss of water from the pool once the stream is in full flood. The marginal plants in particular cannot stand the resultant radical rise and fall in water level if too much water is taken out every time the stream is started.

The size of the stream is also related to the size of the pump delivering water to the top of the stream or waterfall. In many cases this will be a submersible pump, which will be discussed in detail later on; but for now, suffice it to say that it should not deliver in gallons or litres anywhere near the whole volume of the pool every hour. This again would be too much disruption for both the flora and the fauna of the pool. What would be perfect, especially if you wanted to incorporate a biological filter system at the top of the stream, would be the capability of the pump to deliver half the volume of the pool every hour to the required head of the waterfall or the filter.

In the natural scene, where the stream will run is generally dictated by the lie of the land, and this also helps locate the pool. Many people use the mound of soil from the excavation of the pool to run the stream down. However, this will need very careful consolidation, as the soil excavated from the ground will at least double in volume, and it takes a minimum of a year for it to become compressed to its original volume again. With regard to the waterfall at the point of entry to the pool, this will seem a lot more in keeping with the scene if the watercourse enters at a point where the pool has a sharp outward curve, like the 'V' to a delta. Also, the stream should be cut into a cleft in the terrain, as though it has eroded its own path over many years.

The width of the stream is also relevant to the volume of water the pump can deliver to the head of the waterfall: you should estimate roughly for 100ltr per hour per cm of sill or waterfall width (say 60gal per hour per inch) that can be delivered to the height you require. All the pumps carry performance figures and charts on their boxes and in the promotional material on the displays. So bear the waterfall width in mind in relation to the size of the pool.

Once you have worked through this process of elimination with regard to all the practicalities of the site and also the limitations of your budget, the style of the feature will start to fall into place.

'Cumbria in Bloom' by Peter Tinsley at the Chelsea Flower Show 2000 shows how effective a stream is if it is cut into the bank and then emerges into a delta.

DESIGNERS' TECHNIQUES

The next step is to try drawing a scale plan or map of the garden including all the trees and shrubs and permanent features already present. Using tracing paper, try various 'overlays' of various sketched outlines on top of the plan. Try them at different angles.

If the pool is part of a more general view, or enhances a scheme already present, you could try a tracing-paper 'overlay' over a photograph. This is an old technique of the landscape designer Humphrey Repton in the late eighteenth century,

LEFT: *If you have a digital camera you can sketch over a picture turned out on copy paper.*

BELOW: *Preformed pools that looked so enormous on the stands in the garden centre can seem very small once in the ground, so take with you to the centre the dimensions of roughly the area you want to cover with water.*

who showed suggested improvements by sketches on tracing paper that could be overlaid on drawings taken of the original sites. In this way his clients could see what sort of transformation to expect.

Next, see what the scheme looks like traced out on the ground either in dry sand, rope or hosepipe; this allows you to see the proportions of the feature in relation to everything else. You also get to see what it looks like from every conceivable angle; this is more difficult in a very bare or new garden.

Remember, it is also important to establish how much of the water you will see from your main viewing point, so drive a number of pegs in around the

Planning ahead in terms of power supply in the garden will eventually pay dividends: this weatherproof box has obviously served its purpose for many years, and will do so for many more.

modern-day small gardens, there is no reason why we should not create an informal scene that butts right up to our formal patio area. In this way the water garden can form a link between the formal and the wilder elements of the garden.

A tip from the great landscape architect 'Capability' Brown and the Japanese masters, to make a big water garden seem bigger, is never to have the whole of the water feature visible from one point.

The details of pond construction will be covered later, but if at this stage you feel panic if somebody mentions lighting, filters, fountain ornaments or whatever, keep an open mind when considering the site, and plan for them, even if you cannot really afford them at present, or feel as though you will never need them. For instance, include in your design an area for a hidden filter box, and 'plumb' in sufficient electrical cables for lights, pool heater, waterfall, pump and filter pump and an ultra-violet clarifier (UVC).

PLANNING THE PROJECT

Planning is the key to a successful water garden, and the budget is like a multi-levered lock. Plan the project from beginning to end, and cost out the materials to the last penny beforehand: this saves embarrassment when you are at the suppliers and find out the exorbitant costs of the liner and pump you ordered. Good water gardens are not cheap, whimsical creations, and sticking to the plan that has been carefully worked out to a budget may cause your facsimile of Stourhead, the Ville D'Este or the Katsura Villa gardens of Kyoto to shrink a little – but at least you will be able to sleep at nights.

Also, mentally take the project through your mind stage by stage to give yourself some idea of how much effort this is going to take. To get someone in to do the work for you, would double the costs of the project. You may be able to compromise by getting help for some of the labour, and for those skills and trades that are not within your realm. But compromises like this take extra effort to organize, and if they work, they work very slowly, and not always to everyone's satisfaction unless the actual requirements from each worker/contractor/tradesman are clearly delineated.

circumference of the feature to mark what that level will be: this exercise can be very revealing. (*See* Choosing a Site, page 26, and Pegging Out the Site, page 49.)

Very small features need to be utterly in keeping with the ambient style of the garden; the water generally needs to be moving, and the positioning of plants needs to point you to it, otherwise the feature looks like an accident or a small flood.

Formal elements can include anything from the past that involves straight lines and conformity, to the architecture that is apparent on the site. Taking an element from that architecture, such as the regular size of a window or the door, gives you the key to a design that fits like a perfectly shaped jigsaw piece.

In the right context it may be appropriate to allow oriental influences to affect the design. People coming to water gardening through their interest in fish, particularly koi carp, find 'going Japanese' essential.

Informal water gardens cover what we might regard as 'of nature' or 'natural'; then we could lump them in with the 'cottage, 'natural', 'picturesque', 'wild' and 'conservation' gardens. However, in our

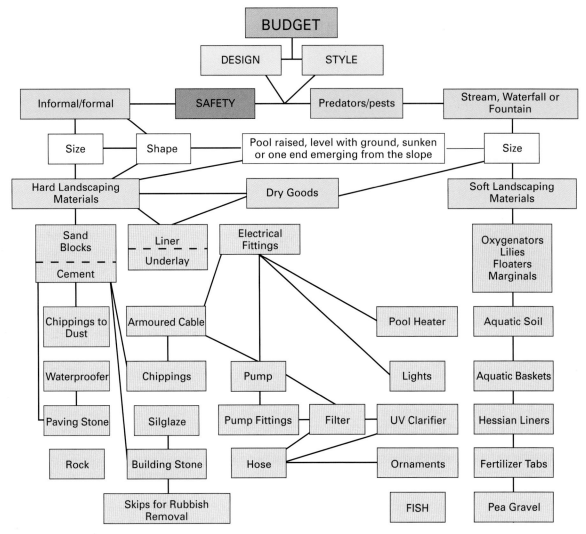

Budget and design, and materials to take into account: the key to a successful water garden.
This diagram shows how all the necessary products and operations are linked in water garden
construction. In other words, if you want one thing, then whatever it is linked to must also be considered.

POOL LINING MATERIALS

Familiarize yourself with what is available on the market, and the effort that might be involved in putting them into place. Try to find out what they look like installed in a garden. Speak to people you know who have had water gardens; their knowledge of materials may be out of date, but their experience is still valid.

For pools, budget for one as large as is appropriate, bearing in mind that the larger the pool, the steadier and more evenly balanced is the environment in it; but also note that there is a false economy in choosing cheaper materials, particularly for the larger project.

Make one dimension of your pool, either its width or its length, plus twice the depth, equivalent to a standard liner width 'off the roll' at the aquatic supplier.

By using flexible liners (made from butyl, EPDM rubber or PVC), as opposed to preformed pools, with care you can create a much more 'natural' environment, with perhaps even a stone facing on the inside. On the other hand, ease of installation and subsequent maintenance might persuade you to choose in favour of a preformed plastic or a fibreglass pool. These are also more dog-resilient and slightly more accident-proof (*see* Preparation and Installation, page 49).

Preformed Liners

If you have mapped and measured the potential area for your water garden at home, you will probably find that those seemingly enormous preformed pools stacked up at the garden centre would look quite small once settled into the ground. On the other hand, there may be a shape and size that fits the space and blends in perfectly with the contours or angles of your garden.

If your design incorporates a beach effect, or if you wanted to obscure the sides of the pool down below the water level with stone, then you would probably not even consider the rigid preformed liners.

On the face of it, preformed pools and streams seem to be the easy option when it comes to installation. But trying to get the top edge of the units precisely level in the ground and to stay that way, sometimes requires the patience of a saint.

High-Density Polyethylene

Preformed or rigid plastic liners made from high-density polyethylene (HDP) or ABS plastic are the 'cheap and cheerful' end of the market. They come with all sorts of useful-looking bumps and notches for cables and pipes, and built-in levels for plants. Properly installed in a suitable situation they represent exceedingly good value for money, but unfortunately they are often badly installed in inappropriate places and soon acquire a cheap and shoddy air. They never look particularly natural, although the most popular shapes are quite informal; but at the same time they don't look out of place in a modern small suburban garden. They have a limitation in size and depth due to the physical limitations imposed in the manufacturing process by the thickness and size of the raw material. Therefore, for a large pool and hence stable environment we need to look at other materials.

Fibreglass

Fibreglass was once the only choice of material for rigid pool liners; however, the advent of rigid plastic liners in the 1980s very quickly took over the market of small pools because they were so ludicrously cheap. The main disadvantages of fibreglass pools are their relative extra expense, and their excessive weight for handling; the latter is also a problem for retailers and distributors, as they take up a huge amount of valuable stock space. The desire for a lighter product, and the competition from plastic preformed pool manufacture, resulted briefly in a decline in fabrication quality in favour of lower production costs, and then a subsequent downturn in the reputation of fibreglass as a viable choice. However, they maintained their presence in the niche of large, deep preformed pools, and in recent years have reasserted their credentials at the quality end of the market.

One sign of a 'quality' fibreglass pool – one that will give a lifetime's service in most situations – is that it would be self-supporting when standing out of the ground on a flat surface, and full of water. If it is too flexible the thickness of the fibreglass is too thin for the size of the design, or the standard of build is not sufficiently high for a durable life.

The advantages of fibreglass pools for the consumer are that they are generally extremely robust, they have a long life, and are easy to repair if damaged. They also come in depths that even koi carp are happy with. Very often they have all the necessary indentations and cambers in the bottom that are necessary to allow for 'bottom drainage' filter systems, and this makes living with koi carp much more worthwhile.

Both fibreglass and plastic pools generally have built-in ledges or shelves that provide varied depths of water for marginal plants and lilies. Some companies have designed troughs around the top edge to create a more wildlife-friendly water garden: the plants in the troughs are allowed the freedom to overrun each other, and under the cover of this protective blanket, wildlife tends to come and go with greater confidence. These troughs also make it easier to blend the pool edge into the surrounding soil landscape if you want, which is particularly effective if you have a bog-garden backdrop. Alternatively you

could create the impression of a beach, by bringing pebbles from around the pool edge into the marginal trough.

On the down side, very often you find that the troughs and shelves are never precisely where you want them, and you never quite get away from that rather Spartan 'swimming pool' look. Either that or the plants run totally rampant in the troughs right from the start; by August they look like a tangled, sick mess, and can only be sorted by extracting them en masse as a giant sausage of root and sawing this up into movable portions for disposal.

Flexible Liners

For those of you considering using flexible liner with the traditional profile of marginal plant shelves and deep-water areas, even in the ground, I always recommend creating a basic skeletal framework out of concrete blocks. This technique will enable you to overcome any construction problems in any type of soil and for any style, formal or informal, and whatever the design, whether it is in the ground, or out of it, or part out of it. It provides even support for the liner in loose, made-up ground and in uneven terrain, whilst at the same time providing a support for the footing for the edging, and a clean, even edge for the marginal planting baskets to butt up to. There is a defined point where water finishes and the terrain begins, and this boundary can be blended away with plants and edging materials, or it can be sharply emphasized as a clean, dramatic line.

Don't worry if simple cement and concrete blockwork seems a little daunting at first. Besides, there are techniques involving flexible liners that don't require the use of cement and concrete blocks: these are particularly suitable for fairly large,

TOP LEFT: *It is cheaper to buy liner off the roll for the larger project. Because it would be inadvisable to buy cheap liner for a big project, it is generally the better quality stock with the long guarantees that is sold in this way.*

MIDDLE LEFT: *In the perfect world, in level compacted soil, just cutting the pool profile into the soil should work perfectly adequately for some situations.*

BOTTOM LEFT: *The completed pool.*

very informal situations with an undefined edge, and also for wildlife and conservation-style ponds (*see* The Conservationist's 'V'-Notch Technique, page 67).

Large projects (say, larger than the largest size of preformed pool) are without doubt easier using flexible liners. Look into what is available, and you will see that the acute competitiveness of the industry has created a range of materials whose price is closely linked to performance and reliability. In general, this applies to most water garden products, so it is easy to gauge a scale of quality based on the price, and to a large extent this also relates to the guarantee. So when you are considering what quality of liner to use, especially for a large project, *always* go for the best, even if it means the project has to be smaller as a result. For large projects, this will also need to be the thickest of whatever material you use. Your estimate for the quantity of liner required will be based on:

the pool length + twice the depth (plus 10%) × the pool width + twice the depth (plus 10%)

The extra 10 per cent is added on by some suppliers as a matter of routine so that you have enough spare liner to tuck under the pool edging.

You will also need to budget for some specialized matting, or a membrane that I will refer to as 'underlay'. This will line the excavation before you fit the pool liner, protecting the latter from the intrusion of stones from the subsoil below. Some people line the excavation with just sand, but over time, small stones do seem to 'float up' from the subsoil as a reaction to the pressure of the water through the liner, no matter how compact the soil was; so the best option is to use sand *and* underlay.

A certain amount of extra underlay may be required if you are considering facing the inside of the pool with stone or brick from the base of the pool, or the marginal shelf level, to protect the liner from the pressure of stone from above. If you are considering lining your pool with soil or (God forbid) pebbles throughout, then you will require enough underlay to line the pool on top of the liner.

Butyl Rubber

Butyl rubber is a good material for all occasions. It is exceedingly flexible, folding into place easily, and has

Where there are variable levels, a raised front edge and made-up ground, a skeletal framework is essential.

A common scenario is shown here, with concrete blocks forming the structural face to a pool that will be raised above the patio and made level with the lawn.

a stretch ability that makes it fairly impermeable to impact penetration. If it does puncture, it is very easy to repair with a patch just stuck into place. It has a long life expectancy of over fifteen years, and often comes with a guarantee of twenty-five years; this may hold good even in exposed situations, if it comes from a reliable source. It is generally sold in sheets that are 0.75mm, 1mm or 1.5mm thick, and of virtually any size. Huge liners can be welded on site from smaller sheets from rolls 2m in width. Folds or creases in the liner soon become obscured.

EPDM Rubber

This type of rubber is a popular robust alternative to butyl rubber, and has made great inroads over recent years into the butyl market. It had a bad start when it was initially being marketed in the UK as an alternative to roofing felt: someone trying to be clever thought it would be perfect for lining large fish ponds, and it certainly would have been, except that some of the compounds used in its manufacture were lethal to fish, and would leach into the water and kill them. However, now there is an 'aquatic formulation' minus the deadly compounds. It is cheaper and thicker than butyl, and has a life expectancy of well over fifteen years. Its look and feel gives it an impression of high quality that gives it a price premium nearly double that of similarly guaranteed PVC. Its minimum 1mm thickness makes it difficult to fold into place neatly in the convoluted shape of a small pool, but it is a perfect option for a large one, when small creases seem magically to 'iron out' as the pool fills with water. In this role it challenges the predominance of butyl.

PVC

PVC has long been considered the cheap alternative to butyl, and it gained a larger foothold in the pond-liner market when manufacturers managed to make it more stable under ultra-violet light. Up until the early 1980s, PVC pond liners had a tendency to disintegrate into crispy bits in sunlight within a maximum of five years. Nowadays, however, liners are retailed with '*lifetime* guarantees'. PVC is still probably the cheapest reliable alternative that can be considered by anybody embarking on a large water-garden project – say, anything over 150sq m (1,600sq ft) – but even then they must use only the best quality, with the longest guarantee, and with a thickness of 0.5mm. PVC liners also come in thicknesses of approximately 0.3mm and 0.8mm, although the thickest is much too stiff for the small pool. Also, do not try to install them in the extreme cold because they can crack.

Although PVC could probably be more easily punctured than rubber liners by a blow, they are definitely more resistant to root penetration, where that may be a problem from trees. Repair is as easy as a bicycle inner-tube puncture, and it can even be carried out under water – the hard part is finding the hole.

The Channel tunnel is lined with PVC above all that concrete, which can only be an argument in its favour. Even cheap PVC really only degenerates when exposed to extremes of temperature and to ultra-violet rays (in natural conditions, sunlight), so those of you still keen to go to the extra expense and effort of a concrete-lined water garden, stretch yourselves financially just a little bit more and give yourselves the added assurance of a cheap PVC liner under the concrete. Concrete ponds are only as strong as their weakest point, which is generally around the rim, or just below the point where ice exerts its most pressure.

Polyethylene Liners

Polyethylene has all the problems inherent in PVC, but liners made of it are more flexible. They are extremely popular all over the world, especially in places such as South Africa and India. The problem with polyethylene is that it comes in a number of forms, and some of the products on the market are not suitable for the rigorous task for which they are marketed, and cannot be worthy of the thirty-five-year guarantee that some retailers put on them. The answer to this problem is to look, feel, and compare visually one product with another. It will be immediately apparent which product is most suitable.

Reinforced Liners

Some liners come as a sandwich of two layers 'reinforced' by plastic or nylon. These emerge as a marketing ploy every few years, but really they are only as good as the thickness of the liner on one side of the reinforcement. It is difficult to know what the reinforcement is for, since it is not a lorry tarpaulin. Sharp or just rough objects can easily penetrate the surface lining, with no more than a slight scuff.

Concrete

If you are considering using concrete, then you should be familiar with the medium. Using concrete is hard work, expensive, and it needs considerable skill to get it right. But if you *do* get it right, then your great-great-grandchildren will grow up beside it. It should be 15cm (6in) thick all over, or 10cm (4in) thick with reinforcement.

Clay Lining

Puddling with clay is more popular on the continent, where suppliers are more common. There is no doubt we have the right kind of clay in many parts of this country, but unless you actually have it on the pool's very site, then the costs of excavating and hauling the correct type of material to the site generally puts it out of the running. Even with clay already present on site, I have only agreed to using it if there has been a permanent stream of water to keep the pond topped up to a point where it overflows back down a pipe and back into the stream; this prevents the clay drying out and cracking through even the driest of summers.

Where clay is sold with the express purpose of lining pools, ponds and lagoons, it is extruded into large tile-like slabs that are designed to be laid overlapping by 50mm in each direction. These should go on in more than one layer to ensure the sealing of the joins, and to build up to a final lining of clay roughly 15cm (6in) thick. This means the excavation needs to be 15cm deeper and 30cm (12in) larger in each direction than your final intention. It is a very messy, labour-intensive process that has many more drawbacks in the preparation and the actual process of puddling than most people can face. It is best to order one third more clay than you estimate you will need, since it will contain a large amount of air that the process of puddling will hopefully remove.

As a sort of 'underlay' to the clay you will need a large enough quantity of soot, ash or lime to line the excavation *below* the liner of clay, in order to deter worms from below and hopefully plants from above.

Bentonite Matting

The bentonite mat is a compromise method, popular with golf-course designers for their water holes, and also reservoir and lagoon builders on a grand scale. Natural sodium bentonite or montmorillonite (aluminium silicate) is volcanically deposited clay found only in the Black Hills of Wyoming and Dakota. It has a unique, silicate crystal, lattice chemical structure that allows it to absorb up to five times its own dry weight of water, and ten to fifteen times its volume in the process, which if it could be seen at microscopic level would be similar to the action of an expanding accordion. This material has been used for many years for lining ponds and lagoons, and in recent decades has been marketed in the form of thin mats. These are simply laid down throughout the smooth, stone- and weed-free excavation, overlapping each other by 150mm (6in). The bentonite is 4mm thick, and comes in a stiff putty consistency sandwiched between two webs of geomembrane to give it some overall strength during construction and installation. A 150mm protective cover of soil, sand or gravel is laid over the surface of the mats, and the excavation can then be filled with water.

When water filters down through the protective layer to the surface of the bentonite mat, the mat begins to swell. The degree of expansion is dependent upon the weight of the material above it. Microscopically, the layers of granules furthest away from the water source will absorb less, and those closest will form a homogeneous gel or skin. If this skin is ruptured, the water will penetrate as far as the next layer of granules, which in turn expand and gel. This makes it seem virtually impermeable. Even complete penetration of a thin sharp object seems to have very little effect, as the 'wound' is effectively self-healing.

The end result looks instantly like a natural pond, and will stand up to the rigours of subsequent maintenance as well as any other liner. If plant life begins to get out of hand, any root intrusion is self-healing. The costs are in the league of the more expensive butyl rubber liners, but with an unlimited life expectancy. It is definitely an option worth considering for the larger watergarden project above 150sq m (1,600sq ft), since the mats come in rolls of a minimum of 1m by 5m (3ft by 16ft), weighing about 22kg (48lb). The reason very little is heard about this material is that it is only available direct from the manufacturers, and they prefer only to supply contractors experienced at installing the material. However, for reasonably large projects they will carry out a consultative site visit, and supervise the beginnings of the installation.

An anchor trench is required to secure RAWMATT bentonite matting at the top of the slope.

The membrane should continue across the bottom of the anchor trench.

The sheets are joined by peeling back the non-woven textile off the lower sheet under the overlap.

Installation of the lagoon with no welding of joints!

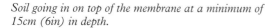

Soil going in on top of the membrane at a minimum of 15cm (6in) in depth.

Golf-course lake created to provide a natural-looking 'golf hazard'.

STREAM AND WATERFALL LINING MATERIALS

Streams and waterfalls for grander water gardens are most effective and reliable when waterproofed with a concealed flexible liner. However, many of the most well known contractors in the country, renowned for the enormous rockscapes they create, just depend upon reinforced concrete without a liner. This is because the sheer weight of the stones that are often used, from five up to even fifteen tonnes, would not only puncture the strongest liner, but would make it exceedingly difficult to place the stone. Bentonite is also used for large displays, but it must be well covered with stone to prevent it from washing away.

For smaller displays, the preformed units you can buy off the shelf are becoming more realistic year by year, and an increasingly attractive option.

To estimate the length of the stream liner: The length on the horizontal + (2 × the height of the head). Although the width is partly governed by the standard widths of the roll of liner material, the width of liner required would be:

Width of liner = width of widest header pool +
(2 × depth)

For instance, a 1.5m- (5ft) wide liner would produce a stream with 75cm (2ft 6in) header pools with 23–30cm (9–12in) outlets. A 3m- (10ft) wide liner gives you 1.2–1.8m (4–6ft) headers with possible 60cm- (2ft) wide waterfalls.

ESTIMATING MATERIALS AND EQUIPMENT

The Excavation

Soil doubles in volume as it is dug out of the ground, and there is always more than you need for further landscaping. The average large skip holds 6cu m, and it takes roughly one day for one person to fill it; digging the stuff out probably doubles the time. If, however, a team of people is doing it, things seem to happen proportionately more quickly, even if there are some standing around drinking

---

METRIC OR IMPERIAL?

Throughout any water-garden project there will be the dilemma of mixing and matching materials and supplies, and the ongoing problem of whether to work in imperial or metric measurements. It is probably best to decide at the outset whether you are going to think in feet and inches, or in metres. If perhaps the construction has to fit in with a metric patio stone, then stick with metric; but if you buy from a supplier who uses feet and inches, then you will have to work in old-fashioned imperial. Where conversions are given in the text of this book, they are only approximate, and to be used merely as a guide to those who may be working in the other measurement system.

---

cups of tea. If you are intending to use machinery (*see* Digging Machines, page 51), budget for the hire of a dumper as well as a digger.

If you want to dispose of the soil, then you will find that this is the largest single expense of the project, a 3cu yd midi-skip being in the region of £65.00 plus, and a 6cu yd £95.00 (at the time of writing). The most popular size of pool for a suburban garden when I was a contractor was roughly 9 × 15ft (3 × 4.5m), and the spoil from the excavation would fill the best part of three '6yd skips', leaving you with a bill of £285 plus VAT, and rising as I write.

The Number of Blocks Required

For pools with liners in the ground: Double the length and breadth in feet and add them together, or just take the measurement from your tape draped around the circumference. Then take two-thirds of this number to get the approximate number of blocks required for the pool. If you are building in support for the marginal shelf, measure this in feet, and add two-thirds of the number to the total.

For raised pools: Measure the height out of the ground in inches, and divide by nine. Then multiply this number with the number of blocks for the circumference (*see* above) to give the number of blocks required for the perimeter. Allow extra blocks for the creation of the marginal shelf areas, and pools set in unstable ground.

For waterfalls and streams created from flexible liners: A commonsense figure for the number of blocks required can be deduced from the 'head' of the stream: that is, its starting height above the pool surface level in feet, added on to its length and then doubled. Therefore: (length on the horizontal + head) × 2. The width is governed by the standard widths of liner.

Other Estimates

Further points to remember using flexible liner materials: Economically it is best to design the pool in one dimension to fit in with the standard widths of liner sizes.

If you have dramatic indentations in pool shapes and streams, measure around the longest contour to take in the extra liner that is required to accommodate this shape.

The liner, no matter how thick, needs to be laid on a 5cm (2in) bed of soft sand or underlay in order to prevent it being punctured by stones from underneath. A metric tonne (1,000kg) will cover (very) approximately 10sq m (107sq ft) at this depth.

The sort of limestone pavement in the north of England once pillaged for its 'characterful' stone.

Underlay: This is cheap material for laying under the liner and on top of the soil or, if you are using sand as well, on top of the sand and below the liner. If the subsoil is in the least bit stony, it is best to have both sand and underlay. In conservation-style pools where soil goes in on top of the liner, the underlay needs to go under the soil, on top of the liner. Allow for the liner size, plus 10 per cent in a simple pool; double that for conservation pools. With pools faced on the inside with stone or underneath beach effects, you will need extra to lay underneath the stones.

Stonework and Rockeries

Rockeries: You can estimate the quantity of stone required for a rockery by multiplying the height by the width in feet, and taking each square foot as accounting for 1cwt or 50kg. This is the same for estimating the rockery surround and the stream face. One of the reasons that rockeries are so out of favour is because of the scar that stone quarries make on our landscape. Also much of the weathered stone that people had preferred to use was pillaged from the beautiful landscapes of the ever-diminishing limestone pavements of the northern counties of England and Eire.

It is possible to buy reclaimed rockery stone or fieldstone picked out of fields on farmland. Good-looking rockery stone is therefore incredibly expensive, and is probably best used as individual stones as features in themselves, rather as the Japanese may use them, in groups of two or three. If you are trying to create a rock bank that is self-supporting, and all but the face of the stone is going to be buried and then hidden with plants, large pieces of 'block stone' straight from the quarry are perfect. Well weathered, water-worn stone can be a nightmare to fit together convincingly. However, even cheap 'block stone' can be expensive, mainly due to the delivery costs and, if it is stored, the room it takes up that could otherwise be used for some more valuable product. Therefore, for the sake of expense and appearance, it must be a local stone. What is more, if it is a stone that looks nothing like any local stone, then it will look perpetually out of place.

Ordinary 'block stone' straight from the quarry is perfectly all right for use in a rockery.

The local stone always blends in well, whether it is used in a rockery, for paving, or in walling.

Natural stone stonewalling: This usually covers about 4sq yd of faced area per ton/3sq m of faced area per tonne. If you have material delivered straight from the quarry you can expect to be left with almost a third of it as waste, unless you can 'lose it' inside the wall. Because of this, expect to use a ton of stone in a double-face wall.

Reconstituted stone or pre-cast concrete walling: This can be priced by the square metre from the retailer. Many styles are manufactured as facing stone, and these have to be priced with a blockwork skeleton. All walling and blockwork needs a footing or foundation.

Footing materials for blockwork and walling: Footings are the foundations to walls and paths, and generally consist of gravel chips of varying sizes down to dust mixed with cement to make concrete in a 6:1 ratio, or 15mm to 25mm gravel chippings mixed with sand and cement in a 4:2:1 ratio. The foundation depth should be between a quarter and a third of the wall height, and twice the wall width. Estimate 2 tonnes to the cubic metre (2 tons to the cubic yard).

Sand for building: Allow two large bags for each 3sq m (4sq yd) of faced walling, but more if there is a lot of backfilling. The coarser the sand that you use, the stronger the mortar will be. The same applies to a concrete mix when chippings, sand and cement are used in the ratio 4:2:1.

Paving and Edging

Natural stone paving: This is much more expensive than reconstituted or concrete slabs, covering about 11sq m per tonne (11sq yd per ton). The site and the style of the pool will dictate whether natural stone edging is the obvious choice (*see* Edgings, page 80).

Preformed slabs and bricks for edging: These are usually sold and priced by the square yard or metre. During the early 1980s the race to imitate natural stone to perfection was a goal all but achieved by a number of pre-cast slab manufacturers; the result was a huge choice of stone types at less than half the cost of the real thing. Competition urged the manufacturers on to even more ambitious aims, and soon 'terracotta', 'wooden sleepers' and even 'log' stepping-stones were being marketed.

Gravel, or gravel to dust for footings: 1 tonne covers about 10sq m at 5cm in depth (1 ton, 10sq yd at 2in).

Cement: Allow one bag for every four of building sand.

Waterproofer for cement: All underwater cement surfaces must be treated with silglaze or pool glaze. In general, a 4-to-1 sand/cement mix is adequate for walling, with the correct amount of waterproofer added for work that will be sub-merged. Use six parts sand or stone dust to one part cement mix for laying paving.

MATERIALS FOR THE ELECTRICITY SUPPLY

The costs of installing an electricity supply can easily exceed the costs of all the actual units and pumps that it is intended to run if the feature is a long way from the mains supply. You can choose to have either a single armoured cable to supply the electricity, or to run an ordinary mains cable through an electrical conduit, but it is important to work out the costs in advance.

Armoured Cable

The size of armoured cable you choose should be capable of supplying 13 amps worth of power at 240 volts. It should be laid at a depth of half a metre, set in a 15cm (6in) deep bed of clean chippings with a plastic tape warning strip lying on top. Check these regulations with an electrician, as they could change at any time. It is possible to have the cable pinned to a wall in a protected situation, such as under capping stones or sills. A two-core cable is suitable for most pumps, since the armoured protection is used as an earth wire. As long as the pump is modest, there is no reason why another pump (say a filter pump) and a UV clarifier might not run off the same cable if the power can be shared out at a weather-proof fused switch box, but they must all be a fairly low ampage. Some manufacturers are producing fairly cheap junction/fuse boxes, with an array of switches if you choose, that can function in this situation on a 'do-it-yourself' level.

For more serious use of power, three-core cable can be used for running perhaps a pump and some other item, because both items can be wired in using the armour as an earth, and they can share the neutral wire. Four-core is a popular choice for those who want to run a pump for a waterfall and fountain, a separate one for a biological filter system, and still have one spare for a UV clarifier or pool lights. Where the armoured cable joins up

with the cable to the unit – for example, the pump – for which you want power, you will need a junction box with the correct waterproof fittings to 'translate' the armour cable to the ordinary weatherproof cable of the unit. It is important to budget for this.

Laying a Conduit

The alternative method is to lay a conduit down to carry ordinary weatherproof domestic cable. There is special flexible electrician's conduit, but for long runs, outdoor alcathene or plastic waterpipe will do; a 25mm-bore plastic waterpipe can take several cables. The trick is to lay the conduit down with a electrician's 'draw cable' or piece of stiff garden wire already in it, because it is much easier to thread anything through a long length if you can jiggle it about a bit as you push the end down. Once this is down through the conduit, you now have the tool installed to pull through your normal type of weatherproof mains cable. Then you can bury the pipe with both its ends rising up to the necessary junction boxes or switch boxes at each end.

You will have to consider where you want the switches. Having them near the pool makes life simpler, because there is less cable to run outside. As with the armoured cable above, one cable can run them all. If you want to run several cables through the conduit, always ensure there is a draw cable in place, because it is virtually impossible to thread more cables through when there is already some cable there. And each time you pull through another cable, ensure there is another piece of wire attached to it, because this will be the 'draw cable' you use to draw up the next cable.

When attaching a cable to a 'draw cable' or wire, make a loop in the wire that is definitely not going to come undone. Thread one of the core wires of the cable through the loop, then twist it up with one of the other wires completely, and tape them all tightly against the side of the cable with insulation tape. Test the join forcefully before you attempt to draw the cable or cables through.

If there is any part of the water-garden project that you really need to be qualified to do, it is installing the electrical supply. Even if you feel

Thread one of the core wires of the cable through the loop. Twist it up with one of the other wires completely.

Tape them all tightly against the side of the cable with insulation tape before you draw it through the conduit.

confident in doing the bulk of the installation yourself, when you come to connect it to your domestic supply, at least get it checked by a professional. All the electrical supply to outdoors should be on a separate 'loop' to your domestic supply, so that if anything fuses it does not affect your home supply.

Junction Boxes and Trip Switches

The electrical supply to outdoors must also be protected from blowing the whole domestic supply by a 30ma RCD trip switch that will shut things down virtually instantly if there is any trace of power 'leaking to earth'. This would occur as soon as any dampness found its way into a connection or electrical unit, or if any current found a way out into the environment. These can seem expensive at the time, but nowhere near as much as a freezer full of meat and frozen food that would unfreeze and spoil when the house end of the electrics blew.

At the pool end, the junction box can be like the one described for the armoured cable (*see* page 44), or it can be a series of weatherproof plugs in a weatherproof box. If you are installing any units that run on a 12-volt supply, such as a small pump or lights, then a junction box large enough to hold the transformer plus any plugs or switches would be useful; this could be fitted into a wall or hidden away with the filter system. With this in mind, if

you are considering installing cheap 12-volt lights for outdoors or under water, try to ensure that they have their own trip switch, since they are much more prone to short circuiting in bad weather than most other outdoor electrical items.

All these electrical items are supplied in several different levels of expenditure. The DIY market in garden centres and aquatic stores caters for the requirements of most people quite adequately, but the products have a limited life and durability. If you enlist a professional electrician to install equipment that does exactly the same job, you will find it to be considerably more expensive, and it looks completely different; however, in time it will prove its value, as it will continue to serve its purpose with minimal maintenance.

The electricity supply must also be protected from blowing the whole domestic circuit by a 30ma RCD trip switch.

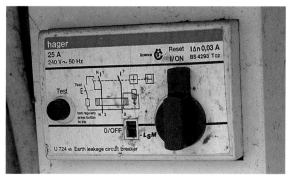

PUMPS AND PIPEWORK

(*See also* Powering the Water Feature, page 98.)
When buying the pipework that will carry water to
a water feature, stream or waterfall, always go for
the largest practical diameter hose with the least
number of fittings; this allows the pump to perform
at its most efficient. Even so, for every 3m (10ft) in
length of hose, it will lose between 270 and 450ltr
(60 and 100gal) per hour in power. The easiest
pipe to use is the type of flexible pipe sold at the
aquatics store. Ribbed pipe is even more flexible,
but is significantly more expensive. Also do not forget the hose clips and any extra fittings.

The performance in pumping vertically (the
head) varies considerably from one make of pump
to another. Manufacturers generally give details on
individual pump performances both in their adver-
tising literature and on their products' boxes: if the
pump performance is in a curve on a graph or on a
table, then choose a pump that has the performance you require right in the middle of the graph
or the table. In this way you will be going for more
power than you think you will need. That spare
power will be easily taken up if you want to run a
fountain from the waterfall pump, which would
reduce its performance by at least 30 per cent. You
should also consider whether you are going to
incorporate a biological filter and an ultra-violet
clarifier in the feed to the stream or waterfall, or if
it is going to be separate. These will slow the water
flow quite considerably, mainly because of the fittings (hose tails and joints and so on) involved in
these items of equipment.

When comparing pumps in terms of their performance, also take into account their running costs,
because it is quite possible that what you might gain
on the price of a pump, you will very quickly lose on
the running costs. This is particularly important if the
pump is running a biological filtration system, since
this will be going twenty-four hours a day. If the costs
are not stated on the box or in the manufacturers' literature, you can work them out from the wattage of
the unit, which provides a sort of mental 'yardstick'.
Another yardstick is the guarantee, which will tell
you roughly what the manufacturer considers the life
expectancy of the pump will be. If the pump has only
a one-year guarantee, I would look elsewhere.

External Pumps

If you are contemplating a very large 'puddled' pond,
or a vast waterfall, or a hugely wide cascade, you will
need to consider an external pump. The volume and
the height to which external pumps can shift water is
virtually unlimited. They have a long life expectancy,
and they are easily repairable in relative comfort –
and for this reason they are relatively expensive. They
do tend to hum, so need housing in a soundproof but
well-ventilated box. Some will also need an arrangement for priming them if they are turned off.

Biological Filters

Biological filters clean the pool water by filtering the
organic matter and algae from it as it moves through
the various types of media. Also, micro-organisms
that build up in the media actually digest this organic matter, breaking it down to its constituent chemical ingredients. If a pool biological filter is required,
a filter pump is also necessary, capable of pumping
a certain amount of solid matter up to the filter
without clogging up. Moreover, for it to be effective,
it must be capable of turning over half the volume
of the pool per hour, with the pump situated as far
away from the filter as possible.

Biological filters usually need a month to become
fully operational in a digesting capacity. Since they
function with the aid of micro-organisms, which
depend upon oxygen, a continuous flow of oxygen-
rich water is essential; this means they must be
operating continuously, twenty-four hours a day. If
the filter is incorporated in the supply to a waterfall
or stream, having the stream running twenty-four
hours a day may not be desirable, particularly in
cold weather – although having said that, it may be
a good idea to have the filter gently turning over the
surface water of the pool if it is not too cold. For
this reason it is best to have the filter system as a
separate entity from waterfalls or fountains. Suffice
it to say that if you are budgeting for a biological filter at this stage, you may as well add the price of an
extra pump and a UV clarifier (UVC) – and don't
forget the necessary fittings and switches.

Biological filters are even more efficient at
keeping water clear when there is a UVC unit

A biological filter with a UVC incorporated into the lid ready for installation next to a pond.

Manufacturers are improving UVCs all the time for greater efficiency and ease of maintenance.

incorporated in the system. Both units need to be installed in a place where they are easily accessible. The UVCs are matched to specific flow rates and filter sizes: depending on your pool volume, you will have a suitable size of filter to choose from, which will relate to a pump capable of delivering the required volume of water via a UVC with the relevant power or wattage.

THE MOST IMPORTANT INGREDIENTS

Plants

(*See also* Chapter 6, Plants and Planting, page 151.) To estimate quantities for a natural balance it must be stressed that 'oxygenating plants', or underwater pondweeds, are the most essential ingredient of the pond; the best example is *Elodea crispa*, otherwise known as *Laragasiphon major* (or 'curly pond-weed'). If your pool or pond is going to have clear water and sustain itself as a perfectly balanced system without the aid of fountains for oxygenation and biological filters, the ultimate aim is to have the pond or pool 60 per cent full of plants that are under water. In this way oxygen, the by-product of photo-synthesis from the leaves of the plants in sunlight, is dissolved into the water from the surface of the leaves. This is why they are referred to as oxygena-tors, as they provide the essential ingredient for all the animal life of the pool, and the bacteria that

digest all the muck in the pool (more of that later).

The oxygenators are then supplemented with a complete range of water-loving plants selected from the different types that will appreciate the different levels in the pool. There will be deep-water plants such as lilies and water hawthorn (*Apono-geton distachyos*), floating plants such as water sol-dier (*Stratiotes aloides*), and marginal plants such as marsh marigold (*Caltha palustris*) that sit in the shallow areas.

Allow one bunch of oxygenators for every 0.2sq m (2sq ft) of surface area to set you off.

Lilies provide pool cover and use up excess nitrates in the water: allow one lily or deep-water aquatic for every 2.3sq m (25sq ft) of pool surface area.

Floating plants use up many excess nitrates in the water and also provide pool cover: allow one floating plant for every 0.9sq m (10sq ft) of pool surface area.

Marginals blend the pool into the surrounding landscape. They use up nitrates, and provide cover for amphibians and other animals around the pool. Allow one marginal for every 0.5sq m (5sq ft) of surface area.

Fish

Never introduce too many fish at any one time, and wait until two to three weeks after planting. As regards stocking rate, allow only 5cm (2in) of fish per 0.09sq m (1sq ft) of surface area.

CHAPTER 3

Preparation and Installation of Pools, Ponds and Bog Gardens

Although it is possible to create a water garden without using cement and/or concrete, your options will be limited. Besides, cement and concrete mixing is really easy, believe me – and if you are a complete novice and would appreciate a beginner's guide, then turn to page 60, 'Mixing It'.

What is probably more of a requirement than practical skills is a certain level of commitment. If there is a deadline, you need stamina; and if you are doing it by yourself, you need a robust physical constitution, and in particular a strong back. For those of you who would still rather try to do the project without any cement and mortar, the 'Conservationists' V-Notch Technique' avoids it (*see* page 67); but you will be limited to the conservation/wildlife/natural style in fairly level ground. However, before you need make a decision, there are still certain preliminaries that must be carried out before you even think of beginning construction.

PEGGING OUT THE SITE

For ponds or pools on uneven ground, peg out the site before you make the final decision. You will need the following tools for this stage:

- 3m (10ft) straight-edge;
- lump hammer, or very heavy hammer;
- a long spirit level;
- several strong square pegs.

OPPOSITE: *'The Blue Circle Garden' by Carole Vincent at the 2001 Chelsea Flower Show was made out of concrete, cement and gravel.*

RIGHT: *The hand tools required for a modest water-garden project. Note the instruction book.*

3m (10ft) straight-edge: This could be a good piece of timber (perhaps 2 × 1in/50 × 25mm) with an uncurved, unwavering edge to it as you look along the edge from one end to the other.

Spirit level: Get as long a spirit level as you can find. A 'Dumpy' or Cowley builders' level can be hired from a tool-hire merchant: these need two people to operate them, but they help you find levels very accurately, and are indispensable for large pool projects. Also, levels that shoot out a laser spot to a level some yards away are a useful new invention for the pool constructor who is on his own.

The little Cowley level can be worth its weight in gold when there is heavy machinery doing the digging, but practise using it before the day of excavation.

This peg has been marked with a line 60cm (24in) from one end, the ultimate proposed depth of the excavation for this pool once the sand and liner are laid in place. It will be driven into the ground to the level at which I want the water level to be, and the mark will then indicate to me that I have dug down deep enough when I reach it.

Strong pegs: Take several strong 5cm (2in) square pegs to mark out the perimeter of the pool area: some of these need be no more than 30cm (12in) long, since they are just going down to the marginal shelf level. Others need to be a few centimetres longer than the depth of the pool, especially if the ground drops away sharply on one side; then those pegs marking the low edge at the marginal shelf will have to be more than the full depth of the pool (between 60cm and 1m/2ft to roughly 3ft).

Mark the short pegs with an indelible line at 23cm (9in): this mark will be an indicator to you when you have dug down to the marginal shelf level. Mark the long pegs with an indelible line near the bottom of the peg that will indicate the final depth of your excavation (adding 5cm for a layer of sand that will cushion the liner to the mean pool depth: thus, for a pool 60cm (24in) deep add 5cm (2in), the total depth excavated being 65cm (26in). If you are keen and/or rich enough to contemplate a concrete- or clay-lined pool, add on an extra 15cm (6in) in every direction.

If the pool is going to be created some way from the house, paint the tops of the pegs with something easily visible so that you can see the pool shape from the house.

Calculating the Planned Position

If the pool has a precise planned position, then this can be calculated by taking readings from precise established datum points, such as the two corners of the house, and describing arcs to the extreme edges of the pool on plan, and then scaling them up to the dimensions of the garden. This is easy with formal shapes where just two measurements can ascertain the centre of a circle, and four measurements can find the side of a rectangle. For a really informal shape you may need up to six measurements. This is called 'triangulation', and is used by garden designers and surveyors all the time to find precise points on grid plans.

Choose one of the long pegs as a datum peg for the pool water level, and drive it into what you consider to be the centre of the pool to roughly the level you foresee. This can be gauged to begin with as being the thickness of the pool edging stone for that side below the average contour of the ground. The top of this peg will mark the level to which you drive in all the other pegs. Keep them less than 2.5m (8ft) apart. As long as you can mark the perimeter with the shorter pegs, save the longer ones for gauging the depth of the excavation later; however, in steeply sloping situations you may need the long ones to mark the perimeter on the low side. Keep them all roughly 15cm (6in) inside the line of your proposed perimeter.

If there is an uneven covering of turf around the site it may be necessary to remove some of it, and even a few inches of soil, in the pool area to get a clearer view of the lie of the land.

At this point you can assess what you have got, and make a firm decision as to whether you are happy to go with what you see. You have not yet dedicated any hard-earned cash to the project, nor made a decision you cannot reverse. You can gauge the size precisely and the amount of engineering involved, and you can also fairly accurately estimate the cost, effort, and hard landscaping required to cover up that engineering. The next step is excavating – and this really *is* the point of no return!

EXCAVATING THE POND SITE

Many people feel that excavating the site is the main part of the project, but if you have done your forward planning you will already have worked out just how much effort will be involved in the whole enterprise.

Remember that the soil doubles in volume once it is excavated, and it is important that you know what you are going to do with those vast heaps of it. You could use some for a rockery area behind the pool down which you could run a stream. Whatever you do, save the loam and topsoil for at least one spit below the soil surface; it will be useful for something, eventually – and the plants will need some of it. Be sure to store topsoil in mounds of less than half a metre (20in) deep, otherwise it will soon revert to being inert, lifeless subsoil at the bottom of the pile.

If you are using skips, find some planks to get you and the wheelbarrow up and over the edge. You can hire front-opening skips that make life easier and less treacherous to begin with.

This may not be a project that you can flash through in a weekend. There is presumably no rush, so just work steadily and mind your back. Try to get some help – perhaps make a social party thing of it; anyone who has a part in it will take an interest in it for ever more. But if no help is forthcoming, then you may have to resort to technology and hire a digger.

Try to get some help. Persuade children to become involved in the project, and they will stay keenly interested for ever more.

Digging Machines

These are surprisingly cheap to hire considering the amount of work they can do *in the right hands*. If you fancy driving one of the mini-diggers yourself, and have never done so before, give yourself a weekend to get the hang of it, and do not expect to get any more done than a good man would with a pick and shovel in the same time. Be aware that access for these machines is a problem for many established gardens, although for narrow gateways, machines less than 1m (36in) wide (but only just) can be found. Nevertheless, in even the most skilful operator's hands, the marginal areas in the pool profile and the top edges need to be finished off by hand.

If your garden is established – meaning that a digger would have to drive across a lawn to get to the pool site – then choose a tracked vehicle (with 360-degree slew) as opposed to a wheeled vehicle (such as a JCB), because tracked vehicles generally cause a lot less damage. Ironically, the larger the vehicle, the less the impression it makes, as proportionately less weight is distributed over the track surface; it can also work from a central point, swivelling spoil from one place to another without having to track backwards and forwards. On the other hand, some of the smaller track vehicles come with rubber tracks, which are even less destructive to lawns, edgings and tarmac.

As the excavation with the machine proceeds, the edges still need to be tidied up by hand. Note the pegs in place as a guide for the final water level.

The complete kit for mechanical digging: a mini-digger with rubber tracks and a dumper with a hydraulic lift for dumping its load into skips.

There is no doubt that for larger excavations – for example, over 100sq m (1,000sq ft) – a good driver hired with his own machine is worth every penny you pay him. For around £200 per day, plus VAT, plus delivery of machine, they can still save you much more time and money. Beware though, supervise them every minute of the day, and don't let them dig too deep, because digging deeper means much more lining material. And bear in mind that it may also be necessary to hire a dumper – another £50 per day, but much cheaper over longer periods (though take note: the handbrake never seems to work on them!).

HAND TOOLS FOR THE EXCAVATION

The following tools will be needed, in order of importance:

- spade;
- long spirit level;
- pegs;
- lump hammer;
- long 3m straight-edge;
- shovel and thumper for consolidating;
- grubber, bar and pick may be useful.

These can be hired from tool-hire centres; it is generally cheaper at weekends.

THE INSTALLATION OF PREFORMED OR RIGID POOLS

Materials required:
Approximately 1 × 50kg of soft sand per 1sq m/10sq ft of surface area.

Construction should follow the sequence of steps as described here:

1. Although the initial stages of construction for water gardens lined with rigid or flexible liners are the same, it would be best, in the case of preformed pools, to try the pool in position. Shift it around to make sure you have planned the best place for it.

2. Once you are happy with the position, with the unit firmly held in position, mark the perimeter of the pool on the ground by using a vertical spirit level or a 'plumb line' moving around the circumference of the rigid plastic shape. Mark the outline 10cm (3–4in) wider and longer than the pool itself.

3. Remove the turf inside the marked area, and put it aside.

4. (a) Excavate the soil in the shape down to the same depth as the marginal shelf, plus an inch or two (to allow for a protective bed of sand), probably 23cm + 5cm (9in + 2in). Also allow for the thickness of the edging stone, whether it be paving or a rock edge, or if it is turf (though this is not recommended), the thickness of the turf.

(b) Save the topsoil. Do not bury it under the subsoil.

(c) Make sure the area is level and firm. You should already be aware that if the ground around the pool is not level, then one edge might have to be set further down in the soil than another. In general this would be the easiest approach, rather than have one edge exposed and faced on the outside with rockery or walling. To do this satisfactorily it would need blockwork support and reinforcement (*see* Practical Considerations, page 27).

5. Bring back the pool to the position you had when you previously marked out the rim, and mark out the shape of the inner section or base in the bottom of the excavation. You now have your marker for digging out the lower section of the pool.

6. Excavate the area 2–5cm (1–2in) deeper than

TOP LEFT: *This is a plastic preformed pool that I have moved from elsewhere and am relocating for the ducks!*

TOP RIGHT: *Make sure the area is level and firm.*

ABOVE: *Position the pool as you had it when you marked out the outer edge, and mark out the inner section or base of the pool in the bottom of the excavation with a trowel or stick.*

you ultimately want, to allow for the protective bed of sand.

7. As the excavation proceeds, keep trying the pool in place to make sure it is a good fit. It is very important to end up with a level base and shelf.

8. Spread an even layer of sand on the base and marginal shelves of the excavation to bring it up to the required final level.

9. Bring the preformed pool back into position and backfill with it in position, using the remainder of the sand to fill up the gap between the liner and the soil. The most effective way of doing this is to wash the sand down the gap using a hose whilst filling the pool with water. Great care must be taken to ensure that the backwash between the pool and soil does not rise above the water level in the pool, otherwise it will float. For the same reason, do not try this in very clayey soils. Meanwhile keep a careful watch on the levels whilst backfilling up to the soil surround.

10. As you fill the pool with water there may be slight movement in its level that can be adjusted very fractionally by extra consolidation of soil at the low point. Otherwise you must empty the pool, remove it and look in the sand layer for the high and low points, and adjust accordingly.

11. You are now in a position to consider the pool surround or the edging (*see* Edging Materials and Types of Edging, page 81).

INSTALLATION OF A POOL USING A FLEXIBLE LINER

With flexible liner pools, there are two further issues that must be weighed up and decided before the excavation proceeds. First, is the soil dense and compact enough to maintain a con-toured and shaped excavation? Clay soils offer no

TOP LEFT: *Excavate the area to a depth 3–5cm (1–2in) deeper than you ultimately want, to allow for the protective bed of sand.*

UPPER MIDDLE LEFT: *As the excavation proceeds, keep trying the pool in place to make sure it is a good fit. It is very important to end up with a level base and shelf.*

LOWER MIDDLE LEFT: *Spread an even layer of sand on the base and marginal shelves of the excavation to bring it up to the required final level.*

BOTTOM LEFT: *Here I am using the soil from behind the pool as a backfill. Because it is quite crumbly it is more than suitable, and it also makes room for the rockery backdrop I had planned.*

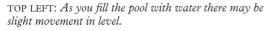

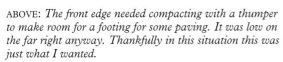

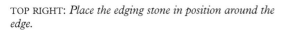

TOP LEFT: *As you fill the pool with water there may be slight movement in level.*

ABOVE: *The front edge needed compacting with a thumper to make room for a footing for some paving. It was low on the far right anyway. Thankfully in this situation this was just what I wanted.*

TOP RIGHT: *Place the edging stone in position around the edge.*

MIDDLE RIGHT (2 PICTURES): *If there is just normal human traffic around the pool, then a 5cm (2in) footing under the paving will be necessary under the edging stones. I have cheated here, and laid the slabs straight onto the concrete before it had 'gone off'. Note the slabs have a slight fall away from the pool. The slabs were left 'unpointed'.*

RIGHT: *If the rockery stone is fairly substantial around the edge, it can be just placed in position and the soil cut down to fill in behind the stones. The ducks and children look on in admiration!*

ABOVE AND BELOW: *This pool has a concrete block skeleton, but is faced on the inside with white lias limestone under the crazy paving and rockery stone on the far side.*

problems, but rubbly or crumbly soils will need skeletal support. Second, if your design sets the pool into a bank with perhaps half the pool having a raised front edge (indeed if the pool is very formal or completely raised), then a concrete skeleton is essential.

As I have said, the techniques are simple and really should not present a problem (*see* Mixing It, page 60). The 10cm (4in) concrete blocks are laid level straight onto a mortar bed (cement/sand, ratio: 1/4) on the consolidated soil that will be the marginal shelf. These blocks will not only define the final water level, but will provide a footing and reinforcement for anything laid down around the pool, be it slabs or rocks around the top, or a stone, brick or wooden facing on the inside. Some landscapers use shuttering and pour concrete to a level to make a framework, rather than use concrete blocks.

Another question to consider is whether you are going to face the inside of the pool with rockery stone or building stone, or just obscure it with plants. In the

Shuttering in place for concrete to establish a firm level edge around this very large pool.

case of facing, if this comes up from the marginal shelf, then the width of the shelf has to accommodate the width of the facing whilst still allowing enough room for marginal planting baskets.

One technique is to excavate the pool to the total length and width, but only down to the marginal shelf level. Then you dig out a ring wide enough and deep enough to be the marginal shelf, and wide enough to support plant baskets and a facing row of edging stones or stonework. This is filled with concrete in the soil, only using shuttering or form-work where it comes above ground. This ring beam (or 'donut', as they call it) then doubles as founda-tion and support for the liner.

As the liner itself is laid in place on top of the 'donut', sand and underlay, so the liner is pulled up to the required water level behind the facing stones that sit on the 'donut' that is now the marginal shelf. This is then backfilled to maintain it in position.

CONSTRUCTION OF A SIMPLE POOL WITHOUT A FRAMEWORK USING A FLEXIBLE LINER

The project illustrated is an example of using a con-crete block skeleton to support the flexible liner to

This pool has been constructed using the 'donut' technique, but the hard level ring is merely consolidated soil instead of concrete. The liner is laid in place, and the edging stones sit on the ring, which doubles as a plant shelf. The liner is pulled up behind the stones – you can just see it exposed – and is held in place with a backfill of pea gravel. This also makes a useful planting medium, because in this style of pool this is where the marginal plants go – a useful technique for a koi pond where the fish are likely to try to uproot the plants.

the required water level, a useful technique in uneven terrain or loose soil.

Materials required:

A flexible liner of a size that takes into account double the width required for any internal facing (not forgetting double the depth in both directions and the width of any skeletal framework).

A number of stout 5 × 5cm (2 × 2in) pegs cut to 20 or 23cm (8 or 9in) deeper than the required depth of the pool, with an indelible mark at the required depth. Also several pegs of roughly 45cm (18in) that have a mark at about 23cm (9in) from the top to mark the depth of the marginal shelf; these will be used in the outer region of the pool.

Underlay to the same area as the pool liner, plus 10 per cent – plus extra for cushioning any facing that might be built up on top of the liner. Or double the whole quantity if the pool is going to be soil-lined.

50kg of sand for every square metre of liner area (1cwt for every 10sq ft).

The Initial Stages of Construction

First, lay down a rope or hose to mark the pool shape.
1. Cut and remove any turf.
2. Drive a peg into the edge or the centre to mark the

Define the pool area using a tape measure and a hose or some sort of marker.

final required water level in the pond. This remains as a datum point for taking other levels. If there is going to be a paved edging around the pool, then the proposed water level is going to be below the thickness of the paving, plus the thickness of the cement bed. Also drive in some of the shorter pegs level with the datum: these will be your guide for the level of the marginal shelf.
3. Dig out the first 23cm (9in) down from this level. This will be the level of the marginal shelf.
4. Using the pegs that are marked with the required depth of the pool, hammer them in level with the water-level marker peg. If the excavation is going to be too large to be accurate with your level and straight-edge, you can hire a site level or surveyor's level. If you get these reference pegs in accurately and they are accessible for reference all around the pool, then everything just falls into place. It may be easier to get the bulk of the excavation completed before you bang in all the level pegs.
5. With constant reference to the level pegs, begin the 'second dig'. Leaving a marginal shelf perhaps half a metre (18in) wide in the required places around the edge, dig down a further 25cm (10in) minimum, or the required depth of the pool plus an inch or two. The profile of the dig ought to be at a minimum of 30 degrees to the vertical in unsupported soil. (Conservation-style ponds to be lined with soil need sloping sides of 30 degrees to the horizontal, maximum.) If the 'second dig' soil looks lifeless, keep it separate from the topsoil.

Cut and remove any turf.

THE WIDTH OF THE MARGINAL SHELF

The final marginal shelf width needs to be 25cm (10in) to support the planting baskets. If you are using a concrete block framework, add this to the excavation. If you are stone-facing the inside of the pool, allow for this also.

For an area where you might want a beach effect, this marginal shelf area needs (I would say) to be at least 1.5 to 2m (5 to 7ft) wide. So that you don't have to have pebbles right down into the base of the pool (where you cannot see them, and where they get in the way when it is clean-out time), they stop at the inside edge of the marginal shelf. There would also be a little bump in the soil or a sausage of cement at the edge to stop any round beach pebbles from tumbling further into the depths of the pool.

6. Remove the pegs, and any sharp stones, and lay a 2–3cm (1in) bed of sand down on the surface of the soil. A plasterer's trowel helps with the smoothing out.

7. Lay down the underlay and fold it into place. Cut to fit, leaving a generous overlap over the edge.

8. Lay the liner into place, gathering all the folds together and tucking it into place. Do not use the weight of water to push it into place just yet, even if everyone else advises otherwise – it is not the best way to proceed. Whilst you are doing this, *check the welds or seams in the liner*: this is where they are at their weakest.

9. Once the liner is in place, then you can fill it with water, smoothing out the smaller folds as it fills. Hold the edges in place with flat stones. Fill it to 10cm (4in) from the top.

10. The edging is the next task; therefore only cut away the right width of turf appropriate for your choice of edging.

TOP RIGHT: *Drive in a peg into the edge or the centre that marks the final required water level in the pond.*

MIDDLE RIGHT: *Also drive in some of the shorter pegs so they are level with the datum; these will be your guide for the level of the marginal shelf.*

BOTTOM RIGHT: *Dig out the first 22cm (9in) down from this level. This will be the level of the marginal shelf.*

MIXING IT (FOR COMPLETE BEGINNERS)

For those of you who are nervous at the thought of mixing cement for the first time, let me assure you that it is easier than mixing a cake. The only difference is the volume, and also it is not very pleasant if you get it on your hands (unlike cake mixture), because mixed with water it is an alkali and very slowly eats into your flesh.

Cement is the powder that, when mixed with sand and water in the right proportions, makes 'cement mortar'. Concrete is a similar mix but with proportionately less cement powder, but it contains aggregate or gravel chippings, which give the resulting mix, once it has 'gone off' (hardened), its added strength.

Cement mixers are an aid to the mixing process even if you are contemplating buying dry 'Readimix' – mixed sand and cement. All tool-hire centres hire out cement mixers, but you must take them back clean. Give yours a stiff brush and wash immediately you finish using it at any time during the project.

A 'mix' is four shovelfuls of sand to one of cement; these can be multiplied up to 'bagfuls'. One 25kg bag contains four generous shovelfuls of cement. There are eight shovels of sand in a 50kg bag (which we used to call a 'hundredweight'). Thus for cement mortar, one 25kg bag of cement will mix with two 50kg bags of sand.

A good concrete mix is four shovels of 15–20mm chippings, two shovels of sand (keep it coarse), and one of cement.

Mixing Cement

If you are mixing by machine you will need a good solid builder's barrow to tip the mix into. If you are mixing by hand, you will need a board at least a metre (4ft) square on which to mix. Initially do not be too ambitious with the quantities. For cement, keep to eight shovels of sand to two of cement.

Mixing with a Cement Mixer

Start with pouring 1.5 to 2ltr (3 or 4 pints) of water from a bucket; the precise amount of water needed depends on the dampness of the sand. Let this slosh around inside to wet the whole inner surface of the mixer.

Then add the cement powder. This should not get more than just creamy. If it begins to get buttery, add more water, but not too much at a time.

If you are making concrete, add the chippings and then the sand to the cement and water.

For cement mortar, add the sand at a fairly even rate. The resulting mixture within less than a minute should be like a buttery cake mixture, stiff enough to be self-supporting, and coming away from the sides as it rolls round.

If it still slops around, it is too wet, so add half a shovel of cement followed by two of sand slowly, one at a time. This is not a precise science at this level, so at any time whilst you are adding extra ingredients it begins to come right, stop it there. Concrete can be slightly wetter if it is being used for footings, but it should be well enclosed; this helps when you are trying to level it out.

If the mixture sticks to the sides, add a bit of water by dribbling it in slowly from the front lip until it comes away from the side of the mixer. Then add small amounts of dry materials to correct your over-correction. Dirty mixers do not help in this situation.

If the weather is likely to be frosty, add 'Frost-Proofer Additive', though with care. You will not need to use as much water because this substance 'plasticizes' the mixture. Follow the manufacturers' recommendations – and if they are hard to follow, then just add a dollop, which is better than nothing at all.

When it is right, tip it out into a well-wetted barrow, or onto a wet board. You now have cement mortar, commonly referred to as 'muck'.

Mixing by Hand

Make a little pile of the heavy ingredients, keeping to a maximum of nine shovelfuls until you get into the swing of it. If you are mixing concrete, mix up the sand and chippings before you add the cement powder. In Somerset we have chippings mixed in their own dust ('chippings to dust'), and these limestone chippings make rock-hard concrete, as you will appreciate as you drive over the new Severn bridge: there is a good bit of the Mendips in those footings.

Pile up the mixture and top it off with the cement dust, encouraging it to cascade down the side. Mix by sliding the shovel in at the base, and turning it over completely onto a new spot. Work through the whole pile until it has all been moved, then do this two more times. By now the pile of ingredients should be thoroughly mixed through, and should be a uniform colour all the way through.

Make a depression through to the board in the centre with the shovel, the width of the shovel wide and long. Half fill this with water.

Imagine this to be a volcano full of red hot larva, and the only way of stopping it from spilling out at any moment is to move the earth up the sides of the volcano and fill in the top with the sides. If you can do that, you save yourself the panic as it does spill out, and then you have to shovel the resultant mess back onto the mountain and poke it in. Work your way round quickly and efficiently. Where a very dry bit is spotted, slice it from the vertical and slice it backwards and forwards on the horizontal. Add water in very small amounts to get the required 'pudding-like' slump. Eventually you should be left with an evenly coloured mix that will flatten out not unlike a giant cowpat, except when you slice off a small piece with a trowel it will maintain its shape. Again, this is cement mortar, or 'muck'.

For a simple PVC- or rubber-lined pond, the procedure would be to establish a perfectly level edge with reference to the pegs that would allow any edging to lie flush with the surrounding turf or soil, as in the picture, page 36, bottom right.

CONSTRUCTING A POOL WITH A CONCRETE BLOCK FRAMEWORK

Tools required:
trowel;
9ltr (2gal) bucket;
lump hammer;
long spirit level and a straight-edge;
possibly a large 10cm (4in) bolster chisel;
a fairly stiff hand-brush.

For pools in uneven terrain, loose soil or made up ground it will be necessary to build a framework for the pool from concrete blocks and cement mortar. The initial stages of construction are as with the 'Construction of a Simple Pool', *see* page 57. However, cut out the marginal shelf 15cm (6in) wider all the way around the perimeter of the pool. This will be the level on which you lay the concrete blocks.

However first of all:

1. Cut and remove any turf.
2. Drive a peg into the edge or the centre to mark the final required water level in the pond. This remains as a datum point for taking other levels. If there is going to be a paved edging around the pool, then the proposed water level is going to be below the thickness of the paving, plus the thickness of the cement bed. Also drive in some of the shorter pegs level with the datum: these will be your guide for the level of the marginal shelf.
3. Dig out the first 23cm (9in) down from this level. This will be the level of the marginal shelf.
4. Using the pegs that are marked with the required depth of the pool, hammer them in level with the water-level marker peg. If the excavation is going to be too large to be accurate with your level and straight-edge, you can hire a site level or surveyor's level. If you get these reference pegs in accurately and they are accessible for reference all around the pool, then everything just falls into place. It may be

Place the level across the block and very softly bang it down at the high end.

Then check that it is both level itself and level with one of your level pegs.

All joints have to be flush with the blockwork in order to make it as smooth as possible.

easier to get the bulk of the excavation completed before you bang in all the level pegs.

5. Lay 10cm (4in) concrete blocks on a 4 sand/1 cement bed of mortar, level with the 'water level' pegs, around the marginal shelf on the inside edge of the pool. These will require a minimum 10cm footing if the soil is very loose, or if this is a half raised pond (cement/sand, ratio: 1/6).

Techniques for Laying a Blockwork Framework for a Pool

Take a bucketful of cement mix and tip it out on a board in the pool excavation. Take the trowel and smooth out, in one stroke, a trowel length from off the circumference. Scoop up a bit about 6cm (2in) wide and deep and the length of the trowel, and slide it onto the spot where you will lay your first block. Press the portion of cement into place with a jerky movement of the trowel running over it; this leaves it with a dimpled cavity running along it, and wide enough to take the 10cm- (4in) wide concrete block.

Place the level across the block and very softly bang it down at the high end. Then check that it is both level itself, and level with one of your level pegs. If it is too low, then use more cement; too high, bang it down, whilst still ensuring that it is itself level. Any excess cement that has oozed out as you banged the block down can be scraped up the face of the block with the back of the trowel, smoothing it out at the same time as collecting the excess. This can be used to fill in one of the vertical joints, or to make up the pile for the next block.

Work your way round the whole perimeter like this, checking and double checking each block in relation to the pegs, the other blocks, and individually. All joints must be flush with the blockwork in order to make it as smooth as possible; this can be done partly with the trowel, and then finished off with the brush at the end of the day. Any excess cement can be dropped in behind the blockwork.

Finally, wash off all your tools, including the barrow and the bucket, with clean water.

LEFT: *Here a sophisticated overflow is also the power supply duct for the submersible pump. Because it overflows out onto a patio area, it falls down a drain.*

BELOW: *The footing dug for the pool retaining wall shown in the pictures left and opposite top left. The small pegs mark the level of the concrete footings, and the tall pegs mark the proposed level of the water.*

ABOVE LEFT: *A common scenario is shown here, with concrete blocks forming the structural face to a pool that will be raised above the patio and made level with the lawn.*

BELOW LEFT: *On this project the second stage of the excavation and the block work are in progress at the same time.*

ABOVE: *Backfill behind the blockwork with soil and consolidate it.*

If an overflow is required a small indentation, perhaps in the pointing of the blockwork, of no more than 10mm (¼in) deep in the most convenient spot (perhaps draining to a bog garden) can be made, to take a 13mm (½in) pipe. This will just lie in the indentation on top of the liner, either under a stone or paver, or wedged between two stones.

If the pool is completely raised, the blockwork framework will have to be the full height out of the ground, in which case it will need a footing.

The footing would consist of a mix of 15mm chippings/sharp sand/cement in a ratio 4/2/1, or 15–20mm chippings to dust/cement in a ratio 6/1. It should be wide enough to provide a base for any facing on the inside and out. For a small pool it need only be 10cm (4in) deep, but for larger pools the foundations should be a third of the height of your wall and twice the width.

If a sound structure for the pool is required on the face of a steep slope, the specifications of the framework can be increased by using 15cm- (6in)

thick blocks laid on their flats, as in the photo top left.

It may be necessary to define the marginal shelving with concrete blocks. These can share a footing with the perimeter blocks if they start at the same level, as in the photo on page 75, top.

With large projects you can use a 'wacker plate' or plate vibrator to flatten the bottom of the pool excavation.

6. Once you have established this structure or framework, if it is in the ground, you can backfill behind it with soil and consolidate it.

7. If you are considering laying paving, it is best to cut out and lay a foundation for it now. This should be a mix of 20mm chippings/sand/cement in a ratio 6/3/2, laid at least 5cm (2in) deep in a slight fall away from the pool, perhaps 1 in 50. This is equivalent to allowing the bubble in the spirit level to stray close to the line on the pool side, rather than dead centre.

8. Before you lay out the liner in the excavation, just make a final check that it will be big enough by actually draping a tape through the excavation. If it looks as though it is going to be a little bit tight, then you can gain a very few centimetres by laying it across the diagonal. Whilst you are in there, check the base of the excavation for any small sharp stones, and consolidate the soil with a thumper.

9. Lay a protective 2.5cm- (1in) deep layer of soft sand on the bottom of the pool. If the sand is wet you can use a plasterer's trowel to smooth it into place even on the sloping areas.

10. Cover the blocks, and indeed the whole excavation, with an underlay of proprietary material or old carpets.

11. Unroll the liner from the middle of one side down into the excavation. A liner for retail sale is generally folded along the seams – which is the length as it came off the roll – and then folded in evenly from each direction along its width.

ABOVE: *Lay a protective 2.5cm- (1in) deep layer of soft sand on the bottom of the pool.*

Cover the blocks, and indeed the whole excavation, with an underlay of proprietary material or old carpets.

12. Once the liner is unfolded into place, *check the seams.*

13. Loose tuck and fold the liner into the excavation. Gather up any folds and creases into as few in number as possible.

In formal pools, gather the creases into the corners, folding them away from view. Ensure that all the folds will be securely held above the water level, preferably lying on top of the blockwork. Don't fold them down over the blockwork. Flaps of excess liner should be cut off to ensure that they don't work as siphons for the contents of the pool when it is full!

ABOVE: *Unroll the liner from the middle of one side down into the excavation.*

TOP RIGHT: *Loose tuck and fold the liner into the excavation. Gather up any folds and creases into as few in number as possible.*

MIDDLE RIGHT: *Cut off any excess liner and underlay that may get in your way.*

RIGHT: *Whilst the pool fills, smooth out the smaller creases and place flat, smooth stones on the liner to hold it in place. These can be the first of your edging.*

Around the base of streams make sure there is enough liner to lie well up the face of the framework or excavation for the stream. Avoid as much as possible any folds on this framework. Any flaps on the face of the waterfall should be folded in towards the stream to contain any sideways seepage. Along the stream length they should be facing in the direction of the flow.

14. Cut off any excess liner and underlay that may get in your way, but not too much until you have filled it with water.

15. Once the liner is folded into position, for many people this is the time to fill the pool with water to push the liner finally into place. It is the moment of truth that shows how precise your levels were.

Facing the Inside of a Liner Pool

If you are going to face the inside of the pool with stone, brick or even soil, this is the stage to start.

16. Those of you who have filled the pool with water now need to empty it again in order to build your facing stone up from the marginal shelf to the water level.

17. First you need to line the pool with underlay where there is going to be stone or soil; this will protect the liner from any sharp edges or chips of stone in the soil. The most suitable material is manufactured specifically for this purpose, being easy to compress and fold into place. Any material that comes up and over the blockwork or framework of the pond must be neatly trimmed back, as it will become an effective siphoning wick once the pool is full of water.

18. If this is to be rockery-style stone facing, avoid using a lot of cement if possible. Therefore lay the stone on a base of waterproof mortar, and backfill the stonework with smooth pea gravel.

If it is building stone, use a 4/1 sand/cement mix with waterproofing liquid or powder. A product called 'SBR Bonding Agent' waterproofs mortar and concrete whilst helping to bond it to brickwork and other stonework or concrete; it can be obtained from a good builder's merchant. Exposed cement and concrete within the pool can be treated with a product called Silglaze prior to filling with water. This will reduce the leeching of lime from the cement.

Do not forget to allow an exit for the pump hose and the power cable. 40mm (1½in) waste pipe or plastic tubing cemented into the stonework can be used as a conduit.

In this part-raised patio pool, the landscaper was trusting that the 1mm-thick rubber liner would be tough enough to take the pressure from the stone wall built on the inside of the liner.

As the wall proceeds, don't forget to build in an outlet where the pipework for the pump can exit the pool. This pool has a large pipe built into the wall through which the hose and the electric cable can be threaded.

Volunteers from BTCV (the British Trust for Conservation Volunteers), a charitable group that organizes conservation schemes, have filled the trench with a heavy sharp sand, such as washed Holme sand.

THE CONSERVATIONIST'S 'V'-NOTCH TECHNIQUE

The following construction method is for larger lined pools or lakes, or pools with a 'natural' look and an undefined edge, where no cement or concrete is required; this is known as the 'conservationist's V-notch technique'. It is a technique employed by many contractors that does away with the absolute necessity for accuracy and precision.

POOL PROFILE OF THE 'V' NOTCH TECHNIQUE

Typical edge-fixing detail for large pool or lakes lined with a flexible pool liner – this gives a natural look and an undefined edge …

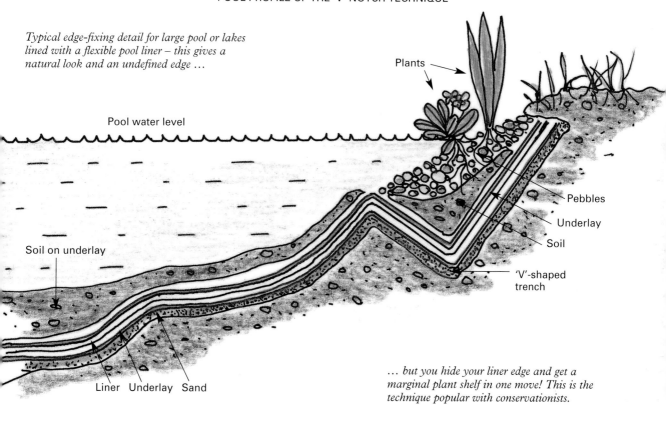

Plants

Pool water level

Soil on underlay

Pebbles

Underlay

Soil

'V'-shaped trench

Liner Underlay Sand

… but you hide your liner edge and get a marginal plant shelf in one move! This is the technique popular with conservationists.

1. Define your water level with pegs, and excavate the site as a shallow dish to the depth required.
2. A 'V'-shaped trench is excavated around the rim of the pool; on the inside of the pool the trench level is below water level. The outer slope of the trench is just a little steeper than the general camber of the inside of the pool, and finishes at a line well above the defined water level.
3. The whole pool area and the trench are lined with sand, and preferably a pool underlay or ceramic felt.
4. The liner is laid on top of this, and pushed into the 'V' of the trench.
5. The trench is further lined with underlay, and can then be filled with sifted soil so that the water level does not wash this away. Then this soil is held in place by a layer of pebbles. The BTCV (The British Trust for Conservation Volunteers), a charitable group that organizes conservation schemes, fills the trench with a heavy sharp sand like washed Holme sand. The sand works as a perfectly sterile planting medium that does not add any pollutants to the water, whilst the rapid build-up and rotting of detritus in the pool soon provides enough nutrition for plant life to get established.
6. Plant marginal plants down through the layer of pebbles. Doing it this way, the trench becomes both the anchor for the liner and the marginal planting area.

USING A BENTONITE MATTING LINER

(*See also* photos, page 40) Excavate your pool with a level edge that will be 15cm (6in) above your proposed water level. It should be smooth and stone-free. The suggested inside slope of the excavation should not exceed 2.5/1 in order that the inside cover material, be it soil or pebbles, does not roll down, exposing the matting to the water. Around the outside of the level edge, a trench 30cm (12in) wide and 30cm deep is cut into the soil. This will act as an anchor trench for the mat.

The mat is placed in the trench, and held in place by compacted soil backfill and extended down into the excavation. All rolls are run down, and fitted into place with the use of a craft knife.

Overlaps at the joints should be a minimum of 15cm (6in). They will seal with each other, but to ensure that debris does not push between the sheets at this stage, a paste mastic can be used to bind them.

Backfill materials such as raw clay or subsoil, gravel or pebbles are placed in the pool to a minimum depth of 20cm (8in). Where practical, this can be compacted to help hold it in place.

CREATING A BOG GARDEN

The temptation is to make a bog garden an integral part of the pool, which you can do if you just stick to 'marginal plants' and give it the *impression* of being a boggy area. The dictionary definition of a 'bog' is 'a wet and soggy area, usually very acid', meaning that the plants tolerant of these conditions would be lime haters. However, for our purposes the conditions will be merely wet and soggy, but not necessarily acidic (although for those of you with limey soil, this is the perfect opportunity to grow those plants you always thought you couldn't). Neither will it be as soggy as those areas tolerated by the marginal plants. It will be an area appreciated by a huge contingent of plants that love damp soil, but which also like the dampness to be draining away: it is merely water hindered around their roots.

It is therefore necessary to construct a bog garden as a separate entity from the pool, where you can grow the plants that are particular to that environment. If the bog is a backdrop to the pond, then with the help of a layer of mulch, the plants will soon obscure the dividing line between the marginal areas and the bog. With a bog garden next to a pool there is the opportunity for the pool to provide the bog garden with excess water via an overflow when there is heavy rain.

The plants for this bog garden would be mostly perennials, so it is unlikely that the excavation for your bog garden need be more than half a metre deep (20in) at the most. You can have shallower regions closer to the pool where you might imagine smaller plants would carpet the area from the pool edge in amongst the taller damp-lovers.

Bog Garden Construction

1. Mark out the site and remove the turf. Save it if it is weed free. If you hit a solid pan of clay, dig a drainage trench through it a spade-width wide and with a 'fall-away' to a part of the garden where it will drain away. Fill the trench with clean rubble, and cover it with a layer of mypex or very well punctured plastic.

2. Excavate to a depth of roughly half a metre (20in) at one end, rising to 15cm (6in) at the other. If the soil is reasonable, as it might be if under a thick, weed-free sward of grass, then save it. Consolidate the sloping sides, ensuring that there is a firm, level edge around the top that will take some edging stones.

3. Line the excavation with cheap liner material, black plastic, the off-cuts of the pool liner. Even an old plastic pool liner will do, because it won't see the light of day – in particular the ultra-violet light from the sun – and so the material is unlikely to further deteriorate.

4. Puncture the base of the pool liner all over with a garden fork.

5. Pour in a layer of clean, inert gravel to approximately 10cm (4in) to help with the drainage. Place the turf on top of this upside down, or perhaps a layer of hessian.

6. Replace some of the soil, mixed half and half with compost or leaf mould. If you are importing soil, the mix should be 7 parts loam (good, chemical-free garden soil), 6 parts leaf mould (or John Innes No.1 equivalent – soilless compost with no nutrients), and 2 parts sand (plus 35 per sq m/2oz per sq yd surface area of bonemeal). If you import sterilized loam you can be sure of avoiding the arch-bane of bog gardens: weeds. You could also

TOP RIGHT: *Mark out the site and remove the turf. Save it if it is weed free.*

MIDDLE RIGHT: *Excavate to a depth of roughly 50cm (20in) at one end, rising to 15cm (6in) at the other.*

LOWER MIDDLE RIGHT: *Puncture the base of the pool liner all over with a garden fork.*

BOTTOM RIGHT: *Pour in a layer of clean inert gravel to approximately 10cm (4in) to help with the drainage.*

Replace some of the soil mixed half and half with compost or leaf mould.

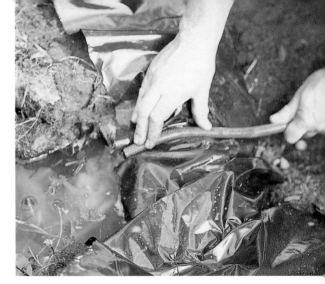

Insert an overflow from the pond down into the gravel.

Make an 'instant bog irrigation device' by drilling holes in a piece of tubing or waste pipe blanked off at one end.

Drape it through the excavation, about two-thirds down, with the open end emerging above soil level at a convenient position to pour water down it.

Plant the bog garden as if you were planting an herbaceous border.

Lay a 20cm- (8in) deep layer of bark to suppress weeds.

Water the plants in, especially from below, using the 'instant bog irrigation device'!

And there you are! Next year it is beginning to look well established.

import some low pH soil and use this opportunity to try some acid-loving plants.

7. Insert an overflow from the pond down into the gravel.

8. Make an instant bog irrigation device by drilling holes in a piece of tubing or waste pipe blanked off at one end. Drape it through the excavation, about two thirds down, with the open end emerging above soil level at a convenient position to pour water down it.

9. Plant the bog garden as if you were planting a herbaceous border (*see* The Bog Garden, page 188).

10. Lay down a 20cm (8in) deep layer of bark to suppress weeds. This is when you begin to con-template duck soup for supper!

11. Water in the plants, especially from below.

12. And there you are! By the following year it will be starting to look well established – and no weeds!

RAISED POOLS

The following staged instructions are for a simple raised pool using a preformed shape or a flexible liner.

Essential tools:
Spade, shovel, level, trowel, pegs, lump hammer.

Materials:
Sand, cement, 15–20mm chippings (to dust), stone or brick.
For capping the edge you might want to use special capping stones, engineering brick, slabs, crazy paving – good for awkward shapes, giving a rustic look – or even wood to soften otherwise hard, stony, formal landscaping.

1. For a preformed fibreglass or plastic pool, choose your pool shape. A formal shape looks best close to the house, either angular to fit in with the patio shape, or round for a wishing-well effect. If it is only partially raised with part set into a bank, then any simple shape will do.

2. Place the pool 'in situ'. Level the site where the pool is to be placed, so that it is sitting roughly at the level you would wish it to be.

For flexible liners, you will need to map out your own shape, thinking in terms of making a complete skeleton that will support your liner level on the inside and your facing stone on the outside. Both the blockwork and the facing will need a footing.

Footings for Preformed Pools

3. Mark out the edge of the pool on the ground using a plumb line or a vertical spirit level. Use this as a guide to dig a trench 10cm (4in) deep for footings all the way round the pool. Take the trench under the pool the same width as the pool rim. It should be as wide as the top of the pool is designed to be. If the top of the pool is going to double as a bench for seating, then it needs to be at least 30cm (12in) wide.

There is a good argument for excavating the whole area underneath the pool and laying a con-crete pad to support the entire pool area. If the material of the pool liner is particularly flimsy or the

ground is loose soil or 'made up' ground, a concrete pad will make the feature a self-contained structure whilst serving as a footing for any concrete blocks laid under the marginal shelves. Always remember that water is heavy stuff, weighing in at 4.5kg (10lb) a gallon (4.5ltr): this means that a modest 200 gallon (900ltr) pond weighs the best part of a ton when it's full of water (so roof gardens, beware!).

If you are incorporating a raised bed, bog garden or filter system, then a second separate trench that takes in all these must run round the planned

ABOVE: *A part-raised pool by the author at Clack's Farm, venue for the Central TV programme* Gardening Time.

This fibreglass liner is placed in position.

Footings for the concrete-block support are in place.

designed area for the feature. This must be wide enough to take the concrete-block skeleton and the width of any facing stone – 30cm (12in) minimum.
4. In the trench, hammer in the pegs level with the foundation for the patio, or 3 to 5cm (1–2in) below the lowest point of the surrounding land around the projected pool. The pegs will all be level with each other, and will serve as a guide to levelling out the concrete for the footings.
5. Mix concrete in a ratio of six shovels of chippings-to-dust to one of cement, or 4:2:1 of 15–20mm chippings, sharp sand and cement. Lay it in the trench level with the tops of the pegs, and tamp it down with a sturdy length of wood to consolidate it and remove any air pockets.

Blockwork for Preformed Pools

6. Once the concrete has 'gone off', lay 10cm (4in) concrete blocks around the shape of the pool, coming up under its rim; they should end up just supporting it when they are in place, sitting on a 15–30mm (½–1in) layer of sand.
7. The support can be made more effective by excavating the soil inside the blockwork construction as

The concrete blocks are laid around the shape of the outside of this fibreglass pool. Some blocks will be laid for support under the marginal ledges. Note the footing for the stream support.

far as is necessary, or building up on the top of the blockwork with bricks or just a fillet of cement.

If you are using a rigid pool liner, which would not be strong enough to support itself when full of water because of its flimsy nature, then a concrete block support must be laid underneath the marginal shelf areas. The blocks around the base should be laid with gaps or pipes or drainage holes within the upright joints every metre to allow for drainage, especially where the blocks are defining a raised planted area.

The blocks around underneath the rim of the pool need to be laid with 5cm (2in) gaps between them. You will use these gaps to feed in the backfill of sand as the stone cladding is built up.

8. You can pour in the majority of this backfill as the blocks go up.

9. If you are considering having a fountain in the pond or a waterfall into it, then you will need to install the electrical supply through the wall of the poolside before it is too late. Place a length of 20mm tubing or electricity conduit pipe next to the blockwork, near to where the electricity supply arrives at the poolside. The cable will run through the conduit up behind the facing of the blockwork to a junction box set within the facing that links up to connections for the pumps and any transformers for lighting and so on.

For the next stage, stage 10, *see* Constructing the Facings, page 77.

Footings and Blockwork for a Raised Flexible Liner Pool

The process for a flexible liner pool is much the same as a pool with a rigid liner, except that the blockwork has to define the marginal shelf areas inside the pool. You are effectively building a complete skeleton of concrete blocks to support the flexible rubber or PVC liner.

Facings

Once all the concrete blocks are in place it is time to face all the visible ones with a material that is more in keeping with what you had planned. This can be brick, stone or wood again, or the concrete blocks can even be rendered and painted. Big square timbers (railway sleepers used to be ideal) laid horizontally were the quickest option for a formal shape. Pinned together well with reed bars (concrete reinforcement bars) running down through them, you could dispense with the blockwork skeleton, apart from underneath the marginal shelves. Upright timbers would need to be set in a trench of their own in front of the blockwork; this

The blockwork complete on the pool; the fibreglass rigid liner is fitted. The blockwork skeleton for the stream is nearing completion.

would need to be tanalized timber set in at least 15cm (6in) of concrete.

Alternatively, I have seen timbers fixed against blocks with holes drilled as for screws and then held in place with 'hammer fixings' – screws hammered into place already in their own 'rawlplug'.

If the wall around the pool needs to be as narrow as possible, then **crazy paving** is effective, applied to a render of a strong mix of 3:1 sand and cement, and a good dollop of SBR bonding.

For a **brick facing**, I would recommend a hard engineering brick that gives a smoothness that is not abrasive to clothing. Specialist brick companies can find just the brick that is suitable, and very often in a variety of shapes for the capping.

ABOVE: *The marginal shelf, 23cm (9in) below the final water level, has to be built in as an added structure in a raised pool. Note the backfill behind the facing stone as it is built up. This is a 'drystone' effect wall.*

Upright timber around a rigid pool on the Federation of British Aquatic Societies stand at Hampton Court Flower Show 2000.

Large pieces of timber, such as sleepers, form the main structure of this pool in a garden by Cherry Burton at the 2002 Hampton Court Flower Show. The liner is obscured in a sandwich of timber on the inside.

The stone facing for this raised 'alpine-style' pool at Blagdon Water Gardens in Somerset is waste stone found in local fields. The stream is lined with the same. The capping around the edge is white lias crazy-paving limestone.

Stone facing can be laid randomly (*see* sidebar), or coursed like brickwork. The stone can be 'dressed' – that is, cut to more or less formal shapes on at least one face – or you can have free stone. The latter is much cheaper, but there is more waste depending on what type of stone it is.

Constructing the Facings

If you have decided to use stone for the facing for your pool, then you can proceed with construction as follows:

10. The stone should be laid on a bed of mortar approximately 10 to 15mm (roughly ½in) thick, and gently tapped into place until the mortar starts to bulge out. Ensure there is a good solid backing of mortar behind the stone. Large gaps can be filled with loose stone put into the mortar; this gives it more strength and saves on mortar. The mortar mix is 3:1 sand:cement, and it is more durable and elastic if one shovelful of builder's lime is added to every six of sand.

11. When the mortar has been allowed to 'go off' for several hours it can be raked out with a blunt trowel and the stone brushed clean with a stiff brush. Or if you were particularly ambitious, you can 'cut away' with a trowel around the stone to give a raised pointing.

RANDOM STONEWALLING TECHNIQUES

The technique of random stonework is to work in your 'mind's eye' in courses, working gradually upwards all along a particular stretch. On a straight flat wall, perhaps for the face of a formal pool, you start with the corners where the best and squarest stones go. These are the quoins.

Next you go on to the base stones. There needs to be a pattern of large stones around the base (remember the gaps or pipes for drainage), and these provide a link into which all the other stones knit – rather like a jigsaw puzzle with no picture. With a little practice you develop an eye for the right stone for the right place.

One old stonemason's rule is that once you have picked up a stone you must never put it down until you've found a place for it: this is easier than looking for a stone for a particular place. If you lose your eye for it, give up and have a cup of tea, or better still a draught of cider. Things will go a lot more swimmingly when you come back to it.

A stone should just look as though it fits. If it wants to tip back or it rocks, then it can be held in place with a small wedge at the back. Minor adjustments can be made to stones that do not quite fit with a lump hammer, or ideally a stone hammer with a scudgeon bit at one end.

Good stonewalling, like this Welsh slate wall by Dougie Knight, can be a work of art.

WHICH TECHNIQUE?

The most suitable technique will probably be one that is in the vernacular for your area. For instance, a particularly rural effect can be achieved if a little extra care is taken with the stones fitting together and making sure that the cement does not show from the front. With a good solid backfill of mortar, a rustic 'drystone' effect can be achieved with the strength of a wall laid with mortar.

Reconstituted stone facing: Using pre-cast or stone-effect concrete facings requires a certain amount of experience to maintain the clean lines and sharp, neat appearance that the products give when well laid. Using cement colouring of the right hue in the pointing allows for a bit of novice experimenting.

TOP LEFT: *Pointing 'cut away' to give a raised finish around this white lias walling.*

LEFT: *Marshall's Stone Products garden at the 1999 Hampton Court Flower Show, 'Garden Through the Ages', showed an admirable use of concrete products for facing a water feature.*

BELOW: *Around this raised fibreglass pool the pointing has been raked out for simplicity. One of the contour paving slabs is used as a guide to ensure the wall does not get too wide. There needs to be an overhang on both sides of about 2cm (1in).*

12. If you want a junction box for the electrics, don't forget it to build it in, and don't forget to build in a tube to carry the pump cable. Leave a strong chord or thin wire lying in the tube to help you pull through the pump cable when you install it.

13. As you work towards the top, fill in the remainder of the backfill of sand behind the blocks supporting the preformed pool liner.

CONCRETE POOLS

Concrete pools need to be 10cm (4in) thick and reinforced; over 20sq m (215sq ft), and they need to be 15cm (6in) thick. A fibre-reinforced waterproof mix helps, but more important than this, for maximum strength you need to render the whole surface of the inside of the pool in one day. The concrete can go down in as many coats as it takes to get the required thickness, as long as each coat is complete. Try to have all the coats laid on consecutive days, or if bad weather interrupts, ensure the surface of the render is allowed to mature as slowly as possible by being protected by damp matting or hessian.

Added insurance for all concrete pools can be obtained at the expense of a cheap liner laid in the excavation before the concreting starts. A geomembrane mat on top of this is a good idea: it gives the liner the protection it needs as the concrete goes in, it also gives the concrete something to stick to, and it provides a bit of extra reinforcement.

Douglas Knight at the Chelsea Flower Show in 1997 showing how to use rock to give a truly natural look; however, his pools are always lined with concrete underneath.

Method of Construction

For an ordinary informal pool set in level, consolidated ground, excavate your pool using pegs as a guide, as you would with a liner excavation; but your excavation will need to be 10 to 15cm (4 to 6in) deeper than the end resulting pool (that includes the edge as well). You will need a datum peg outside the pool to keep you informed of the ultimate water level.

1. Start with a 'lean' mix of cement, sand and gravel at 1:2:4, and lay down a thin 5cm (2in) coat. Take the coat right up out of the pool and around the edge. Leave the surface rough and unfinished.
2. When this has gone off, lay down a reinforcement, particularly round the top edge where the water level will be. Chicken wire has been used for this in the past, but my feeling is that in the long run this might work against the integrity of the cement, since ailing pools always seem to disintegrate down to the level of the chicken wire. Specific concrete reinforcement wire is preferable.
3. Sandwich the reinforcement between the first and another layer of concrete, leaving the surface rough and unfinished. Once the required thickness is achieved, finish off with a topcoat of fibre-reinforced render of sand and cement at 1:3.

For formal pools, many books recommend making shuttering using builders' scaffolding planks and suchlike heavy timber (this is to box in the concrete as it is poured and vibrated into place behind it). However, unless you do this sort of thing on a regular basis, it seems an expensive method of waterproofing a hole in the ground.

An Alternative Method

An alternative method, and for pools in made-up ground or above ground as well as formal pools, excavate your pool 15cm (6in) deeper and 30cm (12in) wider and longer than the required depth. Lay in your cheap liner if you are going to use one.

Pour in a concrete base to the excavation, at least 10cm (4in) thick.

Build a blockwork skeleton as you would with the liner pool (*see above*) out of 15cm- (6in) thick concrete blocks. You will need to build the marginal shelves and backfill behind these with a lean concrete mix.

Finish off the surface with a fibre-reinforced waterproof render laid down in one day.

This is a good technique for koi enthusiasts, who like to fit drainage into the bottom of their pools. They will sometimes finish off the surface with a fibreglass finish.

EDGINGS

Hiding the Liner

The material you choose for finishing off round the top edge of your pool is what instantly converts your 'hole in the ground' into part of your garden again. But a little extra thought can add that look of inspiration, which is everything to the design.

The main practicality is that the liner has to be obscured from view. If there is no facing stone or other material on the inside of the pool, then the liner or preformed pool not only needs to be covered at the top, but it needs to be obscured from view as the water level drops in the summer. This can be done with a strong, luxuriant planting both inside or outside the pond. Alternatively the edging material has to overhang the pool edge, or with flexible liners the edging can be partially immersed with the liner coming up behind the edging stone.

From a design point of view the edging can either blend in with, or contrast with, the other materials used in the garden and pond. If the pond is in a lawn in even the most 'natural'-looking environment, it is best to have some sort of edging of stone or timber. Having the lawn or grass right up to the water's edge is asking for an influx of organic matter and nitrates, and a siphoning down of the water level. It can only be really successful in a large 'Capability Brown' type of scheme with Lakeland proportions. Here the body of water is large enough to cope with a certain amount of organic and chemical intrusion, and is being constantly flushed out. On a purely visual level, the body of water becomes a parallel presence to all the other visible textures of the landscape, and so the edging becomes irrelevant. In fact Lancelot 'Capability' Brown, the great man himself, decried any sort of edging to his waterscapes, and the absolute minimum of planting. This, however,

This thin kerb edging was laid on top of the 'donut' foundation as shown in the photo on page 57 (top left), with the liner sandwiched behind it with a 'haunch' of concrete, and then backfilled with soil.

is a privilege reserved for those of us fortunate enough to have a constant stream or river-fed water supply for our scheme, or a highly efficient filter system.

Edging Materials and Types of Edging

The edge is there to demarcate, and often seems to be keeping the rest of the garden out, as well as the water in. It doesn't have to be obtrusive; it need be no more than a thin layer of lawn edging pegged into place in plastic, wood or concrete. But it does help your eye and ease maintenance if the lawn ends and a new material introduces the beginning of the water – so why not make the most of it?

Patio Ponds and Brick Edging

If your pool abuts a patio or is incorporated into a paved area, then you could use another material for the edging, which links in with another part of the garden or house. A brick or sett style of stone edging can visually break up an expanse of paving, and from a practical point of view, saves you from a great deal of difficult slab cutting around the contour of the pool – in any case, these very rarely look satisfactory.

In a slightly more formal setting, a brick edge can 'hold back' an evergreen planting. Mixing brick and stone is an obvious choice, particularly where the brick edges a patio, and flat rockery stone edges a planting area.

ABOVE: *The end result was a clean line that even 'Capability' Brown would have been proud of.*

The brick edge to the pool of David Steven's garden in the 1996 Chelsea Flower Show is a neat touch in a formal garden.

With a thick brick or sett edging you can bring the liner up behind the edge and so raise the water level up beyond the front bottom edge of the brick or sett. Granite setts are excellent for this purpose.

Slabs and Copings

For informal shapes of a convoluted nature, some manufacturers of 'reconstituted stone' (concrete) slabs do a 'contour' paving slab that can be used as a capping for a wall that travels round a corner; they would be used in conjunction with straight slabs. These provide a quick, simple, clean edge.

Alternatively, if there is a particular rustic style of slab from a manufacturer that you wish to match,

ABOVE: *A simple fishpond excavated, and with its block framework in place waiting for the liner and capping/edging of setts.*

TOP RIGHT: *In the same pool, cutting away the liner behind the setts, level with the top.*

MIDDLE RIGHT: *In this formal garden, where the lawn was not quite level, the thickness of the setts allowed us to make up for the slope. There are three rings of setts, the outer ring following the contour or the lawn, and the inner two following the water level whilst sandwiching the liner at the required height.*

RIGHT: *The contour paving used here for the capping needs to be placed in position before cementing down. If any cutting of slabs is required, then it should be done in the least obvious place.*

quite often the same manufacturer will have created a range of slabs that fit together to make a circular area of paving. Mixing and matching the separate units of these circles gives you scope to follow virtually any convolution.

Natural Stone Paving and Crazy Paving

A good edge to a water feature lends a reassuring air of quality to any garden. Good natural stone, like the best English York stone, does this wherever it is put in the garden, and that is why it is so unashamedly expensive. In recent years imports of thin stone paving from India are being marketed at prices lower than many of the up-market concrete and reconstituted paving stone products. They come in a range of colours and sizes with the same sort of rough surface that fits in well with a natural-looking weathered feature. Their main advantage is that they can be cut to follow the contour of a pond without exposing the telltale aggregate that you would see with reconstituted stone, so it is the concrete manufacturers of paving slabs that have been most affected by these new imports. The quality and softness in the colouring of York stone wins out, blending with anything that is already there, providing a grip underfoot, in even the wettest environment, that is second to none. If local natural

TOP LEFT: Mixing and matching the individual units of some manufacturer's paving circles can make useful 'contour paving'.

The Portland-style stone edge to the Charles Funke garden at the Chelsea Flower Show in 2001 is a fundamental element, directing the eye to a focal point in this formal garden. It therefore needs to be of the highest quality, and laid with utmost precision.

Mark Simmons in his 'East Meets West' garden at Tatton Park Flower Show in 2001 shows a novel method of dealing with the pointing in crazy paving: fill it with gravel.

Although the pool water is not deep enough, the idea of facing and edging the poolside with a withy fence is a technique quite often used around waterways with unstable banks in conservation areas. This is 'The Flower Fairy Garden' at the Hampton Court Flower Show 2000, by Karen Maskell.

stone has already been used in the garden, this is an obvious choice, if still quarried. If not, local reclamation yards may have second hand material.

'Crazy paving', although the most cost-effective natural paving stone, comes and goes in the general public's esteem, but for the rural situation or the 'natural' pool that perhaps has a backdrop of a rockery (another garden feature often shunned by the fashion conscious), the random stone edging or crazy-paving path seems to be the most appropriate edging to have.

Natural paving is generally sold by the square yard locally, and crazy paving is sold by weight. You might think that it is more cost effective to buy stone that comes in thinner layers, but you will generally find that your stone merchant has priced it by the square yard.

Reconstituted Stone or Concrete Edge

There are many high-quality 'reconstituted' stone concrete slabs or bricks that look perfect in the right setting. There is a trend for concrete manufacturers to create fairly convincing facsimiles of natural stone products, and even wooden features such as sleepers or logs set in the ground. In certain respects they are an improvement because they are an even thickness and are easier to lay, and the wood facsimiles are not so slippery

in the wet. However, many of them succumb to the test of time in our climate.

Some manufacturers have completely departed from trying to copy natural products, and instead exploit the fact that concrete is a product that can be moulded into any shape. As a result, imaginative designs and shapes, contours and profiles have been developed. The suppliers of swimming-pool edging, kerbstones and paving stones supply products that may have their uses in a modern style of water garden.

Natural Rock Edge

This is very effective in a natural setting or for a wildlife pond, and is a very practical solution for a pool set in uneven or sloping ground. The rock that you choose can be laid starting from a 'soldier course' from the marginal shelf level, or from the water level, where it would seem to hold back the lie of the land on the up side, and on the down side, would work as low flat stepping stones or rustic paving.

Beach Edge

You may have chosen to have a beach area with a gentle slope of pebbles disappearing below the water level. This is a perfect mask for a variable water level. However, the harshness of this is only

Natural stone sits on the marginal shelf and blends neatly with the natural stonewalling, also built on the shelf. Note the hosepipe conduit for the power supply.

A beach effect around the koi pool, created by Steve Hickling and Steve Day at the Chelsea Flower Show 2002. Credibility is ensured with the varied sizes of pebbles.

'East meets West' by Mark Simmons at Tatton 2001 again. Using a variety of pebble sizes gives a much more authentic look to the beach.

further emphasized by more rock or paving, so the masterstroke here is to introduce decking or a jetty so that you can have a view of the water without having to traverse the beach (*see* Decking and Jetties, page 92). Also, make sure you have a varied size of shingle, because this always seems more natural than a standard size – despite the fact that on many seaside beaches the pebbles seem to be exactly the same size.

To cover the whole of the bottom of the pool with pebbles is pointless and expensive. It's too late now, but did you ensure there was a rise at the end of the margin shelf, perhaps a fillet of concrete around the inside edge, underneath the liner, to stop the pebbles from cascading down into the pool?

Other Edges and Finishes

Plastic and metal are becoming more the choice of designers looking for a dramatic modern effect, but unless they form the cohesive structure of the water container, panels of these materials generally need to be fixed or glued to some structure on the inside of the pool liner, and this should also support the liner, independent of the fascia. The examples shown in the photos here I am sure will be an inspiration – but beware of the impracticalities.

Course Works' design team designed this mixed-medium garden 'Mitsubishi Chic' at the Hampton Court Flower Show 2001.

Edgings for Raised Pools

For raised pools, it is generally wise to have some contrasting material as a coping even if it is just the colour, unless the contents of the pool provide enough of a focal point to lead the eye in.

Constructing the Edging

The following instructions are set out as a guide to constructing edgings in paving, coping stones, capping stones and brick.

Materials required:
Paving, capping or coping stones, or brick; sand and cement; water-proofing powder or liquid silglaze. If a good firm bonding is essential, then use SBR Bonding Solution: this will allow you to dispense with the water-proofer, though it is quite expensive.

Tools required:
Shovel, round-ended trowel, level, lump hammer and stiff brush.

MIDDLE RIGHT: *Regeneration by the Association of British Conifer Growers at the Hampton Court Flower Show 2002 was an experiment in the visual effects of putting water, metal and conifers together, rather than attempting to create a practical water garden.*

RIGHT: *Part of 'The Garden from the Desert' by Christopher Bradley-Hole, in the truly Arab tradition: a reflective pool in a self-supporting metal container.*

An up-market capping for a raised pool in wood. Even the raised bed has it, and it is cut neatly into the natural stone. This would be screwed or glued into place.

Paving

The necessary footings should be in place: these should be a minimum of 10cm (4in) hardcore or 25mm chippings-to-dust mix, compressed with a motorized vibrating plate (known as a 'wacker plate') or a hand-held 'thumper'.

If the area consists of loose, made-up ground, this needs to be a cement and mixed hardcore mix of 6:1, or a cement/sand/chippings mix of 1:2:4. This goes in 3m (10ft) sections around the pool, divided by soft fibreboard; this allows for expansion and contraction in the future. The fall away from the pool should be 1 in 40, or with the bubble on the line on a spirit level. Where it runs above the ground level or through loose soil, shuttering should be used to hold it in place.

Lay out all the stones in place before you cement them down. Yes, even for crazy paving – *especially* for crazy paving!

For Formal Edging

If you plan to edge the pool with very expensive formal paving, it would be best to construct the size of the pool to fit in with the paving. This would minimize stone cutting, which if the stones are precast, always looks slightly untidy. However, if this is not an option, then you will have to do your best with the size of pool that you have got.

Start laying the slabs from the corners and work to the middle, then if they don't quite fit, you will only need to cut the middle one (or two). In this way the formal balance is maintained. Cut the slabs with a disc cutter fitted with a stone-cutting disc. These can be dangerous, dirty machines, and a little daunting for the newcomer who might find it better to mark out the slabs that need cutting and take them down to a friendly local stone merchant. If a slab has a chamfered natural edge, and there is one slab to cut on each side of the pool, it is best to cut both edges of the slabs to maintain consistency. If two slabs each side need cutting, just cut the inside edge and butt them up together.

Laying Informal and Formal Edging

1. Mix a strong sand/cement mix of 3:1, with the correct amount of waterproofing additive.
2. Lay the stones in sections at a time. Lay small units on a 'ribbled' bed of mortar, and larger sections on three or five spots, tamped down to the required level with the handle of the lump hammer. Remember the fall of the stone should be slightly away from the pool.

Be careful not to put too much mortar on the inside edge, and try not to tamp the stone down too hard, as this will force out the moisture from the mortar and dribble down the inside of the pool. On butyl and rubber this will leave a stain that is difficult to remove.
3. Do not forget to insert tubing or conduit to carry power cables. You may need an overflow at the most practical point away from view below the level of the conduit tubing if you don't want the electricity conduit to act as an overflow or siphon.

Stonework or paving is usually pointed once the slabs are set in place. This is time-consuming, and many people prefer to mix up a very dry 3:1 mix of sand and cement and brush it into the gaps between the paving; then either the moisture from

BELOW: *In our simple wildlife pool, the rock edge is placed all around the top and the paving stone for the viewing area is laid out. Note the ramp of stone for wildlife to get out.*

BOTTOM: *The area is compressed with a thumper.*

TOP RIGHT: *10cm (4in) of concrete is laid down lower than the pool edge to allow for the variety of thickness of stone.*

MIDDLE RIGHT: *The stones are laid in place on five spots of mortar each, and levelled with each other. Once set in place they are pointed by 'hatching' in a fairly dry mix of mortar with the edge of a trowel.*

BOTTOM RIGHT: *As the pointing 'goes off', the excess mortar is scraped off and brushed out.*

LEFT: *Once the rockwork and paving are in place, work can start on redistributing the soil saved from the excavation.*

MIDDLE LEFT: *Meanwhile, the bank on the downside of this pool needs support. Rather than a wall, I have opted for a rockery/ruin feature from the Roman occupation!*

BOTTOM LEFT: *Soil is contoured around it.*

BELOW: *When it is planted up, by the beginning of April it is already beginning to blend in.*

BOTTOM: *Now it is a veritable wildlife haven, as the plants provide clear water, oxygen, nourishment and cover.*

the damp below, or a very gentle watering from a fine 'rose' watering can from above, causes the mix to set. However, there are too many 'ifs and buts' with this process, especially at the edge of a pond: the mix is devilishly difficult to clean up effectively, and conditions need to be bone dry to avoid staining.

The best way is the one that is so time-consuming: using the side edge of a trowel and working from the edge of a board, 'hatch' or chop a fairly crumbly mix into the gap between slabs. It should be like the mix of butter and flour for pastry before you add the water: it sits crumbly in the bucket, but will just about smooth out if you trail a trowel through it.

4. When you have filled a gap with the pointing mix, run the trowel along it to smooth it flush with the paving and to make sure it has properly filled the channel. Scrape the loose excess into the next nearest gap and continue.

5. Come back a bit later as the mix is going off, to brush or scrape away any further excess. This tends to dry more quickly than the main strip of pointing, and just rubs away leaving a neat line of mortar filling the gap.

6. Treat exposed cement next to the pool with sil-glaze to neutralize the lime.

Laying Brick or Sett Edging

1. Lay the individual bricks gently on a 'buttery' mix of sand and cement mortar at 3:1. At the same time, sandwich a low pyramid of mortar plastered onto the side of the brick you are laying, and butt it up against the one already laid. The mortar should be 'just too thick' so that with a gentle tap it beds in to precisely the right level. This takes a little practice, but once you get a feel for it, you fly along. On a formal straight-edge, a string line set at the precise level of the top edge of the brick is a useful guide; otherwise 'make do' with a long builder's level, checking for consistency.

2. As the mortar begins to 'go off' or harden, smooth it out with the round point of the trowel, or brush it out with the stiff brush. If it smears, it is still too wet. If it is the end of the day, cover it to protect it from frost or from drying out too quickly, then scrape it out first thing in the morning. This is called 'raking out the pointing'.

On the project with the facing on the inside of the pool, things were beginning to get a bit messy. However, all heavy landscaping projects go through phases like this, and things can look as though they are verging on disaster unless there is an understanding of what happens next and a commitment to get the job done.

With the capping in place, the pointing tidied up, and the waterfall in place, the scene can be knitted together. The waterfall is blended into the landscape with the reclaimed rockery stone.

Brick was traditionally smoothed out or 'raked out' with a wide galvanized bucket handle, but galvanized buckets now being somewhat hard to come by, it is possible to purchase a tool that represents the same thing; however, anything smooth and round and that fits the width of the pointing will do. With practice, you will have laid your bricks with sufficient mortar that will smooth out and double as the pointing, saving a messy job later on.

DECKING AND JETTIES

Decking and jetties allow you a view out into the depths of the pool, which you would be straining to have from the beach. If your pool is quite simply a hole in the ground with a liner draped in, then decking gives you the opportunity to show how much thought has been put into the project. It is also the perfect material to link such an informal scene with the harder landscaping of the rest of the garden, even if it is close to the house. Upright timbers can be effectively combined, and awkward sharp corners can be softened with large pebbles and plants.

Decking as a surface material took a long time to become popular in this country, but sadly this enthusiasm – fostered mainly by the media – is beginning to wane as a result of our damp climate: because of the constantly damp conditions, algae build up on the wooden surface, making it incredibly slippery, and fungi and bacteria eventually break down the preservative effects of the highly toxic tanalizing chemicals, and rot sets in rapidly. Furthermore, cheap imports are flooding the market, and these hardly need to start to rot before they are

ABOVE LEFT: *After the backfill of soil, the plant life soon becomes established around the pool. Although the pool plants were slow to get established here, there is a sense of cohesion in the scene because of the water. (The fishing line is the client's heron deterrent.)*

Cricklade Garden Club at the 2001 Chelsea Flower Show created a memorable image around a jetty and a small piece of water. It shows perfectly the usefulness of a jetty or decking over a beach area, allowing access and a view into deep water.

J. Parker at Tatton Park Flower Show 2003 demonstrates how to make a decking look as though it is hovering magically in his 'Room for Reflection'.

obviously unsafe for human traffic. This sort of product undermines the respect that, not so long ago, people had for decking.

However, the problems of decking can be overcome by buying high quality materials that are tough enough to withstand being power sprayed each spring to strip them clean of the algae, or a wire brushing and an extra coat of preservatives. (If you have gone to the added expense of using redwood or cedar, the preservative may not be necessary.)

For persistent slipperiness under trees and in the shade, there are 'non-slip' varnishes available; however, bodies such as the National Trust or the Royal Horticultural Society, always conscious of 'health and safety' procedures, generally resort to using close-knit chicken wire on horizontal surfaces of wood, stapled into place.

Decking Construction

Decking needs support from bearer timbers, which are in turn supported by pillars or posts. The pillars within the pool itself will obviously be under water,

The routed surface helps prevent slipperiness in the winter, but so does good quality timber that does not absorb water like a sponge.

A jetty that has its supports for the cross-beams down into the water must have a substantial concrete foundation below the water.

Metal grills are a recent innovation exploited by some modern-thinking designers. With these, you can see the action in the water below you, as in this garden 'Le Salon Flotant' at the Garden Festival at Chaumont-sur-Loire 2000.

and these can be either brick columns with a damp-proofing membrane between the brickwork and timber, or substantial wooden posts heavily treated with non-toxic preservative. The liner to the pool must be protected with several layers of liner material underneath the brickwork or wood.

However, by far the best ploy is to try and gain as much support from outside the pool as possible, when fence-post spikes can support the posts. If the ground is too soft or boggy, concrete footings will be required for the posts.

The support posts should be a minimum of 10 × 10cm (4 × 4in), and set in or cut level at anything less than 1.8m (6ft) apart. The posts are spanned by 'bearer' timbers, which should be at least 7.5 × 10cm (3 × 4in), and either coach-bolted to the sides or nailed on top of the posts.

The bearer timbers support the joists (also 7.5 × 10cm), which run at right angles to the decking and support it wherever it changes direction. The joists should be about 1m (3ft) apart. Joists might not be necessary in a very simple low-level arrangement.

The decking itself should be lengths of 2.5 × 5cm planking with bevelled edges. The decking timbers

THE EFFECTS OF BANNING CREOSOTE

The current ban on timbers treated with creosote means that the days of railway sleepers oozing tar or oily preservatives have gone; but with a market niche to fill, good-quality heavy timbers treated with safe preservatives are readily available.

should stick out over the bearers by at least 8cm (3in) to hide them from view. When constructing decking, leave the final trimming until the end. Fixings should be countersunk and should be galvanized or brass, although the main beams can be fixed with self-tapping, bolt-capped screws driven in with a strong power screwdriver manufactured specifically for the purpose.

Timber Edging

This could be an upright timber edging as a facing to a gravel board pegged into place with the liner sandwiched in between. The timber must be treated, so whatever treatment is used ensure it will not have any polluting effect on the water and life in the pond. Oak and Elm do not need treating. The point where the gravel board and the timber edging are fixed/nailed/screwed together must be above the water level.

I have seen an upright timber edging concreted into place in a trench lined with the pool liner. This needs to be done on a large scale to make it worthwhile, since a firm edging needs a good 30cm (12in) footing to hold it in place. This means an extra 60cm (24in) at least added to one dimension of the liner. Also you have to ensure that the wood has not been treated with toxic chemicals.

Alternatively you could have a straightforward timber edging, railway sleeper style: this needs to be self-supporting, and sitting on a level footing situated below the liner. The liner can then come behind the timber, allowing you to have the bottom edge of the timber immersed below the water level. This adds a touch of quality to what would otherwise be an edge of inferior paving stones.

Nicholas J. Boult designed this simple 'Perennial Garden' at the 2003 Tatton Park Flower Show, using simple timber edging that performs as a barrier to the gravel, a face to the decking, and an edge to the lawn. Something more substantial may be more practical in the long term.

CHAPTER 4

Moving Water Features

Those of you who have been fortunate enough to visit the sensationally atmospheric water gardens of the Generalife at the Alhambra Palace in Granada, southern Spain, will appreciate the extra dimension that moving water lends to a garden, even if it is no more than a gentle trickle. The Alhambra was the summer residence of the Moorish Islamic sultans of Granada, and the gardens were designed for contemplation in serenity. They are in fact a series of 'patios', the flow of water leading you through them from one to the next. Water is never concealed and never still in Islamic gardens, busily moving from its source to the exit of the garden, refreshing the atmosphere and murmuring through the vaulted interiors.

For the Moors, the moving water and fountain jets all had their significance and symbolism in the meaning of life. In the West, moving water was later used in entertainment, as in awesome, loud gushing fountains or waterfalls; or in a 'theatre' to drive automata; or simply as moving water features, perhaps at the same time creating sound and power for whistling, chirping robot birds in a metal tree: natural power for technological innovation.

These days we have made certain moves 'back to nature', and try to create something of the natural world in our back gardens, now that we are so far from it in our day-to-day existence. So today, instead of employing the natural resources of the countryside – lakes and flowing streams – to power the technology that illustrates our fantasies, we create a fantasy of nature powered by our modern technology.

Graham Robb created this garden at the 1999 Hampton Court Flower Show, full of fountains, some of them animated, like the metal crows. This was a garden designed to amuse and entertain.

OPPOSITE: *Pumps for fountains with fine jets do need an efficient pre-filter attached to the inlet of the pump.*

Penny Dummit and Jeff Goundrill designed, and the prisoners at Leyhill Prison built, this completely wild water garden at the Chelsea Flower Show in 2003 – a fantasy inspired by nature, and powered by technology.

POWERING THE WATER FEATURE

Whether our intention is to create a fountain or a waterfall, the first thing to consider is the electrical power to the pool. This should have been considered and planned for before any part of the water garden project was actually started (*see* Chapter 2, pages 30 and 44–47). Therefore having reached the waterfall/fountain installation or creation stage, there should already be a 13-amp armoured cable running to the side of the pool, with its own RCD trip, and on a separate circuit to the household electricity. In fact you will have planned as if you were going to include all the possible accessories and features, even if you hadn't really decided to have them or not: a pool heater,

a pump for an 'in-pool' fountain, a filter and filter pump, UV lamp, waterfall, rockery lights, underwater lights – even a squirting frog!

Pumps for Fountains or Waterfalls

You should choose a pump for three main reasons. Its guarantee: is it continuously rated? (That is, does the guarantee cover it for use twenty-four hours a day, seven days a week?)

Its availability locally, from a retailer you like and get on with.

Its performance: this includes its suitability for its purpose. You don't want a pump that needs the protection of a thick foam pre-filter if it is meant to be supplying water to a filter system before it cascades down a stream.

One pump can run a filter system and a water-fall, and these don't need to be in series: they can have separate feeds from the same pump. One pump can also run a fountain and a waterfall, but it cannot run a filter system as well, because for this you need the capability of shifting water with solids in it. If you want a finely jetted fountain or fountain ornament, then to avoid unnecessary maintenance to the fountain (pricking detritus out of the jets) you need a dense foam pre-filter on the pump, and so a separate pump is advisable.

With regard to its performance curve as displayed on the side of the box, ignore the upper reaches of the line, as the volume of water pumped drops off to nearly nothing. See what the performance is along the middle of the curve.

If you are aware of all your requirements before you buy, your friendly local aquatic dealer will be able to advise you on the options.

Quantifying the Power Required

For waterfalls, allow 300 litres per inch, 100 litres per centimetre, 50/60 gallons per hour at the width of the sill at the lip of the waterfall. If the pump is underpowered for the width of waterfall you had in mind, you can stretch it by breaking up the 'mirror' of the flow and having an undulated sill along its width.

Too powerful a waterfall can have an undesirable effect on the plants, so keep the maximum turnover at a lot less than the volume of the pool per hour. The same goes for fountains: for example, lilies cannot abide being anywhere near splashing water – so leave plenty of room for both.

So that it does not spray the total contents of the pool out over the lawn the one night you accidentally leave it on, position it at least the height plus a half of the spray clear from the edge of the pool.

TOP RIGHT: *Foaming fountain jets or 'geyser' jets are not so easily blown about; they make excellent oxygenators for pools, but usually require a fairly powerful pump to make an effective spray. This one is probably working over 1,000ltr (220gal) per hour.*

RIGHT: *Fountain ornaments of even quite modest size, if they are using the pool as their reservoir, require quite powerful pumps to be effective. The small bore of the internal pipework is very restricting. Consult with the manufacturers as to what pump they would recommend.*

Geyser-type fountains or foaming jets have a more solid and less easily blown column of water; they also make very effective pool oxygenators, they are easy to see, and are non-clogging. However, they require a fairly substantial pump to keep them going (check with your dealer whether your choice of pump will run your choice of fountain).

If you want the pump to run a waterfall and a fountain, then you should estimate that the pump's performance at the waterfall will be reduced by at least 30 per cent, and considerably more if the pump delivers less than 1,500ltr (330gal) per hour to a 1m head.

Many pumps come with the fittings for a fountain and a 'T'-piece hose connection for a waterfall, each outlet often having its own regulator. Bearing this in mind, go for a little more performance than you think you need, because you can always restrict flow, but you can never boost it (although the old style of direct-drive pumps are less tolerant of too much restriction); also debris collecting in the pre-filter will soon damp down the performance.

When it comes to plumbing and positioning the pump, remember again that the flora and fauna of

The River Oykel in the Scottish Highlands.

the pool would prefer as little disturbance as possible from moving water. Therefore site the pump as near as possible to the fountain ornament or waterfall, and raised from the bottom of the pool in order to minimize turmoil. This also reduces the pipework, and in turn the friction loss that professional pump suppliers regard as most important. For every length of pipework, every fitting, bend or hosetail, you are reducing your pump's performance by huge amounts. This also means you must fit the widest possible hose that the pump will take.

If you are running a spray fountain directly from the pump rather than to an ornament, then the position of the pump is dictated by where you want the fountain: it should be sitting on a plinth raised off the bottom of the pool in a clear area of water at least one-and-a-half times the height of the fountain away from the side of the pool.

Having said all this, if you are thinking of installing a biological filter into your pool, the pump wants to be circulating the water through the filter from the opposite side. (I will cover this in more detail in Chapter 8, Pond Health, *see* pages 204–211.)

Ensure the pump cable is long enough to reach from its position in the pond to the power-supply junction box. All modern new pumps should be fitted with a minimum of 10m (30ft) of cable, which is adequate for most installations. If the pump needs to be situated in some vast lake, then genuinely waterproof cable connectors can be obtained from electrical wholesalers at no little expense.

WATERFALLS

In nature, as water flows from one level to another, it wears away a course through the terrain it flows over, creating attractive curved banks and cutting into rocks. At other points it will reach obstructions that will hold it back: a relatively still area forms behind the obstruction, and the water spreads as it spills over onto the next level. As it does this, the stream speeds up or falls, and as it strikes the next level its character changes, so that what was a transparent, smooth and silent material gains texture, movement and noise. It is therefore the lie of the land that makes flowing water interesting.

Two water features in gardens built for entertaining: Marney Hall's 'Dinner for Two', Hampton Court 2000 (above); and Mark Ashmead's 'Private Entertainer', Hampton Court 2003 (below). One is nature-inspired, the other modern and minimalist. Despite the contrast, both waterfalls need a header pool to even out the supply from the pump.

A nature-inspired creation by Douglas Knight, with his characteristic double-drop waterfalls. This waterfall has two pumps supplying it with water; you can have it trickling away quietly on one pump to keep everything in circulation and oxygenated, or have both going full bore to impress your visitors.

The Japanese have contemplated the various forms of waterfall and stream in nature, giving them symbolic meaning and working out formalized methods of constructing them. In England today the most renowned waterfall builders display their talents at the great English flower shows, builders such as Douglas Knight and Peter Tinsley, who get their inspiration from places like the Lake District and the Yorkshire Dales. Now it is up to you to do the same.

Now this is not as difficult as it may seem, it just means that you will be building something that although unseen, will result in a creation that was as if nature had intended it. By following examples in nature, you will find that you can create stupendous effects with modest amounts of water, whilst the drain on the resources of the pool is also kept to a minimum. As I said before, the waterfall and stream should be in proportion to the size of the pool they are flowing into: if they turn over more than the total volume of the main pool every hour, it will cause too much disruption. Half the volume is adequate, and then it would also be possible to incorporate a biological filter system.

In order to limit the demand for water from the final pool, design any waterways, streams or waterfalls so that they are effectively a series of pools running from one into another. The most important is the pool immediately after the outlet from the pump at the top of the stream: this is the header pool, and it forms a reservoir for the rest of the water feature, and evens out the forceful spray of the outlet from the pump in the bottom pool.

Having water retained in the waterfall feature means that any fresh water pumped into the waterfall does not immediately flow out into the next section or back into the pool, thus minimizing the draining of the bottom pool. Despite this though, the waterfall and a stream will take a certain volume of input for it to begin flowing throughout. This could mean the addition of 10 to 15mm over the surface of the stream and pools, and much more than this if a powerful pump is delivering large quantities of water to a series of waterfall header pools with narrow outlets. Add on all the water moving within the pipework, and the hidden nooks and crannies the water finds as it rises, and you will find that a considerable gallonage is taken from the surface of the bottom pond before you get back water into it from down the stream. A large series of waterfalls or a long stream can suck a small pool dry, and many water plants are particularly sensitive to radical water-level changes that intermittent running would cause. Eventually you will be able to work out the volume of water the stream or waterfall uses by measuring the time the outlet of water takes to fill a 10ltr (2gal) bucket, and then timing how long it takes to build up and flow down to the bottom of the stream; then divide one time into the other.

Preformed plastic or fibreglass units will put the above theory into practice, and are generally fairly straightforward.

INSTALLING PREFORMED WATERFALL AND STREAM UNITS

These units allow you to create a gentle waterfall almost instantly for any distance that you may dare to go or can afford. Although they seem unsympathetic with the environment to begin with, a bit of a 'roughing up' with some emery or sandpaper will soon help to 'weather' them in. Milk, honey, cow muck or a concoction of all three sloshed on will speed that up as well.

The height you can go to is limited only by the power of the pump. The plastic and fibreglass units can generally only handle about 1,500ltr (300gal) per hour, so gauge the pump to suit the height of the top unit. The concrete versions can handle a bit more volume.

Some of the modern concrete units, such as the Rockway designs, fit together in an impressive but pre-ordained design. The main visual let-down of the plastic preformed units is the view of the lip from which the water flows, but these modern concrete ones have improved on this. With the plastic units, the temptation is to have the units resting one on top of the other to camouflage it, but this often allows water to seep along surfaces by surface tension out of the designated stream area.

It is also better to avoid having too great a fall from one unit to another. I would say a fall of 25cm (10in) is a risky maximum: 15cm (6in) is safer.

Choose units of a colour that fit in with the local stone.

Start from the bottom and work up. You must finish at the top with some sort of reservoir or header pool that will even out the flow of water from the pump. Excavate roughly the shape of the waterfall units into the bank next to the pool. Cutting them down into the bank to give the impression that the water has cut its way through over time instantly gives a great deal of extra credibility. Also dig in the hose from the pump, travelling the shortest possible route.

Next, bed the units into 25mm (1in) of sand within the excavations. To make a slightly more permanent job of it, and to prevent the erosion of the sand by rainwater, one shovel of cement powder

Preformed waterfalls and streams are getting better all the time, and they save on the exploitation of a depleted resource, namely water-worn and weathered stone from our diminishing rocky landscapes.

to every six of sand will eventually 'go off' to form a hard, immovable base.

Rockery stone lends a certain amount of extra support and holds back the soil and bedding from washing into the pool. This is placed in front of and around the top of the unit, blending it into a rockery. Where there is a waterfall face at a certain level, this should be the level from which you create a strata or terrace of stone left and right from the waterfall, coming out initially towards you, the viewer, emphasizing the cut-in effect. Putting pea gravel into the bottom of the units and around the top edge between the units and rocks also helps.

The pump hose as it exits the pool to go to the top of the waterfall can be disguised with a well-placed basket of marginal plants. At the outlet into the top waterfall the hose can be disguised with some flat stones placed upright in the unit.

Check with a small builder's level whether the outlets from the units are level. Try to gauge whether there is plenty of leeway around the back edge for holding the water within the unit.

The units should be shedding the flow of water well into the unit or pool below. Run the system as soon as possible to make sure you have got it right, waiting a good ten minutes or so until the flow has got up its full steam.

If the units are sitting in made-up ground from the spoil of the excavation, over time this is quite likely to sink further and the units to tip backwards: so watch out for this in the future.

BUILDING NATURAL-LOOKING WATERFALLS INTO COMPACTED SOIL USING A LINER

This is definitely a do-it-yourself method, and the secret of getting it right is the same as with most building projects: it is in the preparation – that is, all the work that goes unseen.

Materials:
This stream uses a liner. The pictures from page 105 show me using a cheap, light-coloured (and now obsolete) brand. I would normally use butyl or rubber, which are much tougher and easier to hide, but this one was given to me. After you have done the excavation, measure the hole by draping a tape measure through it from well down into the pool, to right over the top: this will give you the length of liner required. Take a width measurement at the widest point. Liners come in standard widths, and

A natural-looking waterfall using just a liner, a bit of sand and cement, and natural stone and gravel – though the soil had to be firm and stable.

for economy's sake it is wise to keep within one of these; but at the same time you must allow for plenty of overlap.

You will need a considerable amount of stone for even a small feature. The stone I have used has all been dug up in the garden since we have lived here, otherwise this would have been the major expense of the project. For a steep waterfall like this, think in terms of 100kg (220lb) of stone for every square metre of visible face (include the flat). By the time this is landscaped into a rockery, you are using much more. This project probably used the best part of two tonnes of stone.

Liner underlay (I used damp newspaper, but that rots away in less than a year) and sand are necessary for cushioning the liner.

Cement will be needed to seal the stonework to the liner: overall I used 200kg (440lb) of sand and a 25kg (55lb) bag of cement.

A submersible pump to go in the pool, which will be connected to the mains through a conduit under the pool edging via a waterproof junction box. Allow a performance that relates to the height of the inlet to your topmost header that will give you 300 litres per hour for every 25mm of sill width (that is the outflow width from the header pool).

The pump requires a flexible hose of the maximum bore that can fit onto it, through which to supply water to the head of the waterfall.

Tools:

Spade, thumper, stone hammer, cement trowel, shovel for mixing cement, scissors or sharp knife.

Site and Site Preparation

A waterfall or stream should enter a pool on an outward curve of the pool shape. This gives it immediate visual credibility, because it looks as though it has helped to shape the pool by wearing into it over a long period of time.

Clear the area of any weeds. (This is something you may observe I have been very remiss about. This was to my continual frustration at the time of construction and, without doubt, will be for the future.)

In loose soil areas, or where the ground has been made up, I would build up the waterfall or stream shape using concrete blocks. However, since in this case the soil was well compacted, I was happy to work with the shape dug out of the soil.

Method of Construction

1. Dig out the steps for the waterfall. The soil is fairly stable and holds the shape cut into it.
2. Dig a dish shape to the base so that the waterfall will hold water. This makes for an even and consistent flow. Using a cement mortar mix (3:1 sand:cement), reinforce the outlet from the pools

Digging out the steps for the waterfall.

Using a cement mortar mix of 3:1 sand to cement to reinforce the outlet from the pools.

Laying the pool liner on top of the geomembrane and sand.

Laying down a bed of mortar for these first stones.

in a scooped shape. Sweep out the dished header pools and brush the mortar smooth, and consolidate the soil in the base of the headers. Render them if the base is particularly stony.

3. Smooth out a layer of 'pit' sand with a trowel over the header pool bases, 25mm (1in) deep. Also smear a thin cushion over the outlets. Line out the whole excavation with a geomembrane or underlay.

4. Lay the liner in place, gathering up the folds into larger folds, ensuring there is plenty of excess material all round, including down into the pool.

Large folds on the flat should be lapped in towards the centre of the waterfall. Large upright folds should be folded flat at the point farthest from the flow, and faced away from it. Try placing stones that you will see – the facing-stones – in position before cementing them in place.

The most important rule is: work from the bottom to the top.

5. Lay down a good bed of mortar for these first stones and bed them in, backfilling well behind the base stone. Be generous with the mortar on this

Trying a flat sill stone in place on the outflow.

The base stone to a waterfall needs to be cemented into place on a bed of mortar. The rest of the base of the stream can be filled in with gravel.

Here I have found a sill stone for the main face stone, and also flanking stones at the bottom of the waterfall. If you spot an ideal stone for any situation, use it before you forget.

inside face, as this will hold back the water. Excess mortar can be cleaned up later as it 'goes off'. Beware that it does not go into the pool if there is water in it.
6. Try a flat sill stone in place on the outflow. This will give the water a fall, rather than a stream effect. Bed it in place, filling in around the edges. Make sure it is level, or at least that the outside edges are, and that they are above the middle.

Continue to work up the visible face of the feature.
7. The base stone to a waterfall needs to be cemented into place on a bed of mortar. The rest of the base of the stream can be filled in with gravel.
8. After backfilling behind the back of the base stone, carry on upwards. To keep it simpler, if not quite as realistic as true nature, keep the stonework level. You will find your 'eye' for spotting stone develops as the project proceeds – it is like doing a jigsaw puzzle. 'Africa' and 'India' shapes are particularly useful.
9. Before you get too carried away with the stonework, don't forget the hose that will feed your water supply from your submersible pump to the back of the top header pool. This will emerge unobtrusively from the water near the fall and disappear under the rockery to emerge at the back of the header pool. Also ensure there is a little 'way out' or conduit (a piece of hosepipe is adequate) for the power cable for the pump.
10. Having gone upwards, work out. Try the flanking stones for the main waterfall in position.
11. Bed them on mortar and backfill behind.

Trying the flanking stones in position.

12. The liner must be supported up to a level at which it will contain the water flow. Backfill behind the liner, so that it is permanently fixed at this level.

13. As the side stones go into place like a jigsaw, infill and support with smaller stones.

14. Gravel is trailed into any exposed mortar joints to disguise them – and all of a sudden, things look as though they are coming together.

15. Now is the time to cut off the excess liner material.

16. At the final outlet of the waterfall, fold the side edge of the liner back in on itself to catch any seepage of water under the stonework and to channel it back into the pool.

17. Cut off the bottom of the liner, leaving enough to shed any seeping water well into the pool. Placed stones, built up from the pool marginal shelf, will eventually hide this.

18. Now the insides of the header pool and around

ABOVE: *Working out, after going upwards.*

TOP LEFT: *The flanking stones are bedded on mortar and backfilled behind.*

RIGHT: *Backfilling with mortar behind the liner.*

Infilling with smaller stones.

Trailing gravel into exposed mortar joints.

Cutting off the excess liner material.

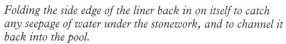

Folding the side edge of the liner back in on itself to catch any seepage of water under the stonework, and to channel it back into the pool.

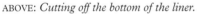

ABOVE: *Cutting off the bottom of the liner.*

TOP RIGHT: *Landscaping the inside of the header pool.*

RIGHT: *Making final adjustments.*

the top need careful landscaping. Whilst keeping the liner well up at the back, the hose needs to be obscured. Strata or terraces of rocks can be laid by cutting into the bank, laying stones and filling in behind. The strata look most convincing if they move out from each drop in level.

19. Towards the end some stones will need a bit of judicious adjustment in order to get them to fit. Also, make sure you save some good bits for the end, as it will be obvious if the rockery or the stream peters out into rubble at the top or sides. With the outlet hose now hidden, ensure that end is not too low in the pool otherwise when the pump is turned off, it siphons the pool empty, often sucking small pieces of gravel back down into the pump

20. Fit the pump to the hose at the pool end. For the initial trial a clamp won't be necessary.

21. The only things left to do now are to turn it on and to plant up the rockery. The ducks were not sure that they approved.

Fitting the pump to the hose at the pool end.

NATURAL-LOOKING WATERFALLS WITH LINERS AND A CONCRETE BLOCK SKELETON

Whereas the last project was essentially 'do-it-yourself', this one demands the professional touch. This is a technique to be used in made up or unstable ground, or in loose, sandy soil. You will be using all the techniques in the previous project, but you will be reinforcing the rockwork by using a blockwork skeleton.

Start from the bottom, working up. Imagine, as you are excavating into the bank down which you wish this cascade to run, the water coming down in a series of drops. Even if there is only one drop and it is vertical, or if the scheme is near horizontal and looks simply like a stream, regard it as a series of pools flowing from one into another for the initial skeletal construction.

This project is intended to be permanent, and a considerable amount of stone will be involved, with

Finally, just turn it on and plant up the rockery.

some quite heavy individual pieces; it is therefore best to create a construction that will hold everything in place, with the liner at the right level and the water being contained where necessary, even if there wasn't any stone there.

For the series of waterfalls, leave enough room to lay a skeleton of 10cm (4in) concrete blocks. These effectively face the soil with a hard framework that supports the liner and the stone facing that covers the liner.

This stream will have a series of waterfalls cascading down at some speed. Already there is a blockwork pool at the bottom, and a line of bricks will raise the face of the other two drops to contain the water. When they are filling with water, the lower front edge will allow water to cascade from one pool into another.

WATERFALL CONSTRUCTION

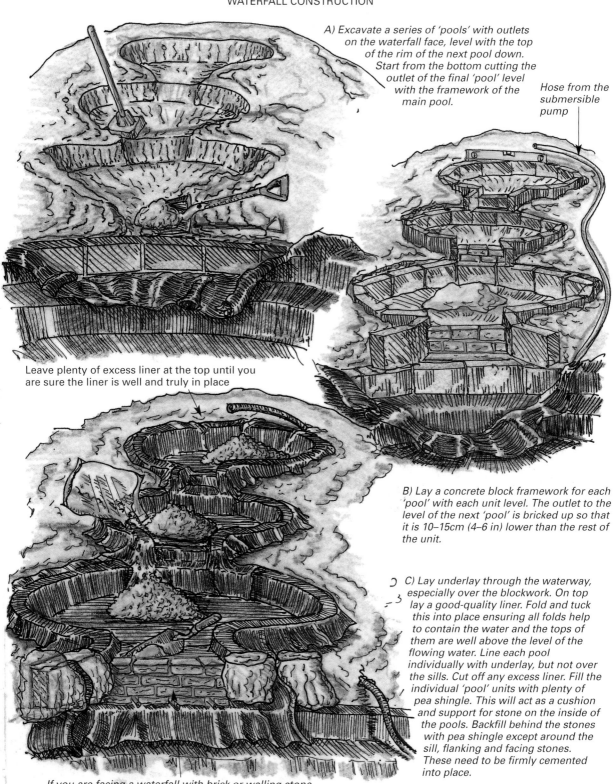

A) Excavate a series of 'pools' with outlets on the waterfall face, level with the top of the rim of the next pool down. Start from the bottom cutting the outlet of the final 'pool' level with the framework of the main pool.

Hose from the submersible pump

Leave plenty of excess liner at the top until you are sure the liner is well and truly in place

B) Lay a concrete block framework for each 'pool' with each unit level. The outlet to the level of the next 'pool' is bricked up so that it is 10–15cm (4–6 in) lower than the rest of the unit.

C) Lay underlay through the waterway, especially over the blockwork. On top lay a good-quality liner. Fold and tuck this into place ensuring all folds help to contain the water and the tops of them are well above the level of the flowing water. Line each pool individually with underlay, but not over the sills. Cut off any excess liner. Fill the individual 'pool' units with plenty of pea shingle. This will act as a cushion and support for stone on the inside of the pools. Backfill behind the stones with pea shingle except around the sill, flanking and facing stones. These need to be firmly cemented into place.

If you are facing a waterfall with brick or walling stone, drainpipes taking seepage water from the face of the liner will help reduce the tendency for it to be forced sideways

The blocks must be laid level, apart from the outlet at the front, which will be at least 10cm (4in) lower; this is where the water flows into the next section, and the outlet must be low enough to allow for the thickness of a 'sill' stone cemented into place on top of it. These pools I often describe as 'armchairs', where the 'arms' of the 'chair' contain the water as it flows over the 'seat' until it reaches

ABOVE AND BELOW: *The stream and the waterfall from the same feature: you can see the effect that is created when the pools are lined with stone in the same manner as the small waterfall construction.*

TOP: *This stream will have a series of waterfalls cascading down at some speed. Already there is a blockwork pool at the bottom. A line of bricks will raise the face of the other two drops to contain the water. When they are filling with water, the lower front edge will allow water to cascade from one pool into another.*

ABOVE: *The completed feature.*

the water in the next pool. Make sure that the face of the waterfall is well back behind the end of the side blocks at that level – that the face of the 'seat' is well behind the 'arms'. In this way the blockwork projecting out beyond the sill and the fall, whilst supporting the liner up the sides of the waterfall, will also contain any sideways seepages.

The blocks are laid on cement on a well consolidated soil base. A footing would be ideal, but is not always practical.

After the cement is dry, the blocks are backfilled with soil. The bases of the pools are smoothed out and consolidated gently.

A 3cm (1in) layer of sand can be laid throughout the system with an underlay over the blocks.

Lay the hose from the pump along the most sensible route. Excavate a trench for it, but save the backfilling for when you are finishing off the rockery.

Lay the liner over the blockwork and underlay with a large overlap right down into the pool, making sure that the stream liner is *on top of* the pool liner (people do get it wrong!).

Carefully push and fold the liner into place, gathering as many creases together as possible, whilst fitting it right into the contours of the blockwork. Thoughtfully trim off some of the excess where it obviously won't be required, though leave plenty spare at the top until the last possible moment.

The side and base of the pools and stream can be lined with pool underlay to lend the liner a bit of protection from the stone that will be used to face the inside of the pools. Be careful not to have this underlay folding over the top of the blocks, either at the sides or down through the stream or series of waterfalls, because it will work as a wick and siphon

TOP RIGHT: *In this example the landscaper has cast a series of steps in concrete, and will lay supporting blocks at the side later to contain the water sideways. This will make a great cascade, but it will not hold water because there are no individual pools as such.*

MIDDLE RIGHT: *The pool liner lies over the stream liner.*

BOTTOM RIGHT: *Because this stone has so much character, the landscaper is trying to use the individual stones in such a way that they lend their character to the stream at the same time as guiding the flow. This is very difficult, since according to Murphy's Law these stones will never fit together. He is infilling as he goes.*

ABOVE: *After some time the project does seem to come together, though because of the thickness of the stone the ground will have to be made up at the side.*

BELOW: *As the cascade nears completion, the blockwork is added round the sides, now that he knows how high the liner needs supporting. Note that there is a distinct header pool that will even out the flow from the submersible pump. The pipe will be inserted behind one of the stones in the header pool.*

The rockwork from the sides is built up and backfilled with soil. The end result in full flow is the waterfall in the photo on page 92.

the water out of the stream pools into the surrounding soil or down into the bottom pool, which may cause it to overflow. Remember, you want the waterfall/stream pools to stay as full as possible, even when the stream is not running, so that when you turn the stream pump on, there is a minimal amount of water taken from the main pool at the bottom to get the stream flowing again.

Line the pools and stream with stonework. Start from the bottom and work up, laying base stone on a thick layer of mortar; save the best flat stones for the sills. Concentrate on the face of each waterfall, and work outwards and slightly forwards into the rockery or wall retaining the soil at the side of the waterfall. Always think in terms of how the water will be retained within the stream liner as it comes over the sill and falls down the face.

On the whole, particularly around the sides of the stream and waterfall, try to lay the stone as it would have lain naturally in the ground, following the general strata of the rockery if there is one. Having said that, this is a rule that can be broken, because as you will see in nature, very often a waterway cutting is

Rules can be broken with Douglas Knight around. With his 'Rock and Water Garden' at Tatton Park Flower Show 2003, a sublime natural scene shows echoes of a prehistoric geological turmoil.

strewn with rocks and boulders heaved up and cast aside in more violent times, geologically or meteorologically speaking.

Pull out the liner between the side facing stones (not so much that it can't be disguised), enough to prevent water travelling out sideways behind the stone.

In order to use the minimum amount of mortar, the best technique for the long term is to make the stonework as self-supporting as possible, and only to use mortar around and behind the outlet, the sill stones and usually the facing stones on a large fall. Using cement mortar gives you a really solid

SEALING THE STONE TO THE LINER

There is no point in trying to seal the stone to the liner with cement. In the longer reach of time water will find its way between the liner and the cement, and will seep down, sideways and, with the pressure of flowing water from behind, can seep upwards, thus creating a hidden seepage you had hoped to deter by using cement. The pea gravel behind the stone works as a gentle cushion, a growth medium and a filter medium, and it holds the water static. Moving water – the water that we see – flows over it.

Hamilton's romantic, multi-tiered cascade at the outlet of the lake at Bowood House. A large liner on a block face built up in tiers could achieve this.

finished feature, but it will add lime to the water, so a waterproofing agent in the mortar mix may help. Fill in the gaps and backfill behind the stone with smooth pea gravel. You will use a lot, but it is much more healthy for the pool environment than cement, and often doubles up as a biological filter bed if the stream or waterfall is in operation for long periods.

When placing the sill stone on a bed of cement it is very often best to project it over the lower facing stone, unless this is very rough and patterned. The result otherwise is that the water sticks to the facing stone surface and the effect of the fall is lost.

Stones cemented into place on top of the sides of the sill stone contain the water as it flows over. They can be on the stone if it is wide and reach right across the width of the outlet, or they can be cemented to the side of it with the gap between sill and side stone, pointed up with cement and dressed with pebbles or gravel. You will find it possible to 'fine tune' the flow with strategically placed small stones once the feature is finished and in full flow.

RIGHT: *At Furnace in west Wales many years ago a small waterfall was dammed with boulders within the cleft of some very large flanking stones.*

BELOW: *A scenic waterfall built in Edwardian times in north Somerset as part of a 'Swiss scene'. Water let out from a large header pond of fresh water from the hill is allowed to tumble in commotion over steps covered with boulders. When the water is stopped (bottom picture), the construction techniques are revealed.*

RIGHT: *I built a miniature version of the Furnace Fall for a garden for Bristol Water, whose company logo is a cleft stone issuing water. The plant is* Saponaria ocymoides, *a soapwort, which loves being next to flowing water.*

To add intrigue and interest to the garden in the photo on page 26 (bottom) we start with a seeming source like the wall fountain …

… and end with a flourish over a static waterwheel into the final pool.

OPPOSITE: *A stream in Yorkshire in a wood near Malham Cove.*

CREATING AESTHETIC STREAMS

Creating a stream involves rather more than cutting a sloping trench in the ground, lining it with butyl or PVC, and disguising it with a few stones or pebbles: this would be merely a ditch or, with pebbles in it, a 'French drain'. These are devices engineered to shift as much water as quickly as possible from an area that needs draining to an area where it can be dispersed. Here, function rules over aesthetics: we want the reverse.

A stream has a timeless quality that makes you feel as though it has always been there. In fact it is ever changing with the seasons and the years, and in that time it would have etched itself into the landscape, deeper and deeper. So even if the simplest concrete or plastic preformed stream unit is set down in a valley or a cleft, it would instantly look right.

Streams always lead to somewhere, preferably from somewhere. Where they go to, and when they arrive there, is usually something of a visual treat. Where your stream emerges into your pool, it should widen out and enter with a flourish that is a fitting focal point for the whole of your water garden.

A stream will always find the course of least resistance. Every now and then an obstruction will hold it back, and the water will back up behind it, widening and deepening and flowing more slowly in the process until the obstruction is surmounted or breached. After this it will probably speed up and perhaps become shallower, making a noise as it rattles over the stream bed and pebbles, which accumulate in swathes, creating beaches on the curves.

PLANTS AND STREAMS

In nature, we see streams that have evolved from vast, unbridgeable, valley-wide rivers, to quiet, wending backwaters cut into a rich sediment deposited from a former majesty. The surrounding undergrowth is lush, and if it is not food for grazing animals, it hides a treasured atmosphere of blissful calm. So plant up your stream edges, paying as much attention to them as you would the marginal zones in the pool. There is a whole host of plants adapted to stream sides, plants that will even enjoy the occasional flood, such as *Iris ensata*, *Saponaria ocymoides* and *Veronica beccabunga*, to name only three.

Plant up the stream itself, too. This is an ideal opportunity to do a little extra biological filtration and oxygenation. Grasses such as *Acorus gramineus* and *Carex* Bowles Golden always look happier out of the flow, but oxygenators such as *Ranunculus aquaticus*, crowfoot – the true water buttercup – and *Potamogeton crispa* with its ruddy crinkled leaves, waft and sway dramatically, adding extra movement to the action of the water.

Dunster Castle in Somerset. Some plants relish being next to water. As a stream wends its way through the landscape, small gravel or pebble beaches build up on the curves.

When creating a stream, the main limitation to the possibilities is cost: of the liner, the stone, the pump, and the installation of the power to the pump. But if you already have a pool into which the stream is proposed to flow, there is also the limitation in the volume of water the pool can provide to keep the stream flowing without detrimental water loss in the pool. So there is a feasible limit to how big the stream could be for any particular pool; and apart from that, long streams give rise to a radical increase in the evaporation of the water from the stonework. In shallow streams the water readily heats up, and this, combined with the lime content from cement work, makes the whole system very prone to blanket weed.

Method of Construction

If you have decided to line your stream with a flexible liner, you will need to vary the speed of the flow of water in order to give your stream character, and a closer resemblance to the real thing. To this purpose it will be necessary to fashion a number of

In this example a huge stream is being built using only the existing clay in the subsoil to line the steam, but the principles are the same as if we had used a liner. 'Sleeping policemen', or physical barriers to the water, are laid across the stream at intervals along the fall of the stream, positioned so that the base of the barrier upstream is not higher than the top of the next barrier downstream.

PROFILE OF THE WATERFALL CONSTRUCTION

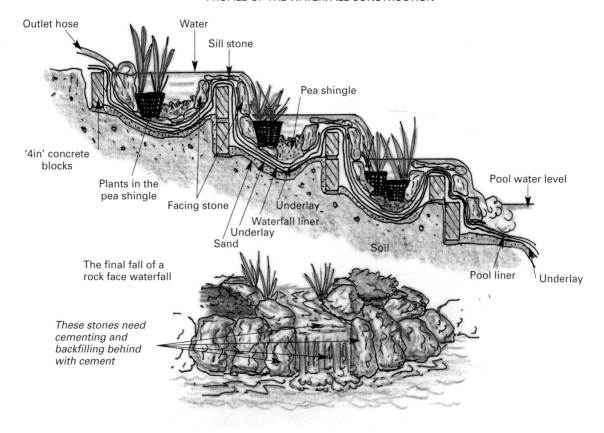

'sleeping policemen', similar to those used in urban areas to slow down the traffic. In our case they are risers of brick or concrete laid right across the width of the stream under the rubber liner, and they will effectively slow the water down and cause it to become a wider expanse, with a greater sideways spread; otherwise it will rush down the middle at high speed under the gravel and stone in the base of the stream. At other points you may wish to constrict the flow to make the water deeper and faster.

The principles for stream construction are the same as waterfalls, but the effect is different. A good level is essential, preferably a Cowley level at least. For a large project it is best to drive in pegs that mark the rise and the course of the stream; these should be in pairs, level with each other, marking the height of the concrete block skeleton at the point where they are laid.

Start from the pool end, and work upstream to a level header pool area at the top; a low brick ridge

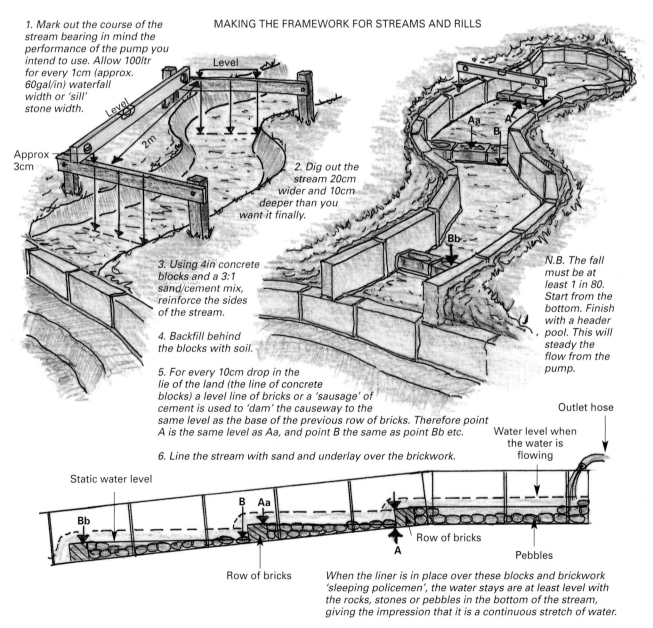

MAKING THE FRAMEWORK FOR STREAMS AND RILLS

1. Mark out the course of the stream bearing in mind the performance of the pump you intend to use. Allow 100ltr for every 1cm (approx. 60gal/in) waterfall width or 'sill' stone width.

Level

Approx 3cm

2m

2. Dig out the stream 20cm wider and 10cm deeper than you want it finally.

Aa   A
B

Bb

3. Using 4in concrete blocks and a 3:1 sand/cement mix, reinforce the sides of the stream.

4. Backfill behind the blocks with soil.

5. For every 10cm drop in the lie of the land (the line of concrete blocks) a level line of bricks or a 'sausage' of cement is used to 'dam' the causeway to the same level as the base of the previous row of bricks. Therefore point A is the same level as Aa, and point B the same as point Bb etc.

6. Line the stream with sand and underlay over the brickwork.

N.B. The fall must be at least 1 in 80. Start from the bottom. Finish with a header pool. This will steady the flow from the pump.

Outlet hose

Water level when the water is flowing

Static water level

B   Aa

Bb

A

Row of bricks

Row of bricks

Pebbles

When the liner is in place over these blocks and brickwork 'sleeping policemen', the water stays are at least level with the rocks, stones or pebbles in the bottom of the stream, giving the impression that it is a continuous stretch of water.

is the outlet into your stream. The stream itself is a channel (of concrete blocks if the soil is loose or soft) cut down into the contour of the ground running down to the pool, very gently winding if you want. As the ground rises, lay a fillet of concrete or a row of bricks at regular intervals. These intervals are governed by the fall of the ground, which should have an absolute minimum fall of 1 in 80. If the fall was 1in in 80in (2.5cm in 200cm), and we were using 4in (10cm) bricks to create our humps, then we would need a hump within every 320in (4 × 80in) or 8m (10 × 200cm). The idea is to create a shallow pool that runs from the top of the obstacle back to the base of the next obstacle upstream. The stone, gravel and even a clay base can sit in this static water as visible surface water flows over it.

Working up from the bottom, take a level from the top surface of the lower hump to the point that it is level with upstream. The next hump must be laid before this point, but not too much before. In this way you are making static pools of water over which a visible moving sheet of water flows.

If the humps are laid on top of the liner they lose their effectiveness over time, and the water that should be contained within the stream when the system was not running would all seep back down into the pool.

Lay in underlay, and then the liner. Each section of stream can be protected with more underlay – but remember, don't make it continuous because of the wick effect. Gravel or fine round pebbles make a handy cushion and backfill for the bigger stone to come.

Use rockery stone or large pebbles or boulders to bring in the sides, constrict the flow and make it deeper. If pebbles are a dominant feature, try to use a variety of sizes. You can get river-washed pebbles that come in the perfect mix. Medium-sized pebbles can be laid in a swathe as though they have been washed up to a particular level in a violent flood. Rocks are used to drive the flowing water from left to right against stone facing the inside of the liner. Large stones in the flow curl the water around, and in groups can create 'white-water rapids' effects even in the most sedate flow. Most of this can be placed in position and backfilled with smooth gravel, except at the high points of the 'sleeping policemen', or where an awkward shape needs to neatly seal with the side; here, a backfill of cement will be necessary.

It is probably better to constrict the flow at the high spots, working upwards and outwards from a low sill area. A little trial and error is sometimes necessary. Keep a stone hammer handy to adjust

Large pieces of stone are used to face the lumps. In this case they protect it from wearing away, particularly on the down side at the base. This needs substantial foundation of at least twice the height of the barrier.

As the water builds up you can see that the number of drops, and the amount they drop, is governed by the fall of the land.

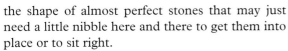

the shape of almost perfect stones that may just need a little nibble here and there to get them into place or to sit right.

Alternatively you may wish to spread the flow over a rise, splitting it and breaking it up into ribbons of flow; but essentially it is still a constriction of the flow behind which water gathers, widens and deepens.

After a constriction you can make it wider and shallower, and with the right size pebbles in the base you can create patterns on the surface and a proper 'babbling' brook.

Puddled Clay Streams

For this type of stream there must be a heavy stone or concrete foundation extending out on the 'fall' side of what effectively is a weir. It must be twice the height of the 'fall' to stand up to the effect of the turbulence caused by the obstruction.

ABOVE: *In shallower areas you can use large groups of boulders to restrict the water and make a 'white-water rapids' effect. This deepens the water upstream slightly.*

TOP RIGHT: *Even in fairly steep terrain, the water will build up and a lot of the stone will disappear.*

MIDDLE RIGHT: *Adding interest and constricting the flow behind the dam with stepping-stones.*

BOTTOM RIGHT: *This man-made stream from the mid-1700s at Hestercombe has little stones wedged in it to liven up the water, creating sound and movement.*

WATERFALLS AND STREAMS OF ENORMOUS PROPORTIONS

Those of you who have been to the Chelsea and Tatton Park Flower Shows have probably stared in admiration at the big rock-bank displays, and wondered how those enormous boulders were moved into place, and made an integral part of such natural-looking landscapes. The truth is, the project is done slightly backwards, because when the digger comes in for the major excavation, its other important task is to move the really big main stones into place using chains attached to the bucket arm. These are not generally part of the face of the pool itself; the stones for this are moved in later. The chains sometimes have a simple pincer device that grips more fiercely the heavier the weight it is lifting.

All the levels are done by eye, and putting the stones where they look right is just a matter of experience. Ledges are created for smaller stones – though 'small' is relative, they are still huge – that face the scene later, and concrete – usually fibre-reinforced – is then laid thickly through the waterfall and stream. This is effectively the integral stream and waterfall liner. Stone is placed on top of this, and

With chains looped round the ends of the relatively small stone, the digger is ready to move it.

in front on the face of the stream. Facing stone is backfilled with concrete, but a great deal of effort is then made to completely obscure the concrete.

MODERN-STYLE WATERFALLS AND CASCADES

The 'letter-box' cascade or the stainless-steel chute is nowadays more than just a passing fancy of the minimalist garden designer: these water features can actually last as long as fashion dictates. Once upon a time, trying to prevent water from seeping out between materials when more than two different materials were employed in a feature was never successful, and the only foolproof method of controlling leaks was to have a hidden liner underneath the materials, directing any leaking water back into the main reservoir. The problem was – and still is – that different materials expand at different rates when they heat up to different temperatures in our variable climate; so, for example, a stainless-steel chute directing water through a concrete wall would soon come adrift either at the height of winter or summer. There were bituminous sealants, but these would tend to lose their adhesion at extreme temperatures, unless they were laid so thickly that they were obviously and unsightly. Now there are various forms of silicone and other sealants that will seal and glue any combination of materials for any length of time, and can be transparent or in any colour. However, in a permanent display I would still, where possible, try to use a continuous liner under the flow of water.

RILLS

The slow-flowing or static rill is inherited from the very roots of garden design, when irrigation channels carried water to all parts of the garden; thus they became an essential ingredient for all Islamic gardens. They do make an excellent guide through a garden, and can be used to 'point' to an item of interest. From Victorians Jekyll and Lutyens at Hestercombe, they have featured regularly in gardens created by the Victorians with a strong architectural feel to them, and particularly now in modern garden design.

'Through the Glass Ceiling', by Miriam Book at Chelsea 2002, was a 'no-holds-barred' display of modern design techniques, complete with letterbox cascade and perspex chutes.

BELOW RIGHT: *In 'The Theatre Garden', Chelsea 2001, Xa Tollemache and Jan Kellet used a host of dramatic techniques to add vitality to clean lines.*

In construction they are little more than very long, narrow pools with an outlet slightly lower than the sides. The concrete block technique, as in the pool construction techniques, lends itself perfectly to rill construction by forming a support for a liner or fibre-reinforced render, and also a footing for edging or stonework.

Faster-flowing rills on sloping ground are also simple. Constructed as very formal streams, regular hindrances are positioned in the base of the flow to agitate the water to make it visible and audible, and also to slow it down.

WALL FOUNTAINS

These can be self-contained, and as such can be the very smallest to which a water garden can shrink. They can also give an imaginative purpose to the start of a stream or rill; in the long tradition from Roman times, we almost expect to see every spring-head or outlet, even just a conduit of fresh water, to be adorned with a figure. Originally it was perhaps

TOP LEFT: *One of the dramatic rills in the formal garden at Hestercombe.*

ABOVE: *The rill as a 'focal pointer' in a Chelsea Flower Show garden by Lingard and Styles.*

LEFT: *This pebble-lined rill acts as your guide when you enter the Welsh Botanical Gardens near Camarthen in South Wales.*

OPPOSITE:
TOP: *A Tatton Park Flower Show garden by Liz Roberts and Mary Macgregor, 'Dreaming of Italy', shows the simple use of a preformed stone drainage channel to form a rill to a formal pool from a simple wall fountain.*

BOTTOM: *The pipe comes up behind and is linked to the wall fountain with 'Quickfit' plumbing fittings.*

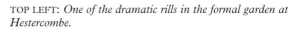

to remind us which god we ought to thank for this life-sustaining fluid, but the effect of the water spouting is to bring the ornament itself to life. It is easy to see why waterspouts with figures attached became popular.

Although the theory of adding a waterspout to a pool, or a wall fountain to a wall, is quite simple, it does in the first instance require a wall through which the pipework from the pump must be threaded, and in the case of a wall fountain, the cable for the pump in the feature reservoir needs a conduit to the mains.

The most professional approach for the waterspout is a double-skinned wall with the spout on one side and the pipework travelling between. If the wall with the spout is only viewed from the front, then the pipe from the pump can run through the base of the wall almost at pool level, and connect up with a pipe from the spout higher up.

An alternative is to build a wall in front of your existing wall, building the fittings and the pipework in behind. This can be formally rendered, or plain brickwork, or perhaps a grotto effect with rough, water-worn stone or tufa.

For myself in the past I have used just trellis and evergreen plants to hide the pipework. With some strong trellis fitted to the wall with screws and rawlplugs, I could then hang the wall fountain from that, running the pipework behind the trellis into the reservoir below. Plant a vigorous ivy under the trellis and in no time at all, trellis, pipework and fixings are invisible. What the eye does not see lends magic to the mundane.

This Haddonstone ornament could be self-contained, or fed from a pool.

The grotto effect has a strong appeal across the ages. This is a Haddonstone ornament again.

Triton Castings self-contained wall fountain uses the water-worn stone to add to the ancient atmosphere it creates. Note that carefully placed stones conceal the tiny pump in the reservoir.

A brick facing suits this terracotta wall fountain, and hides the pipework.

My home-made gargoyle beginning to blend into the foliage. The trellis that it hangs on is not quite obscured below yet.

FOUNTAIN ORNAMENTS

A fountain ornament in a formal pool gives the pool purpose, especially if it is raised. Traditional materials have been stone, concrete, cast iron, lead or bronze: the choice is yours, and depends only on your budget. Nowadays the choice has expanded even more, with resin-moulded ornaments that are frost-resistant and look almost unnaturally finely detailed. Metal ornaments, too, have a more delicate and refined look.

A heavy stone ornament in a pool is best erected on a pedestal that brings its base up to water level. The pedestal can be created with brick or blocks, and should be treated with silglaze for its lime content; it will double as a hideaway for fish, and a place to hide the pump.

Be prepared for the fact that installation might be quite a struggle – getting a heavy ornament to the edge of your pool, then persuading it on top of what now seems to be a thoroughly inadequate liner, only to find that nothing seems to fit together like it should. So be mentally prepared to dismantle the project if everything seems on the kilter after all your efforts, or that essential clamp is not threaded onto the hose at the right point.

Start from the very base, ensuring that everything is level as far as you can. If the ornament is 'in pool', start with a large concrete slab (as large as

This elegant formal garden at a Chelsea Flower Show has been given movement, height and grace by the cast-iron fountain in the formal raised pool.

Large stone fountains need a solid plinth to sit on in a pool that in turn sits on a large slab on a cushion of underlay to spread the load. Ideally there is a 10cm (4in) concrete footing below the slab on the other side of the liner.

FOUNTAINS: THE THIRD DIMENSION OF WATER GARDENING

For artists and designers alike, it is the fountain that has really captured the imagination. Art and artistry abound with ideas and gimmicks that demand your attention, from the amazing to the amusing, from leaking taps to wild wicker women, even gushing computers and swirling birdbaths. Also the way in which the water is sprayed can be manipulated to stunning effect, particularly if it is picked out by underwater lighting. The latter has come within a sensible budget in recent years, particularly in the safe 12-volt ranges. These units are as easy to place and fit as the submersible pump, though make sure they take their power supply from a separately fused source, since their reliability will still not be up to the standard of the other power-consuming products you might use in and around the water garden.

An early garden by Paul Dyer at Hampton Court in 1994, with a wicker woman holding an ever-watering watering can.

Brian Toms for Chenies Aquatics at Hampton Court 2001. Part of '2001: A Garden Odyssey'.

A Dennis Fairweather sculpture has come to life.

you can get) on a cushion of underlay on the liner. Arm yourself with some wedges of plastic – loose change or credit cards will do in an emergency – and pull plenty of tubing up through the ornament as it goes together.

Ensure maximum flow by having the pump as close to the ornament as possible, and the pipework to a minimum.

If the ornament has a big bowl, get plenty of help and allow yourself plenty of time to get it right. If it is made from concrete it comes from a rubber mould, every one is different and each presents a unique challenge to get it looking right and flowing right. A small triangular file, felt-tip pens and nail varnish have their uses.

TOP LEFT: *A Humphrey Bowden copper fountain.*

LEFT: *A Ben Pike fountain in a Garden Guy's garden at the Bristol Flower Show in 2000.*

ABOVE: *Underwater lighting under a copper fountain by Waterstones.*

OPPOSITE TOP: *Oase showing off their fountain technology at a trade show and demonstrating the effects of lights under their fountains.*

PEBBLE FOUNTAINS

Pebble fountains are my generic term for the huge plethora of ornaments and gushing water objects that sit on a layer of pebbles spouting water from dawn to dusk. Originating from a modest spring-style fountain set in a circle of pebbles, this style of feature is constantly evolving, fitting in with a modern life style, and following the fads and fashions as they arrive. The pebble pool is an important focal point in a small garden, and they are usually child-safe. Indeed, children love them because of their constant movement and companionable sounds – and this is where their real purpose lies: they are in fact the vestiges of the water garden concept, fitting into the modern, small, enclosed garden that functions more as an outdoor room than an area to commune with nature. Everything therefore needs to be safe and easy to maintain.

What You Will Need

The main requirement is a sump of reasonable size that can carry a good volume of water to keep a small pump supplied with water. The pump will need as safe an electricity supply as would a larger

A Ben Pike pebble fountain in amongst grasses. This is easy to maintain because the pump in the reservoir of water is not immediately below the ornament, so you can service the pump without touching the ornament.

pool construction, with the relevant trip-switch and connection boxes (*see* Chapter 2, pages 44–5). If there is an ornament involved, then the manufacturer of the ornament may have a pump that he recommends for the desired effect. For something with a moderate spurt of water less than a metre high, a 1,500ltr (300gal) per hour supply should be more than enough. For a straight fountain effect directly from the ground, or for a small fountain ornament, then 900ltr (180gal) per hour is adequate; and for a very small, gentle fountain ornament, even less.

For the jets from pebble fountains, one manufacturer states that you should estimate 1ltr/min per cm diameter of the pebble fountain ornament; thus for a boulder 40cm (16in) across, the pump will need to deliver 2,400ltr (550gal) per hour (60 × 40). This would only be possible with a good wide hose through the ornament, ideally not less than 25mm (1in).

For small ornaments there are several manufacturers that supply excellent robust sumps or pebble pool reservoirs. Look for one with a good large reservoir and a lid that allows you access to service the pump with the minimum upheaval to the surface pebbles. If the ornament is concrete there is a risk that it will be too heavy for many of the cheaper reservoirs and will cause them to cave in; so ask for one that actually states the weight of ornament it will support.

If the ornament is tall or you wish to have a high fountain of water, you must expect to have quite a bit of splashing and subsequent water loss. It is therefore important to have as large a reservoir as

possible; you can also extend the collection tray by means of a liner, and collect the water and divert it back to the reservoir. The tray lies over the reservoir and has a hole in it so that water can drain back into it; this also allows access to the reservoir. The surrounding area that is covered by the liner should have a gentle fall down to the reservoir.

If there are several ornaments (for instance, spouting boulders) – and this is especially relevant if they are too heavy to move once they are in place – they can share the water supply from a single sump, to which the water supply drains back along a liner (*see* below).

Constructing a Luxury Pebble Pool

1. Choose the site near the house.
2. Excavate the soil to 10cm (4in) below the level of the surrounding paving – that is, the proposed finished level of the display. Place a pebble fountain reservoir in a fairly central position. Scribe a line in the soil that marks the position of the base, and also describes a shape around the outside edge of the unit.
3. Dig out a hole for the base of the unit, and carefully excavate an area within the line around the reservoir 10cm below soil level at the edge of the reservoir, and rising almost up to the level of the surrounding soil. The bubbling boulders are intended to sit at the higher end of this excavation, and the water that flows out of them will drain back down into the reservoir. Ensure the reservoir is level within the excavation. Make sure the unit is

This ornament or 'pebble fountain' reservoir allows you to place the ornament away from the main reservoir because you can collect water from quite a large surface area. It also has space for a few bog plants.

well supported by an inch of sand, but will still lie low in the excavation.

4. Lay out everything in place to see how it might look. Drill out the boulder with a stone hammer drill. Drill a 'pilot' hole with a thin drill bit first, and work up to a bit large enough to make a hole that will take at least a 12mm hose.

5. Lay a concrete scree that effectively reinforces the slope in the soil down to the reservoir, ensuring the fall is adequate and that the slope is dished towards the centre. As the concrete 'goes off', brush it smooth.

6. Place a good piece of liner over the concrete and the reservoir, and cut away a hole for the water to drain into the reservoir. Fit the pump in the reservoir with as large a diameter hose as it will take. Also fit a triple hosetail that will supply water to three drilled boulders.

7. Fit a water-resistant plug to the pump cable; this will be hidden under the pebble mulch. The picture

TOP: *The excavation for the pebble pool reservoir is 10cm (4in) below the surrounding soil and cushioned with sand.*

TOP RIGHT: *Lay a concrete scree that effectively reinforces the slope in the soil down to the reservoir.*

MIDDLE RIGHT: *Place a good piece of liner over the concrete and the reservoir, and cut away a hole for the water to drain into the reservoir. Fit the pump in the reservoir with as large a diameter hose as the pump will take.*

RIGHT: *A water-resistant plug is fitted to the pump cable.*

The stones are cemented into place.

Plants are planted and a mulch of pebbles is added. Large paddle stones are for the centre.

The final scene. Note the water level looks fine.

shows what should be fitted onto the cable before the wires of the cable are fitted to the plug itself. Everything is then screwed into place using the waterproofing cap to the plug.

8. This pebble pool will have an added accessory: a water-level indicator for the sump. Drill a hole into the plastic lid, and insert a clear plastic tube obtained from an aquatic store, in which is a thin fisherman's float. Two rubber 'O' rings from a garage hold the tube in place. Insert 12mm tubing into the stones, and test with a hose connected to a tap to see if the water will flow down the liner into the sump.

9. Cement the stones into place, ensuring the thin pipes are virtually in position for connection to the big pipe by the triple hosetail. The pipes need to be as short as possible to ensure maximum water flow.

10. Fill the sump with water, and connect the pump to a power supply that has been inserted in the pointing of the paving. Test the system with the utmost scrutiny.

11. Lay out the plants and plant them. Lay paddle stones, and washed and tumbled slate, in the central wet area, along with a few bigger pebbles; a mix of smaller river-washed pebbles provides the infill.

OPPOSITE: *A pebble pool using a large stone ornament at the Bristol Water 'Water-Saving Garden'.*

A pebble pool with a difference. There was a time when overflowing urns of water seemed to be everywhere. This magical effect with the chain took the idea a little further.

CHAPTER 5

Decorative Structures for the Water Garden

Having created your water garden, you could now embellish it with some sort of decorative structure. How about a pergola? For potential koi keepers, a pergola over at least part of the pool provides a framework for supporting shade nets for the pool. This could come in the guise of a ruined temple that harks back to ancient classical times. Or you might feel like creating a fragrant arbour with a seat where you can contemplate in peace and tranquillity.

A decorative structure will also exploit the reflective qualities of the water. If your pool is of a reasonable size, then the dimension that the water adds by reflection creates the illusion of another space, with light and added movement. A structure next to the pool can only enhance the scene, particularly if its effect is echoed in the water surface, creating the romance and mystery of 'the other world in reflection', just as in *Alice Through the Looking Glass*.

It is important that the structure is in keeping with the water garden, and that it further emphasizes its style. Pavilions, pergolas and pilasters may seem obvious additions in the more formal environment, but they can also be used as a transition between the wild, informal outer reaches of the garden, and the more formal areas. It might be that the water garden is so large that parts of it are inaccessible, so a bridge is essential.

Japanese bridges, pagodas and teahouses are definitely oriental – and if that also means an interest in koi carp, then they will have a dual function: to

OPPOSITE: *Mark Davies's rustic bridge in 'Still Waters', Hampton Court 2000.*

Andrea Parson's 'Help the Aged Garden', Chelsea 1996, has a pavilion with a shingle roof as the focal point from which the water runs – a well-used design ploy.

Ian Taylor's 'Zen-Inspired Garden', Chelsea Flower Show 2000, has a pergola over a pool that would be perfect for koi keepers.

A sense of 'otherworldliness': a place to view, and to view from, and a place that is reflected in the water. Hampton Court, Hereford.

shade areas of the pool, and to hide filter systems. They also provide an opportunity to go wild with the paintwork. A more rustic and natural setting, on the other hand, will be better suited by less garish effects: understatement in colour would be more fitting in this case.

Jetties, boathouses and bridges will all blend in with their surroundings most effectively if you use the dominant material of the setting. Thus in a natural landscape, buildings would be best rustic or 'ruined' – although this does not mean inferior craftsmanship. In fact rural and vernacular craftsmanship produces some extremely stylish constructions in 'green' oak and other home-grown materials, such as willow and wattle, generally used for fencing. Although these products can be expensive, they never look out of place, inappropriate or out of fashion.

Purpose-made craftsmanship may be too expensive for your budget, and you may wish to embellish the scene with something you have made yourself. Structures in wood, or with a light metal framework, may be bought in kit form from a garden centre or wood merchant.

It is to be hoped that you have planned for this addition to your water garden or scene, and have already put in place the foundations essential to their construction. For instance, stepping stones need footings underneath the liner (*see* Stepping-Stones, page 148) and bridges need a foundation in the pool bank. And if you have not planned ahead, then it is time to work out the practicalities, and also what is required in material terms as regards what you must buy, and how much energy you will have to commit to the project.

'A Taste of Japan', designed by Terry Hill at the Hampton Court Flower Show 1999 has a Japanese teahouse from which to contemplate your creation; it is also a convenient place to hide the filtration system.

This pergola construction at Bodnant echoes Victorian steel bridge construction; while light, this seems overcrafted for modern tastes.

PERGOLAS

Originally the pergola was constructed as a support for vines, but it has evolved into a structure whose purpose is to provide shade for paths and support for quick-growing climbers. If for your purposes the emphasis is on plant life, then a simple modest structure is adequate, as plants will quite quickly cover this over.

Grander affairs with brick or stone supports need to be built in proportion to the space outside the pergola. A limiting factor in their construction is the size of the horizontal beams, which can only be as long as their section is wide and deep enough to prevent any tendency to warp. The supports also need to be stout enough to support these.

Variations on a Pergola

A good pergola accentuates distance by its continuous tunnel effect that draws us down its length to the light at the end. An arbour is a short pergola; it is used as a focal point, and usually has a seat in it, making it both a place to view and a place to view from. Taking this a stage further, a loggia is a pergola or an arbour with a roof or some sort of cover; and a summer house is an arbour with a roof and sides, the latter generally predominantly glass, facing the sun.

Method of Construction

Many landscapers now support the upright timbers – either 7.5 × 7.5cm (3 × 3in) or 10 × 10cm (4 × 4in)

– for pergolas in metal stirrups that are set in a 30 × 30 × 30cm (12in cube) pad of concrete. This keeps them off the ground and saves on timber, concrete and labour. Otherwise the posts need to be set in the ground at least 45cm (18in) deep, and preferably 60cm (2ft), in 30 × 30cm concrete. Another alternative is the ubiquitous Metpost timber support.

If the posts have to go on an area that is already paved or is decked, then the 'bolt-on' Metpost is useful, using small rawlbolts in paving, and coach screws in decking. A 'bolt-on' version of the stirrup keeps expensive rawlbolts to a minimum.

Once set in place, the uprights need to be between 2m and 2.7m (7ft and 9ft) apart across the structure, 1.8m (6ft) apart along the length, and approximately 2.2m to 2.4m (7ft 6in to 8ft) tall. Allow for a stylistic 15cm (6in) of timber to show above the cross-members of the pergola/arbour.

PERGOLA CONSTRUCTION AND UPRIGHT SUPPORTS

A method of pergola construction, and techniques for securing the supporting uprights.

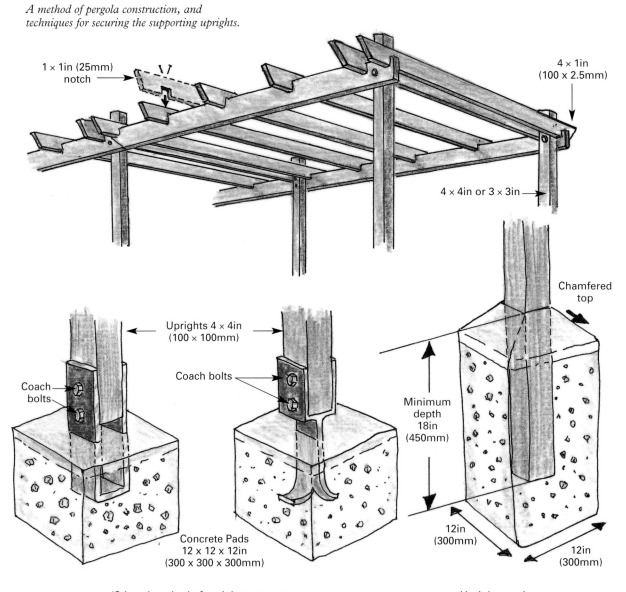

'Stirrup' method of upright supports

Uprights set in concrete

METRIC OR IMPERIAL?

When setting out on a project like this, it is best to decide at the outset whether you are going to think exclusively in feet and inches or metres, since mixing and matching does not make life very easy. If the construction has to fit in with, say, a metric patio stone, then stick with metric. It might be that you want to fill in one side of the pergola with a trellis from a supplier who uses feet and inches, in which case you would be as well to work in old-fashioned imperial.

The uprights along the length of the structure are linked by a run of 10 × 2.5cm (4 × 1in) timbers, secured to the uprights by coach bolts or just galvanized nails at between 2m and 2.2m (7ft and 7ft 6in). The height is what looks right to you, and that will be in proportion to the width of the pergola.

Most people will link these 'bearer' timbers at the point of the upright with a cut of 45 degrees. This will allow you to nail both horizontals to the upright and to each other. Alternatively you can make a scarf joint or a half lap, which will allow you to coach-bolt the timber to the upright. At each end of the run the timber projects the width of the crossways horizontals in order to support the last one.

Keeping it simple with pergola construction.

The crossways horizontal timbers are also 10 × 2.5cm (4 × 1in), although they can be deeper – if they are 15 × 2.5cm (6 × 1in) the structure looks more oriental. These timbers sit on top of the long run of the bearers at regular intervals of around 45cm (18in). Allow at least three cross-members per section, and two to sandwich the uprights. They should extend 15cm (6in) further out than the bearer timber in each direction. Very often they are cut back at an angle of 45 degrees, and are notched into the bearer horizontals by 5cm (2in).

If this pergola were set on decking, then with forethought the upright supports for the decking could extend through it to become the uprights for the pergola. However, if they do not, and the pergola is just going to be bolted to the surface, whether decking or a patio, then it will be necessary to add some bracing to the structure to give it strength laterally in order to withstand windy conditions when laden with plants. These can be nailed or screwed in short lengths between the uprights and bearers, giving a sort of cloistered effect.

There are many variations on this theme and you may have your own design, but if ever you are in any doubt about some fancy woodworking, the golden rule is to keep it safe and simple.

Construction Point for Summer Houses

The main concern with a summer house is to get the roof right. As well as making it watertight, it needs (effectively) to be its own self-supporting structure, so that when it is sitting on the frame or uprights of the building there is no force either inwards or outwards on the main points of support. The only force on the vertical structure of the building should be pressure straight down, therefore the beams or joists that support the roof must be 'tied' across the structure by other beams or metal rods. It might be helpful to go out 'technique spotting', looking up into the vaults of summer houses, sheds, gazebos and even your own loft space to get a feel for how roofs are structured, and the ways in which the structure gathers the divergent forces and neutralizes them.

For the purposes of this sort of project, wooden or 'felt' tiles help to keep down the weight of the roof.

In this building that serves as a central feature in the Bristol Water 'Water-Saving Garden', the roof is supported by rafters with the added strength of tie rods across the inside roof space.

BRIDGES

Quite apart from its inherent practicality, a bridge that spans a pool of calm water also looks great in reflection. A curved arch over the water is the perfect focal point to a pool that doesn't seem to be going anywhere, and a 'sham' or 'faux' bridge can be used to great effect at the end of a water garden, giving the impression that the pool flows on behind. Capability Brown constructed one to this effect at Audley End in Essex, and there is also one at Prior Park in Bath.

Sometimes nowadays in a very small garden a clever designer will put in a mirror under a bridge so that it really does look as though the pool is twice its real size as you view its reflection 'through' the bridge.

Essentially a bridge provides that focal point in a garden that draws you to it, offering an aspect and an outlook that cannot be seen from anywhere else, and an uninterrupted view of any fish in the water below. (Because it will be used in this way, it would be appropriate to have a good solid handrail with a pattern of rails underneath – particularly if there are children around.)

A bridge over a stream can offer a close-up view of a waterfall, and the concomitant thrill of being 'close to the action' – there is nothing more exciting than being close to white-water torrents, if that is what you have managed to create. The simple 'clapper'-style stone that rests horizontally on other stones provides all that is needed for that view, without spoiling the one from further downstream. An even simpler alternative is stepping stones, nevertheless still an exciting lure or challenge, and a very symbolic feature for Japanese water gardens (*see* below).

Buying Your Bridge

There are dozens of manufacturers keen to sell you their bridges, and between them they offer a huge range of designs, mostly in wood, but sometimes of steel or reinforced steel. Prices are competitive, but they still seem very high, and once the projected span exceeds 6m (20ft) the cost is really serious – so be prepared.

This bridge at Weston Park in Staffordshire was built by James Paine, as a complement to the 'Capability' Brown landscape, at the end of the Temple pool mainly as a focal point; very little of the lake exists beyond it. It also provides a splendid view back towards the main house.

A simple clapper-style bridge in front of a waterfall in the 'Waterwheel Garden' (see page 26).

An attractive Japanese-style bridge. With an arch like this you need a good foundation to prevent it 'turning turtle'.

The dilemma for the manufacturers and designers of bridges is whether to go for durability or weight: they can't know that you only want a bridge for your plastic gnome fisherman, and produce structures with a minimum guarantee of twenty-five years and up, not knowing that after few years, you intend filling the pond in and moving anyway. Most large bridge makers build bridges that will be safe for generations – which is just as well, because most people would need a mortgage to pay for them.

A bridge can be purchased complete, then you will have to install it. Large, strong, level footings on each side are essential, especially for a curved bridge, since these have a strong tendency to 'turn turtle'.

Constructing a Wooden Bridge

1. First of all, use timber that has been pressure-treated with non-toxic preservative (tanalith is now out of favour in situations where people or animals may come into contact with it), or green oak or elm if it will be in contact with water.

2. Planking for the surface needs to be substantial, 10 × 5cm (4 × 2in). It can be grooved, covered with chicken wire, or varnished with a new abrasive varnish such as Hicksons, in order for the feet to maintain traction. Mixing sand with ordinary varnish might help, and there are stick-on sandy treads available too. Chandlers and yacht suppliers are a good source for the latest in non-slip surfaces.

3. Keep the spans to roughly 3m (10ft), or less for a single span bridge. If it is more, then consider upright supports, brought up from the bottom of the pond (*see* below).

The span timbers, or joists, should be 10 × 10cm (4 × 4in) minimum; they can rest on a bearer 10 × 15cm (4 × 6in), supported by posts 10 × 10cm (4 × 4in) driven into, or concreted into, the bank. If the timber needs further support as it reaches out across the pool, then make an 'H'-frame structure of treated 10cm posts bolted together; this can rest on slabs smooth side down in the bottom of the pond on a protected liner. If there is a likelihood of any lateral movement, then the upright supports will need to be set in a flat concrete base 30cm (12in) deep. This can be disguised with plant life.

4. Handrails need to be substantial and at a minimum height of 1m (3ft 3in). If children are about, fill in the space below with a pattern of more rails, either vertically or horizontally. The main upright handrail supports should be at least 7.5 × 7.5cm (3 × 3in), and should have a good, secure double bolt into the substantial spanning joists below.

The National Trust solution for a slippery bridge at Westbury Court in Gloucestershire.

BELOW: *A simple bridge construction at the Chelsea Flower Show 1999.*

Constructing a Stone Bridge

If there is not too much stone in the landscape already, but enough to make it seem appropriate, then a stone bridge will impart an air of perpetuity and tranquillity. A little arched stone bridge can be made in two ways: it can be just a façade, a stone dressing to a bridge that is essentially RSJ concrete lintels running over the water with concrete laid on top; or it may be made completely of stone. In either case you will need to make a wooden former.
1. The wooden former is made out of two arcs of plywood battened together at the required width of the bridge. The shape of the arc is the projected shape of the inner circumference of the arch; this will sit supported by beams and blocks, with the base at the level of the footing for the bridge.

If the bridge is going to be all in stone, the former needs to be given solidity by tacking a sheet of ply over the top of the shape. It doesn't need to be too securely nailed together, as it may need to be bashed apart to get it out from under the arch.
2. Sort out the best, most even and square stones for the stone around the arch. If they work out as roughly two different sizes, alternate them evenly. If this is something that is fairly new to you, have a 'dry run' of building the facing arch, working up from each side to the middle, and saving a large, wedge-shaped stone for the middle.
3. If these stones were just wedged in, square to the radius of the arc, with small bits of stone or wood, they should be self-supporting even without mortar. So mark the position of the stones on the former and perhaps number them, and then rebuild the arch or arches using mortar (4:1 sand to cement with waterproofer, or treat them with silglaze a few days later). At the end of the day as the mortar goes off, rake out the joints.

Work away, building with stone in horizontal courses from the arch, up and outwards from the footings, up to the height and shape of the bridge you envisaged.
4. If you intend to face the inside of the arch, try to keep the construction self-supporting, as before; in this case work up from one corner of the arch at footing level, filling in the gaps between the stones with mortar as you go. Work up over the plywood sheet on the former in a diagonal from one side at

Jackie Knight has made her little stone bridges her landscaping trade mark, as in this garden at the 2003 Tatton Park Flower Show.

A stone-faced culvert by Douglas Knight.

the front and the other side at the back, so that you are gaining support from front to back as well as from side to side. Therefore the last stones that you put in will run from one side to the other as you go from front to back.

5. After three or four days knock out the former, and if you have bricked or blocked the interior of the arch, 'point up' the inside. If this all seems unnecessarily difficult, then you could effectively leave the former in place – that is, if it comes in the guise of a concrete culvert. You will need a small piece of wooden shuttering to make a concrete seat for it; this would treble as a seal between the pool liner and the concrete ring, and also as a footing for the culvert and a footing for the bridge structure.

A stone face can then be constructed up and over the ring in the same manner as using the wooden former, backfilling behind the culvert up to bank level with concrete.

STEPPING-STONES

There is a great deal to be said for keeping things simple, just like the Japanese-style wooden staggered boardwalks or stepping-stones, which are decidedly low key. These were designed to confuse bad spirits that can only travel in straight lines, and are not able to traverse clear water.

Stepping-stones are unobtrusive and seem an easy option, but they must be planned for, particularly in a pool. They can be pillars of concrete blocks or stone, capped with a paving stone with the bottom edge set just below the mean water level. Ideally each stepping-stone should have a smooth 10mm footing of 6:1, 15mm chippings-to-dust and cement, measuring twice the diameter of the pillar, situated below the liner and the underlay. If footings have not been made, ensure that the base of the pillar is twice the width of the column

Deep stepping-stones across a stream at Bodnant allow for the variation in water level.

Paul Cooper designed these wooden 'stepping boards'.

at water level in order to cope with any lateral movement caused by people carelessly stepping from one to the other. Also cushion the liner from the concrete blockwork with underlay and a large paving slab. The blocks of the piers should be sealed with mastic or treated with silglaze; cement with waterproofer should be used.

If you have a large stream or waterfall coming into the pool, it is best to use thick stone to take account of the variable water level in the pool. A stepping-stone looks best when it seems to be floating on the surface of the water. The stepping-stones should be set at 66cm (26in) apart, centre to centre, and they should be chosen for their individual character.

CHAPTER 6

Plants and Planting

When your new pool fills with water a whole new environment is created in the garden. Here indeed is a place for new possibilities – though if left to its own devices it would very quickly turn into a noxious lagoon of pea-green slime. This goo is caused by microscopic single-celled plants called algae. Although algae are also responsible for the production of most of the oxygen on this planet, and hence have a place in the cycle of life in every pond, they do need to be restricted. Like any bare piece of ground in a garden, if the gardener does not put in his own plants, then nature takes over and it becomes overrun with what we usually regard as weeds. Algae are effectively the 'weeds' of water, and the only way to inhibit them is by encouraging the growth of other plants so their environment is more competitive. These 'higher' plants have other functions, too, and they all work together to ensure a healthy environment in which all the animals and plants themselves can flourish.

Any plant that grows below the surface of the water will produce oxygen as a by-product of its natural photosynthesis. This is the process by which the plant manufactures sugars for its own growth and sustenance, namely when the green chlorophyll in the plant's leaves reacts to sunlight. One of the most important uses for this oxygen is to break down organic matter in the bottom of the pool. As plant detritus, fish muck and uneaten food sinks to the bottom of the pool, it is decomposed by fungi and bacteria. A lot of this would be broken down to poisonous ammonia compounds were it not for the *Nitrosomonas* bacteria, which, with the use of oxygen, convert these chemicals to nitrite compounds. These are still poisonous, but hopefully there are *Nitrobacter* bacteria on hand, which can,

again using the presence of oxygen, convert nitrites to nitrates. Nitrates are the perfect food for plants, and if there are plenty of plants present to make use of them, they take them up before the opportunistic algae use them. The plants flourish, and then die, and so the cycle continues. Meanwhile these other plants provide cover to the water surface, restricting sunlight to the algae and providing somewhere to hide for fish and animals.

PLANTS – THE ESSENTIAL INGREDIENTS

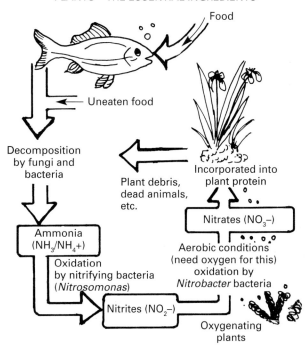

As can be seen in the diagram all plants in the pond form an essential link in the ecosystem. More importantly the oxygenating plants or pond weeds help provide the necessary oxygen for the conversion of ammonia to nitrates. If the plant life fails to maintain the link in the chain, anaerobic conditions and denitrifying bacteria cause the pool to become stagnant.

OPPOSITE: Iris pseudacorus, *yellow flag.*

Nitrosomonas and *Nitrobacter* are oxygen-dependent and are described as 'aerobic bacteria'. There is a process by which the results of their activity, the nitrates, can be broken down further to oxygen and nitrogen in a much slower process; this is by bacteria that are not in fact oxygen-dependent – they are anaerobic – but as nitrates are readily taken in by most plants and used for growth, then it is as well to have in residence efficient plants for doing this.

This is in fact a subtle balancing act. Some plants are really good at taking up nitrates, but they do tend to be very strong growers, to the point of being rampant; because of this it is best to have as wide a range of species as possible to inhibit those of more rampant habits. Unfortunately the pool must begin to look completely overgrown before a reliable balance is achieved, because to keep the water in your pool clear, altogether there must be two thirds of the pool surface covered with plants or oxygenators just below the surface. If you feel too much plant life will obscure your view of the fish, then I am afraid, if you want to guarantee seeing them, you will have to resort to technology (*see* Chapter 8, page 203).

If you intend filling your pond with tap water, note that it is dead, inert stuff, with plenty of mineral nutrition for algae, but not much else. Therefore leave it for two to three days for the chlorines to waste away, and a few of the other additives and minerals to drop out. The process can be accelerated with pond treatment chemicals, which can help encourage the essential bacterial life into action. Also, if you have a neighbour or friend with

Adding pool water conditioners helps neutralize the chemicals in tap water; it can, therefore, 'naturalize' much more quickly.

a perfectly clear, well balanced pond, then ask if you might borrow a couple of gallons, to act like a 'yoghurt starter' for your pond.

These things will help to discourage the almost inevitable algal bloom that will appear after three to ten days, and lasts for about a month. Do not be discouraged by this, however, since at least when it happens you know the water will sustain life. To make doubly certain of this, and before any fish are put in the water, it is important to check the pH with a water-testing kit (available from any aquatic dealer). If the pH remains high above the level of the ordinary tap water, and the hue has an almost creaminess in the green, then there may lime leaching in from cement or stonework. Several changes of water may be necessary before you can keep this down, but it is better to do it now, before you have all the prospective residents of the pond lined up ready and waiting to go in. Also, there is nothing that the dreaded blanket weed, the cotton-woolly filamentous algae, appreciates more than a 'limey' pond.

PLANTS ESSENTIAL TO A HEALTHY POND

If a pond is to remain in good order and maintain a healthy balance of aquatic life, it is essential that it contains four basic classifications of plant: oxygenators, deep-water aquatics, marginals and floating plants.

Oxygenators are properly known as submerged aquatics, and include any plants that are happy with their foliage submerged. Usually these plants will absorb all they need in terms of carbon dioxide, oxygen and nutrients directly from the water through the surface of their leaves, and often through the whole surface of the plant. During the daytime they absorb carbon dioxide from the water, and give off oxygen – hence their life-sustaining role as regards the fish, fauna and bacteria in the pool.

Deep-water aquatics have their roots in the bottom of the pool and their leaves floating on the surface. Generally speaking these include the water lilies, *Aponogeton distachyos* or water hawthorn, and the *Nuphar*s and *Nymphoides peltata*, close relatives of the water lily. All of them provide very useful surface cover for the pool, thereby inhibiting the

Plants are so effective at keeping water healthy and fresh that Anglo Aquarium Plant at the Hampton Court Flower Show in 2001 proved it by introducing this country to the 'Swimming Pond', where water is kept clean and good enough to swim in just by the right mixture of water plants. These are incredibly popular in Europe, especially Austria.

sunlight that would encourage algae to proliferate, and at the same time providing protective cover for fish and other animals.

Marginal plants provide protective cover too, especially for animals going to and from the pool. Their other uses in the pool environment are that they are great users of nutrients, and also serve to 'landscape' the pool into the garden scene. Their name derives from the fact that they are generally planted around the margins of the pool, although many of them are in fact tolerant of quite a range of water depths, and in some cases even dry ground. For our purposes they thrive in depths of water between 5 and 15cm (2 and 6in) above the soil they are planted in. This tolerance distinguishes them from bog plants, in that they will only tolerate moist soil where the water is draining away from them; they do not like standing in a static slop.

Floating plants also provide cover to the pool surface, and use up nutrients. Some of them have an almost magical effect on water clarity.

Finally, animals and insects come of their own accord whether you want them to or not – but are nevertheless part of the very essence of a healthy pool or pond. But they won't feel welcome if the plants are too invasive.

OXYGENATORS (SUBMERGED AQUATICS)

The plants that live below the surface of the water of the pond produce essential oxygen in the daytime as a by-product in the process of photosynthesis. From the energy of the ultra-violet rays in sunlight and by absorbing carbon dioxide they manufacture sugars that are used for growth, amongst other things. The carbon dioxide available in the water is produced from the respiration of the animals and fish in the pond, and from the plants' own transpiration at night. These submerged plants also provide cover and a spawning mat for fish (and food for snails).

By far the most efficient oxygenator is *Elodea crispa*, also called *Lagarosiphon major* and commonly called 'curly pondweed'. It is not a native plant to the UK, but came originally from South Africa; it is easily kept under control, even in small pools.

A close relative is *Elodea canadensis*, sometimes referred to as *Anacharis alsinastrum*, 'Canadian pondweed', 'drain devil' or 'Babington's curse', after the Cambridge professor who introduced it to this country in 1847. It has smaller leaves than *Elodea crispa*, and is extremely vigorous, particularly in new ponds; it always seems to fill a pond with vegetation more quickly than you can ever remove it. In its favour, it is said to be excellent at removing toxins from water. The Australian swamp stonecrop *Crassula helmsii* has no redeeming features. It merely depletes any habitat to which it is introduced of all resources. Avoid it at all costs.

LEFT: *Bunching up cuttings of* Elodea crispa *with lead wire.*

BELOW LEFT: *Submerging a basketful of gravel and* Elodea crispa *cuttings.*

BELOW: Elodea canadensis *or Canadian pondweed.*

Callitriche autumnalis *or water starwort just below the surface of the water. Other plants include the wet meadow plant ragged robin,* Lychnis flos-cuculi.

On the left is hornwort, Ceratophyllum demersum, *on the right the less stiff-textured* Myriophyllum spicatum, *water milfoil.*

Callitriche autumnalis, or 'water starwort', is indigenous. It is a good oxygenator and is grazed by fish. It sends bright green growths up to the surface in starry masses.

Ceratophyllum demersum, or 'hornwort', is very hardy and survives in great depth and shade; it can be just thrown in to fend for itself. Despite being slender and brittle, it grows to great lengths.

Hottonia palustris, or 'water violet', is native and has tiny little whorls of flowers that emerge up to 20cm (8in) above the water surface in early summer. It dies back completely in the autumn after forming little buds that sink beneath the mud. In the following spring it re-emerges from these buds.

Myriophyllum spicatum, or 'water milfoil', is a good oxygenator for small pools, preferring calcareous or 'limey' water. It has a little flower spike that emerges from below the water surface.

Myriophyllum proserpinacoides, or 'parrot's feather', is often sold as an oxygenator but in fact is apt to float its foliage on the surface. It is a plant to avoid, especially in large pools in mild areas, as it tends to choke up the environment in very little time.

Potamogeton crispus, or 'curled pondweed', is an excellent plant for slow-moving streams where its colour and leaf shape are shown off to their best. Beware of other species of *Potamogeton*.

Ranunculus aquatalis, or 'water crowfoot', is another flowering oxygenator. There are ten different types that grow in this country, some very particular about their habitat. They all have fine

RIGHT: Myriophyllum spicatum *or water milfoil, in flower on the surface of a pond.*

Hottonia palustris *or water violet in the shallows, with the little water lily* Nymphaea odorata *var.* rosea.

TOP LEFT: Myriophyllum proserpinacoides *or* Myriophyllum aquaticum *or parrot's feather.*

MIDDLE LEFT: Potamogeton crispus *or curled pondweed is an excellent plant for slow-moving streams.*

BOTTOM LEFT: Ranunculus aquatalis *or water crowfoot.*

feathery leaves below the water surface, and sometimes buttercup-like ones above the surface. The early spring flowers are like buttercups with white petals. It is a perfect plant for streams.

These are just a sample of some of the many oxygenators or submerged aquatics available.

Planting Oxygenators

Allow one bunch for every 185sq cm (2sq ft) of surface area. A bunch will consist of four to six strands of plants 10–13cm (4–5in) long, tied together with lead wire.

Because of the weight of this lead wire, many people assume that it is quite acceptable just to throw the bunches of oxygenator into the pool, and let them settle at random at the bottom and root in the accumulating mud. This is all very well until the weed needs to be cut back, and then you find there is no geographical central point of growth to cut back to. The result is that it all comes out in one big lump and you have to start again.

Instead, push as many bunches as you can into medium-sized aquatic planting baskets full of smooth pea gravel (usually about twenty-five bunches). Place the baskets so the oxygenator cuttings lie at not much more than 30cm (12in) below the surface. Once they seem to be growing strongly, you may move them to depths of up to 60cm (24in) below the surface.

DEEP-WATER AQUATICS AND LILIES

Of all deep-water aquatics, the lilies in particular are the main reason why so many people want a water garden, where 'garden' is the operative word, rather than a 'water' garden because they want fish. Lilies are plants of exceptional beauty, and dark mystery surrounds them even to this modern day. They are also gross feeders, and so effectively use up a lot of the excess nutrients in a pool. Because their leaves lie as big flat pads on the surface, they provide the most efficient cover and shade on the pool when it is most required – when spring burgeons into summer.

Allow one lily to every 2.3sq m (25sq ft) of pool surface, if it is classified as a 'moderate to vigorous' grower.

Lilies come in all sizes and colours apart from blue in the UK; some are suitable for growing in tubs or the shallow margins of the pool, such as the small *pygmaea* hybrids that are quite happy in a mere 15–20cm (6–8in), through to the hardy giants such as *Nymphaea* 'Collosea', a cream-coloured lily, and *N.* 'Gladsoniana', a white: both of these are happy in depths up to 1m (40in), and have a spread of up to 2.5m (8ft).

Yellow Varieties
Vigorous and reliable yellow lilies include *Nymphaea* × *marliacea* 'Chromatella', bred in 1881 by the first water-lily breeder of all time, Joseph Bory Latour-Marliac. *N.* 'Moorei' is another reliable plant, in my experience, although *N.* 'Colonel A. J. Welch' tolerates the greatest depth of the yellows, with a spread of up to 1.5m (5ft).

The prolific Nymphaea × marliacea *'Albida' has more petals than the basic indigenous* N. alba; *the flowers stand above the foliage.*

Nymphaea × marliacea *'Chromatella', the first hardy coloured lily bred in 1881.*

Nymphaea *'Rose Arey'.*

Pink/Red Varieties

The most common pink lily is the very free-flowering *N.* × *marliacea* 'Carnea'. It is meant to be fragrant, but looks a bit insipid when it first begins to flower. However, the colour becomes more positive after it has become truly established, and then the colour is amplified by the dark purplish leaves. More instantly strong pinks are *N.* 'Rose Arey', *N.* × *marliacea* 'Rosea', 'Mrs Richmond', 'Fabiola' and 'Formosa', all of which are very reliable at a medium depth. *N.* 'Rose Arey' is the best known, with its incurved petals and fragrant flowers. Some people consider it a small plant, but it is nevertheless very free-flowering.

N. 'René Gerard' makes a transition from crimson to pink as the flowers age.

Nymphaea 'Attraction' is the hardiest and most readily available red, but until it gets established it often flowers pink, or the colour seems to be more washed out towards the outer petals of the flower. The edges of the petals always have white flecks.

For extremely large crimson blooms in deep water, another popular lily is *N.* 'Escarboucle'. It has a vividness of colour that seems impossible to capture on film. If, however, you are planting into depths of less than half a metre, *N.* 'James Brydon' is probably the most spectacular and free-flowering red.

Nymphaea *'Rose Arey'*.

Nymphaea *'Attraction'*.

Nymphaea *'René Gerard'*.

Nymphaea *'Escarboucle'*.

WARNING TO SMALL-POOL OWNERS

If you are being offered a variety of lily for next to nothing, find out exactly what the variety is. It is quite important if your pond is either small or quite deep, as lilies perform much more impressively if they are planted at the right depth for that specific variety. The most robust and vigorous varieties are some of the whites. The only indigenous lily is the white-flowering *Nymphaea alba*, which seems to prefer to produce leaves on a grand scale rather than flowers. It is happy at anywhere around 1m (40in) in depth, as are the hybrid varieties *N.* 'Colossea' and 'Gladstoniana'. The minimum depth required for these would be 45cm (18in).

Some lilies are fragrant, such as *Nymphaea* 'Gloire de Temple-sur-Lot' – although you are not likely to appreciate that fact when is out in the middle of a 60cm (2ft) deep pond. It is, however, considered by many to be the most beautiful hardy lily. It is a 'double', starting off creamy pink and turning to white later on. It is slow to get established, but it is certainly worth the wait.

Other fragrant lilies that you may find more easily available are the *odorata* hybrids, such as *N. odorata minor* (white), *N. odorata* 'Sulphurea' (yellow) and *N. odorata* 'Rosea' (pink). These tend to be on the small size, and are suitable for small pools – where at least you can get close enough to smell them.

More vigorous fragrant flowerers might include *N. marliacea* 'Albida' (white) and *N.* 'Masaniello' (pink). There are no reds that I know of.

When a hardy lily flowers, each flower lasts for three days, emerging initially at the water surface and opening in the morning, to close as dusk approaches. On the fourth day the flowers sink. In some varieties, as they open on subsequent days, flowers are seen to change colour, often from white to pink but usually from yellow to orange. Many of these are classified as 'sunset varieties' (*see* below, 'Lilies for Small Ponds').

Lilies for Small Ponds

Smaller-growing lilies for smaller water gardens are more expensive because it is more time-consuming to propagate them in volume. The *odorata* forms are all fragrant and relatively small, fitting in with the proportions of most preformed pool sizes. Most of them are happiest at depths of between 20–50cm (8–20in). Some of the *pygmaea* varieties probably would not be able to hold their own space in any but the margins of the quietest tiny pools, and are best preserved for a half-barrel or tub water feature.

Other quite small, popular hybrids include *N.* 'Albatross' – not so easy to find nowadays, with large white flowers, and the young leaves have the added attraction of starting purple – and *N.* 'Hermine', pure white and star shaped, that stands up out of the water.

The corkscrew rush, Juncus effusus *var.* spiralis *with* Nymphaea *'Masaniello' in the background.*

Some of the small yellows have flowers that gradually turn to orange day by day, and in some cases crimson as the blooms age: *N.* 'Aurora', *N.* 'Indiana' and *N.* 'Sioux' are popular examples. These are known as the 'sunset varieties'.

Pink/Red Varieties

Amongst the small pink varieties is one of the first lilies to flower: *Nymphaea* 'Sumptuosa'; it has a huge number of petals and is very fragrant. Unfortunately it is not commonly available.

Nymphaea 'Froebelii' is the most commonly available small red that is generally recommended for small pools. *N.* 'Vesuve' is as bright as its name suggests, and *N.* 'William Falconer' is extremely dark – even its young foliage is dark red.

Maurice Laydeker, Latour-Marliac's son-in-law, had a whole range of lilies named after him. They were all pink or red, and they reward a fairly shallow planting with a very long flowering season. *N. × laydekeri* 'Fulgens', *N. × laydekeri* 'Lilacea' and *N. × laydekeri* 'Purpurata' are all red. The variety *Nymphaea* 'Maurice Laydeker' is also red, and is a true miniature, only requiring 7cm (3in) of water to flourish. Some catalogues describe it as having a 'somewhat poor constitution'.

Planting Lilies

When you are buying lilies, do not necessarily choose the plants that are flowering unless you are unsure of the variety. A lot of energy goes into flower production that could be reserved for

TOP RIGHT: Nymphaea pygmaea *'Alba' likes 15–30cm (6–12in) of water where it will spread on the surface 40–60cm (16–24in). This can be propagated from seed, and may be a form of* N. tetragonal. *This means the rhizomes should be planted vertically.*

MIDDLE RIGHT: Nymphaea odorata *'Firecrest' has fragrant flowers. This flower is opening early in the morning. Eventually the petals lie widely open, and the stamens become red-tipped.*

BOTTOM RIGHT: N. × laydekeri *laydekeri 'Lilacea' is happy in 25–50cm (10–20in) of water where it will give a spread of nearly a metre. The soft rose-to-carmine blooms are fragrant.*

Take your growing tip of tuber and slice off the thick, white, fleshy anchor roots. I have lined a lily basket with a hessian liner, and started to fill it with good soil. I have taken the precaution of using a liner, because I am trying to introduce lilies into a koi pool, and they will persistently bump the basket with the result that the silt in the soil will sieve out.

Place the lily in position and fill in around it.

getting established in a new environment, and the flower will usually abort itself by the time you get it home anyway.

May and June are the best months for lily planting. If the plants are not already planted in a suitable basket for putting straight into the pond, note the style of growth. Some, like the *odorata* or *tuberosa* groups, have rhizomatus or tuber-like growth across the surface of the soil. *Marliacea* varieties have a gnarled appearance, and are more upright in growth, whilst the roots appear all around the tuber.

Rhizomatus varieties should be planted horizontally about 2.5cm (1in) below the surface of the soil, but not covering the growing tip. The radially rooted upright stocks should be planted upright, with the root tip similarly exposed.

To prepare the tuber for planting – if the retailer has not already done so – cleanly slice off a growing tip that is about three times longer than it is wide. Cut off the thick, white, fleshy roots used for anchorage, leaving the black hairy ones.

Take a plastic lily basket of an appropriate size; it has fine meshed sides. Vigorous lilies need a large basket, otherwise it will be torn apart in a matter of months. Fill it with good, chemical-free, heavy (clayey) loam or proprietary aquatic soil, leaving enough room for a layer of pea gravel on top.

Take your growing tip of tuber and place it in position, and fill in around it. If it seems that the lily should start into strong growth immediately, insert a slow-release aquatic plant food pellet. In the old days this may have been a pellet made of clay rolled in bone meal.

Tuck the hessian in around the basket and top off with pea gravel to keep fish out and the soil in. These are quite large pebbles in an effort to deter the delinquent urges of koi carp.

Tuck the hessian in around the basket and spread a 13mm (½in) layer of pea gravel around the top of the basket, to help hold the soil in and to deter fish from foraging around in the basket.

Lower the basket into the pond immediately. Let it acclimatize at 20cm (8in) below the surface for a couple of weeks on a pedestal of bricks. As its growth gains momentum, move it to its final resting place.

Other Deep-Water Plants

The water hawthorn, *Aponogeton distachyos*, is an essential plant for the water garden, perhaps because it flowers from the dawning of the spring to the end of November. The vanilla-scented flowers can be appreciated from a considerable distance, and it is said it will tolerate a planting depth of up to 75cm (30in); however, I have seen it flourishing in pools twice that depth. It may be more

Aponogeton distachyos, *water hawthorn, is a native of South Africa, and down in the Cape Town area there is a popular stew-type meal that uses the flowers as a major ingredient.*

difficult to get it established in a pond with a high snail population, so introduce it at a shallow level of between 10–20cm (4–8in) until it builds up vigour and momentum, before introducing it to the depths of your pond. Once it is established it never poses any threat of taking over, unless there is literally no competition whatsoever.

One deep-water plant that *will* take over is *Nuphar lutea*; it always surprises me when I see it down canals and rivers because it does not look like a native plant. It is often referred to as the 'common pond lily', although it is nowhere near as spectacular as a proper lily. The 4–5cm (1½–2in) yellow flowers sit high above the water level, whilst oval leathery leaves float on the surface of the water. It will survive depths of more than 2m (6ft), in which case its foliage is submerged and more feathery. *Nuphar japonica* and *Nuphar pumila* are less invasive.

One plant usually included in the marginal plant list is *Nymphoides peltata* or *Villarsia*, commonly referred to as the 'yellow fringe lily'. This has a strong creeping habit, and makes excellent cover with its small, lily-like leaves. It produces a profusion of small, yellow, star-shaped flowers all summer long. Planting depth should be 10–60cm (4–24in).

The planting procedure for all these deep-water aquatics is the same as for lilies.

LEFT: Nuphar lutea, *sometimes referred to as 'the brandy bottle', perhaps because it has a slight brandy-like fragrance, or because the seed-head looks something like the old-fashioned brandy bottle.*

BELOW LEFT: Nymphoides peltata, *the yellow fringe lily, can seem rampant, but it is easy to control on a small pond.*

FLOATING PLANTS

Floating plants are perhaps not quite as important as the other vegetative ingredients to a pond, and some varieties can be a scourge, particularly in slightly warmer climes than Britain. But if your lilies are slow to get their heads up and get moving, floating plants provide invaluable pool cover and prove exceptionally efficient competition to algae. However, definitely beware of duckweed (*Lemna minor*). Fairy moss or *Azolla filiculoides* is also regarded by some as a nuisance, but it has a spectacular colour in the colder months, and is often finished off by icy weather. Fish like to eat it, too, and so it is not the universal problem that duckweed is, once it gets into your water garden.

Less rampant, but frost-tender, are water hyacinth (*Eichornia crassipes*) and water lettuce (*Pistia stratiotes*), hated in South Africa and the USA for clogging up dams and waterways. These need to be overwintered indoors.

Trapa natans (water chestnut) only overwinters if it sets seed and is then allowed to germinate the following spring.

The two native floating plants frogbit (*Hydrocharis morsus-ranae*) and water soldier (*Stratiotes aloides*) survive the winter by sinking to the bottom of the pond. The frogbit looks like a white miniature pygmy lily and sinks to the bottom as a small nut-like food-store, easily missed in a very late season clear-out. The water soldier looks like the top of a pineapple plant; it is now rare in the wild, only to be found in Norfolk.

Planting these floating plants is just a matter of throwing them in. Don't be disappointed if they sink to the bottom: they will re-emerge when they recover. Allow one floating plant for every 1sq m (10sq ft) of pool surface.

TOP LEFT: *Duckweed and pebbles make an annoying mixture!*

LEFT: Azolla filiculoides *or fairy moss, despite its brilliant autumn colour, is regarded as a menace in the milder parts of the country.*

TOP RIGHT: Eichornia crassipes, *the water hyacinth, rarely flowers in this country, but it has a magical effect on clearing the water in some pools.*

ABOVE: Pistia stratiotes, *water lettuce, is very frost tender.*

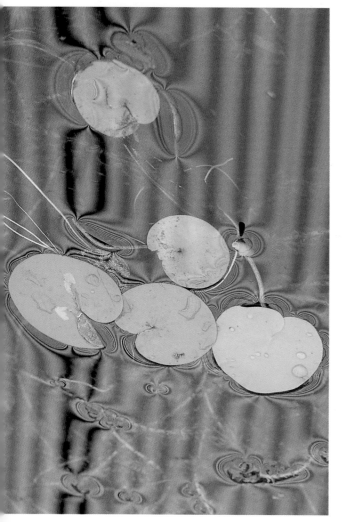

ABOVE LEFT: Trapa natans, *water chestnut, overwinters as a nut.*

LEFT: Hydrocharis morsus-ranae. *Frogbit has a little white flower.*

ABOVE: Stratiotes aloides, *water soldier, floating just below the surface. It stays at the bottom in cold weather. It mostly propagates itself by side shoots. One can just be seen on this plant.*

MARGINAL PLANTS

When the marginal plants start to emerge, spring can really be said to have arrived, the marsh marigolds, *Caltha palustris*, being the first to flower. Marginal plants help to use up the nitrates in the pond, and some of them – rushes and reeds in particular – are very quick to absorb many of the toxins that might otherwise permanently pollute our waterways and wetlands. They provide valuable cover for the continuous traffic of wildlife in and out of the pond. To the pond constructor they can help hide the weaknesses of the design, such as the intrusive pipework or the little bit of visible liner. Visually, they soften a hard paved or rock edge to the pool.

For the garden as a whole, they can help blend the pool into its setting. Many marginal plants are happy to double as bog plants or even ordinary border perennials, so using some of them outside the pool in a separate boggy backdrop can disguise the precise margin of where the pond ends and the dry garden begins.

ABOVE: *A fine mix of marginals in a Peter Sims-designed pool for World of Water at the 2002 Hampton Court Flower Show.*

Brian Toms and Chenies Aquatics demonstrating at the Hampton Court Flower Show 2002 how to use leaf colour and variegation in the water garden.

Even though many marginals are spring flowering, their period of interest can be continued with the range of variegated and coloured leaved varieties. For instance, there is the variegated form of the sweet flag or scented rush, *Acorus calamus* 'Variegatus', or the miniature version for smaller ponds, *Acorus gramineus variegatus* (*gramineus* means 'grass-leaved'). There is a yellow clumping golden grass, *Carex riparia* 'Bowles Golden'; a variegated form of the yellow flag iris, *Iris pseudacorus variegata*; and the blue *Iris laevigata variegata*. There is a conversation piece in the 'zebra-striped rush', *Scirpus lacustris* ssp. *tabernaemontanae* 'Zebrinus' (often referred to just as *Scirpus zebrinus*) that has horizontal variegation. And for a bright splash of lush, variegated colour there is the water figwort, *Scrophularia auriculata variegata*.

The aristocrats of the marginal plants are the irises, particularly the *ensata* hybrids, previously all under the banner of *Iris kaempferi*. These are the clematis-flowered iris, with colours varying through white, blue, red, violet and crimson, often with bold and elaborate markings.

Those of you who are keen on the perennials of the herbaceous border may be surprised that *Houttynia cordata*, *Lobelia cardinalis*, *Iris sibirica* and even some *Hostas* appear on the retailers' lists of marginal plants. The latter two may survive in very

---

MARGINAL PLANTS: PART OF OUR HERITAGE

If we were to investigate the history of herbalism and medicinal plants, these 'marginals' – plants of the marsh and soggy wetlands – must have provided more cures for ailments and diseases than any group of plants from any other habitats. And not only that, but many of those indigenous to this country, particularly the reeds and the rushes, were an essential raw material for man's service and comfort: from thatching for roofs to lights at night, as materials for baskets, beds and pillows, and even for food, it is hardly surprising that many tribes of early man lived near or amongst these plants that did so much to sustain them. Even today we still use them, in particular the Norfolk or common reed, used to clean and extract pollutants from the water effluent from domestic and commercial premises. This is an important and sustainable method of dealing with raw sewage, particularly for landlocked counties that have rivers and waterways to conserve.

---

marshy conditions, but they won't flourish. Rockery plant enthusiasts will spot the all-terrain *Sisyrinchium californicum* and *S. burmudianum*, and the multipurpose 'creeping Jenny', *Lysimachia nummularia*. Flower arrangers will be surprised to see the stately arum lily, *Zantedeshia aetheopica*, whilst herbalists will find water mint and chives.

NATURAL PLANTING

Those who are keen to establish a conservation style of water garden with indigenous plants should choose these carefully. Don't turn your back on them for too long, as they will all very quickly become overgrown and intertangled. Be wary of 'give-aways' and bargains, and always try to see what a mature clump looks like (a four-to five-year-old plant). This will give you a much better idea of its real characteristics.

A marginal planting that has got out of hand after only three years. The rampant indigenous reeds and rushes have to be sawn apart, despite starting off in baskets.

Planting Marginals

Allow one marginal for every 0.5sq m (5sq ft) of pool surface area. Instead of planting them in a line all round the edge of the pool, try to get some depth to the planting by having some in front of others. If the shelf is only wide enough for one basket, is there room to plant outside and behind the pool, like a backdrop? Otherwise use the groundcover characteristics of plants such as creeping Jenny (*Lysimachia nummularia*), brook-lime (*Veronica beccabunga*), *Mimulus* and even water forget-me-not (*Myosotis palustris*). Plant one of these in the same basket as a taller-growing plant. However, having said that, some marginal plants do not make very good bedfellows, so if you do this, don't be surprised to find only one in residence after twelve months.

The rules and techniques of planting are roughly the same as for the lilies. Choose plants with strong, fresh growth, which are not in flower. Plant them at the same level as they were in the container you have taken them from.

Line an aquatic basket with a hessian square – unless you can acquire the make of aquatic basket known as 'Finofil' which is lined with a very fine mesh, thereby doing away with the need for the hessian liner. They are also designed to allow plants to outgrow their containers without too much hindrance.

Fill the baskets with chemical-free fibrous loam or aquatic soil to roughly 5cm (2in) from the top of the basket. Plant the plants or offsets in the loam, and top up the soil level to almost the top of the basket, allowing enough room for a layer of pea gravel. If it is early in the season, the new growing tip should be just showing at the surface.

TOP RIGHT: *A good chemical-free heavy loam is perfectly adequate for planting marginals. Fill the basket to about two-thirds full.*

MIDDLE RIGHT: *By planting up in the corners I can get two plants to share this basket – for a while, at least.*

BOTTOM RIGHT: *Top off with an inert grit or pea gravel.*

As a general rule, marginal plants are happy sitting up to their necks in water – that is, the water can just cover the top of the basket by a little more than 13mm (½in). If there are areas that are a little deeper (5–10cm/2–4in), then *Alisma plantago* (water plantain), *Calla palustris* (bog arum), *Menyanthes trifoliata* (bogbean), *Orontium aquaticum* (golden club), *Pontederia cordata* (pickerel), *Sagittaria sagittifolia* (arrowhead) and *Typha latifolia* (reed mace) will all happily exploit these conditions. *Zantedeschia aethiopica* (arum lily) will thrive in a depth of 15–23cm (6–9in).

The baskets or marginals in this pool are having to be placed on bricks in order to maintain them at the right level for these marginal plants.

Spring is here and the plants are raring to go.

Directory of Widely Available Marginal Plants

The following directory is provided as a guide to what is good and what is to avoid. These plants can be safely planted in the shallow waters of your pool margins, and it is in this respect that they differ from what we consider as 'bog' or 'marsh' plants. However, most of these 'marginals' wouldn't mind such 'bog' plant conditions, either! Thus the 'depth of water over the soil' figures are only a rough guide.

***Acorus calamus* 'Variegatus'** Variegated version of the scented rush. It has an aromatic rootstock and leaves like an iris, with an insignificant horn of a spadix, which is the flower, that emerges from the leaf in summer. It has been in this country since Norman times, and is therefore regarded as indigenous. Height 50–80cm (20–32in); spread 1m (40in); depth of water over the soil 0–15cm (0–6in).

***Acorus gramineus* 'Variegatus'** A foliage plant, it has small, grassy, yellow-striped, lanceolate leaves. It grows happily in solid clumps, and looks good for most of the year. It thrives in nooks and crannies in streams. It only gets out of hand if it has no competition at all. Height 25–35cm; spread 50cm (20in); depth of water over the soil, 0–5cm (0–2in).

***Alisma plantago-aquaticum*, the water plantain** Indigenous. The arrow-shaped leaves come before a huge spray of tiny white/grey flowers in July/August. It remains fairly contained if it is prevented from setting its seed. Height 50–80cm (20–32in); spread 50–80cm; depth of water over the soil, 0–20cm (0–8in).

***Aponogeton distachyos*, water hawthorn** Often grown as a marginal. It flowers from March to May, and from September to December (*see* Deep-Water Aquatics and Lilies, page 156–64). It has oval leaves and scented waxy flowers that appear on the surface of the water. Spread 1m (40in); depth of water over the soil 10–75cm (4–30in).

***Butomus umbellatus*, flowering rush or pride of the Thames** It has triangular sword-shaped

Acorus calamus *'Variegatus'*.

Alisma plantago-aquaticum, *the water plantain*.

Acorus gramineus *'Variegatus'*.

Aponogeton distachyos, *water hawthorn*.

Butomus umbellatus, *flowering rush,
or pride of the Thames*.

leaves, red in the spring, turning to green. Rose pink flowers are produced in umbels from June to July. Height 60–100cm (24–40in); spread 1m (40in); depth of water over the soil 2.5 to 25cm (1–10in).

***Calla palustris*, bog arum** A pioneering plant growing on the water surface out into the pond, but it presents no problem. It has waxy, heart-shaped leaves and little arum-like flowers in June or July, followed by bright red seed heads. Height 15–25cm (6–10in); spread 1m (40in); depth of water over the soil 2.5 to 25cm (1–10in).

***Caltha palustris*, marsh marigold, king cup** The herald of spring, flowering from March/April to May with yellow flowers and slightly serrated leaves. It is indigenous. Height 30–50cm (12–20in); a contained hummock, of spread 60cm (24in); depth of water over the soil 0–15cm (0–6in).

***Caltha palustris* var. *alba*, white-flowered marsh marigold** Flowers sometimes in October, but usually early spring. Height 25–40cm (10–16in); spread 50cm (20in); depth of water over the soil 0–10cm (0–4in).

***Caltha palustris* 'Plena', double marsh marigold** Flowers in early spring, and often again later in the summer. Height 25–50cm (10–20in); spread 50cm (20in); depth of water over the soil, 0–15cm (0–6in).

Caltha palustris* var. *polypetala It has large, serrated leaves with large, single flowers that appear in late April/May. Less of a hummock, it behaves more in a 'leap-frog' fashion, growing to a height of 60–90cm (24–36in) and falling down amongst other plants, or out into the water and rooting. Therefore its spread is up to 1m (40in), but it is easy to control – a lovable rogue. Depth of water over the soil 5–25cm (2–10in).

***Carex riparia*, great pond sedge** It has coarse leaves and brown spikelets for flowers. Beware, it is a vigorous native, and not a plant for a small pond. It also creates problems if it sets seed after flowering, in May/June. Height 90–120cm (36–48in), and it will quickly spread to 1m (40in). Depth of water over soil 0–25cm (0–10in).

***Carex riparia* 'Bowles Golden'** It is much more reserved in habit than its basic cousin. Seen here by the iron wheels (*see* page 173, bottom left) it makes an attractive foil for other foliage in the water garden, and is usually attractive all year round. It flowers from May to August. Height 30 50cm (12–20in); spread 50cm (20in); depth of water over the soil 5–20cm (2–8in).

***Cotula coronopifolia*, brass, or golden buttons** An annual with a creeping habit which flowers from May to September. It sets seed well, and can colonize a muddy space if left to its own devices. Height 20–40cm (8–16in); spread 40cm (16in); depth of water over the soil 0–20cm (0–8in).

Calla palustris, *bog arum.*

Caltha palustris, *marsh marigold, king cup.*

Caltha palustris *var.* alba, *white-flowered marsh marigold.*

Caltha palustris *'Plena', the double marsh marigold.*

Caltha palustris *var.* polypetala.

Carex riparia, *great pond sedge.*

Carex riparia *'Bowles golden'.*

Cotula coronopifolia, *brass or golden buttons.*

***Cyperus longus*, sweet galingale** A tall native that can get out of hand if not checked every three or four years. Attractive, dark green, pendulous foliage; because it can grow in the sun or the shade it is a very useful filler and cover. It flowers in summer. Height 60–120cm (24–48in); spread 120cm (48in).

Dichromena colorata An unusual-looking plant that displays five green/white bracts around an insignificant flower, producing a white star shape from July until September. Height 40–60cm (16–24in); spread 60cm (24in); depth of water over the soil 2–5cm (1–2in).

***Equisetum* 'hyemale', horsetail** This plant sends out echoes of a prehistoric age. Beware, however, because the horsetail can swamp most competition. Height 60–100cm (24–40in); spread unpredictable; depth of water over the soil 0–15cm (0–6in).

***Eupatorium cannabinum*, hemp agrimony** This plant has mid-green lanceolate leaves, reddish stems, and reddish purple florets in rounded heads; it is 12cm (5in) across from July to September. Height 60–120cm (24–48in); spread 60cm (24in); depth of water over the soil 0–10cm (0–4in).

***Glyceria maxima* 'Variegata', striped watergrass** This will run everywhere if it likes the conditions. It has pinky-red grass-type foliage in spring, maturing to yellow and green later, with pendulous inflorescence in June and July. Height 30–60cm (12–24in), with an unpredictable spread; depth of water over the soil 2.5 to 25cm (1–10in).

***Hippurus vulgaris*, mare's tail** Beware, because it is invasive. The stems stand stiffly out of the water, and have densely packed whorls of narrow foliage. Height 25–30cm (8–12in); spread is unpredictable; depth of water over the soil 2–15cm (1–6in).

***Houttynia cordata* 'Chamaeleon'** This plant has red, yellow and green tricolour cordate leaves with red stems. It has single white flowers from August to September. Height 20–50cm (8–20in); spread 50cm (20in) if kept contained; depth of water over the soil 0–10cm (0–4in).

***Houttynia cordata* 'Plena'** Seen here growing with the orange-yellow *Trollius chinensis* (*see* page 175, bottom right) it has bluish-green cordate leaves with a red edge and red stems. The white semi-double flowers have flecks of red on the end of the petals in August to September. Height 30–50cm (12–20in); spread 50cm (20in); depth of water over the soil 0–25cm (0–10in).

LEFT: Cyperus longus, *sweet galingale.*

Dichromena colorata.

Equisetum *'hyemale'*, *horsetail.*

Eupatorium cannabinum, *hemp agrimony.*

Glyceria maxima *'variegata'*, *striped watergrass.*

Hippurus vulgaris, *mare's tail.*

Houttynia cordata *'Chamaeleon'*.

Houttynia cordata *'Plena'*.

***Iris ensata (Iris kaempferi)*, the clematis-flowered iris** It comes in a huge variety of colours, often with elaborate markings, in June to July. In order to thrive it needs to be in fairly dry conditions throughout the winter. Height 60–90cm (24–35in); spread 15–20cm (6–8in); depth of water in the summer only 0–10cm (0–4in).

***Iris laevigata*, water iris** This has rich blue flowers in June. Height 60–90cm (24–35in); spread 30cm (12in); depth of water over the soil 0–20cm (0–8in).

***Iris laevigata* 'Variegata'** Can be difficult to establish, but once it is, the bright green and white foliage is on show for most of the year and with blue flowers in June. Height 50–60cm (20–24in); spread 60cm (24in); depth of water over the soil 2.5–10cm (1–4in).

***Iris pseudacorus*, yellow flag** The most vigorous iris, with broad green foliage; it flowers from May to June. Height and spread 60–100cm (24–40in); depth of water over the soil, 0–25cm (0–10in).

Iris siberica These are excellent as cut flowers. They will grow anywhere from the herbaceous border to the wettest bog, flowering in June. Height 60–100cm (24–40in); spread 60cm (24in); depth of water over the soil 0–10cm (0–4in).

***Iris versicolor* 'Roy Elliot'** An ornate variety of *I. versicolor*. They are similar to *I. pseudacorus* in habit and in their ability to spread. Height 60cm (24in); spread 60cm (24in); depth of water over the soil 0–25cm (0–10in).

***Juncus effusus*, soft rush** A native plant used by poor people in the past as a substitute for candles. It has dark green stems and brown inflorescences from June to August. The pith within the stem is continuous. It stays in its own clump, but seeds all around. Height 30–120cm (12–48in); spread 1m (40in); depth of water over the soil 0–25cm (0–10in).

***Juncus effusus* var. *spiralis*, corkscrew rush** Very popular with designers as a 'spot plant' or central feature in a small pool because of its twisted, corkscrew stems. Height 25–45cm (10–18in); spread 45–50cm (18–20in); depth of water over the soil 0–10cm (0–4in).

***Juncus inflexus*, hard rush** Another common native with bright green grass-like foliage and dark brown inflorescence from June to August. Height 55–75cm (22–29in); spread 55cm; depth of water over the soil 0–15cm (0–6in).

Lobelia cardinalis This has purplish-red foliage on stalks bearing brilliant red flowers from August to September. Height and spread 80–100cm (32–40in); depth of water over the soil 0–5cm (0–2in).

Iris laevigata, *water iris.*

Iris laevigata *'Variegata'.*

Iris siberica.

Iris versicolor *'Roy Elliott'*.

Juncus effusus, *soft rush.*

Juncus effusus *var.* spiralis, *corkscrew rush.*

Juncus inflexus, *hard rush.*

Lobelia cardinalis.

Lobelia siphilitica This has lanceolate light green leaves, and bright blue flowers 2cm (1in) long from July to September. Height 45–90cm (22–36in); spread 45cm (36in); depth of water over the soil 0–5cm (0–2in).

Lychnis flos-cuculi, **ragged robin** This plant has ragged, rose-pink flowers from June to August. Height 50–75cm (20–29in); spread 30cm (12in); depth of water over the soil 0–10cm (0–4in).

Lysichiton americanus, **American skunk cabbage** Has bright yellow, arum-like flowers in March to May, followed by large, dark green leaves. *Lysichiton camtschatcensis* is similar, but has white flowers. Height and spread 40–100cm (16–40in); depth of water over the soil 0–30cm (0–12in).

Lysimachia nummularia **'Aurea', golden creeping Jenny** A familiar plant to most gardeners as a groundcover. Like the ordinary creeping Jenny, this golden-leaved version has bright golden flowers from June to August. Height 10–15cm (4–6in); spread 1m (40in); depth of water over the soil 0–15cm (0–6in).

Lysimachia thyrsiflora, **yellow loosestrife** A native and a popular border plant that also thrives in the wet. It has spikes of golden yellow flowers throughout July. Height 50–70cm (20–28in); spread 1m (40in); depth of water over the soil, 0–20cm (0–8in).

Lythrum salicaria, **purple loosestrife** A native plant of variable height with spikes of small, reddish-purple blooms from July to September. Height 90–150cm (36–60in); spread 1m (40in); depth of water over the soil 0–15cm (0–6in).

Mentha aquatica, **water mint** A native plant that never seems to stay where it is put. It has egg-shaped, serrated leaves with a purplish tinge to the new growth. The flowers are lilac whorls around the stem in late summer. Height 30–60cm (12–24in); spread is unpredictable; depth of water over the soil 0–20cm (0–8in).

Menyanthes trifoliata, **bog bean** Has trifoliate, olive-green foliage, and pink-tipped, delicate small white flowers in April/May. It is a surface rambler, softening the orderly edges of the pool. Height 30–40cm (12–16in); spread 100–150cm (40–60in), but easily controlled; depth of water over the soil 5–30cm (2–12in).

Lobelia siphilitica.

Lychnis flos-cuculi, *ragged robin.*

Lysichiton americanus, *American skunk cabbage.*

Lysimachia nummularia *'Aurea', creeping Jenny.*

Lysimachia thyrsiflora, *yellow loosestrife.*

Lythrum salicaria, *purple loosestrife.*

Mentha aquatica, *water mint.*

Menyanthes trifoliata, *bog bean.*

Mimulus luteus, **monkey musk** Serrated leaves with yellow flowers from May to August, variably marked with maroon and brown spots. Height 20–40cm (8–16in); spread 40–100cm (16–40in); depth of water above the soil 2.5–15cm (1–6in).

Mimulus luteus × *M. guttatus* **hybrid, *M.* 'Major Bees'.**

Myosotis palustris **or** *Myosotis scorpiodes,* **water forget-me-not** This plant is indigenous. It has elongated, hairy, spoon-shaped leaves and clusters of little blue flowers in May, and sometimes again in August. Height and spread 20–30cm (8–12in); depth of water over the soil 5–40cm (2–16in).

Petasites hybridus A perennial with thick stems topped with many pink flower heads in March to April. These are followed by large, very wide leaves. Height 100–125cm (40–50in); spread unpredictable; depth of water over the soil, 0–5cm (0–2in).

Phalaris arundinacea **var.** *picta,* **reed canary grass** A grassy aquatic with green and white striped leaves. It can be vigorous, so small pool owners should treat it with care. Height and spread 75–150cm (30–60in); depth of water over the soil 0–15cm (0–6in).

Phragmites australis, **common reed or Norfolk reed** Indigenous to this country, this plant has travelled the world over and has innumerable uses, including for thatching. It is a strong-growing grass, with purple to violet plumes of florescence from July to October. Height 180–300cm (70–120in), spread unlimited; depth of water over the soil 50cm (20in).

Pontedaria cordata, **pickerel weed** This plant has heart-shaped green leaves with clusters of closely packed blue flowers borne on a spike from August to September. Height and spread 60–80cm (24–32in); depth of water over the soil 10–30cm (4–12in).

Ranunculus flammula, **lesser spearwort** This plant has small lanceolate leaves with branching stems that hold large numbers of small yellow buttercup-shaped flowers from June to September. Height 20–30cm (8–12in); spread 30–40cm (12–16in); depth of water over the soil 5–20cm (2–8in).

Ranunculus lingua **'Grandiflora', greater spearwort** Indigenous. It has long, ovate, deep green leaves with buttercup-type flowers. As is often the case with native plants, it is fairly rampant. Height 60–90cm (24–35in); spread as large as the pond; depth of water over the soil 10–30cm (4–12in).

Mimulus luteus, *monkey musk.*

Mimulus luteus × M. guttatus *hybrid M. 'Major Bees'.*

Myosotis palustris *or* M. scorpiodes, *water forget-me-not.*

Petasites hybridus.

Phalaris arundinacea *var.* picta, *reed canary grass.*

BELOW: Phragmites australis, *common reed or Norfolk reed.*

ABOVE RIGHT: Pontedaria cordata, *pickerel weed.*

Ranunculus flammula, *lesser spearwort.*

Ranunculus lingua *'Grandiflora', greater spearwort.*

***Sagittaria sagittifolia* var. *leucopetala* 'Flore Pleno', double arrowhead** This is the double form of the arrowhead, flowering from July to August. Height and spread 50–80cm; depth of water over the soil 10–20cm (4–8in).

***Saururus cernuus*, lizard's tail** Green, heart-shaped leaves with white pendulous flowers in July. Height and spread 40–90cm (16–36in); depth of water over the soil 0–20cm (0–8in).

***Scirpus angustifolius* or *Eriophorum angustifolium*, cotton grass** A native plant with stiff, grass-type foliage. In summer, fluffy heads of white cotton-like flowers are carried on tall stems. Height and spread 30–50cm (12–20in); depth of water over the soil 2.5–10cm (1–4in).

***Scirpus lacustris* ssp. *tabernaemontani* 'Albescens', variegated bulrush** This is the variegated form of the bulrush. Beware of the non-variegated form. This one has tall, cylindrical foliage with green and white vertical variegations. Height and spread 90–120cm (36–48in); depth of water over the soil 5–30cm (2–12in).

***Scirpus lacustris* ssp. *tabernaemontani* 'Zebrinus', zebra rush** Has cylindrical foliage with green and white horizontal stripes, and brown flower heads in July to August. Height 75–110cm (30–44in); spread 100cm (4in); depth of water over the soil 5–30cm (2–12in).

***Scrophularia auriculata* 'Variegata'** This has tall, heart-shaped, nettle-like leaves on a square stem. Grown mainly for its foliage early in the season, it has insignificant flowers from July to August. Height 60–90cm (24–36in); spread 50cm (20in); depth of water over the soil 0–10cm (0–4in).

***Sisyrinchium* 'E. K. Balls'** This will grow anywhere, from a rockery to water margins. It is a clump-forming, semi-evergreen perennial with linear leaves. All summer it produces a succession of star-shaped, mauve flowers 2cm (1in) across. Height and spread 25cm (10in); depth of water over the soil 0–5cm (0–2in).

Sisyrinchium californicum Another adaptable plant that self-seeds prolifically; slightly smaller, at 20cm (8in), with yellow flowers. Depth of water over soil, 0–5cm (0–2in).

Sagittaria sagittifolia *var.* leucopetala *'Flore Pleno', double arrowhead.*

Saururus cernuus, *lizard's tail.*

Scirpus angustifolius *or* Eriophorum angustifolium

Scirpus lacustris *ssp.* tabernaemontani *'Zebrinus', zebra rush.*

Scirpus lacustris *ssp.* tabernaemontani *'Albescens',*
variegated bulrush.

Scrophularia auriculata *'Variegata'.*

Sisyrinchium *'E. K. Balls'.*

Sisyrinchium californicum.

***Sparganium erectum*, branched burweed** An indigenous plant with a stiff, erect, branched stem, it flowers from June until August, leaving these remarkable seed-heads. Height 60–100cm (24–40in), spread 30cm (12in); depth of water over soil, 5–40cm (2–16in).

***Typha latifolia*, great reed mace** The flower and then seeds are in a close cylindrical spike that becomes brown and velvety. This is everybody's idea of a pond plant, but great consideration should be made before including it on your list of plants for your pond. It grows upwards and outwards at a phenomenal rate, and once established will send underwater runners across a 4m (13ft) pond in less than a season. If it sets seed, each seed-head can contain upwards from 175,000 viable seeds: no wonder it can be found all over the world! Height 120–240cm (48–96in); spread 240cm (96in) minimum; depth of water over the soil 10–50cm (4–20in), but once established it will float its stems in any depth.

***Typha minima*, miniature bulrush** The safe alternative to the above, with a much more reserved spirit. It flowers from July to September, and has small, almost cylindrical, velvety seed-heads. Height 40–60cm (16–24in); spread 80cm (32in); depth of water over the soil, 5–20cm (2–8in).

***Veronica beccabunga*, brooklime** A native and a spreading plant with almost succulent stems, ovate leaves, and clusters of small, bright blue flowers all through summer. Height 20–30cm (8–12in); spread 100cm (40in) if it enjoys its situation; depth of water over soil 0–15cm (0–8in).

***Zantedeschia aethiopica* 'Crowborough', arum lily** This variety is always considered the most hardy of the arum lilies. It has glossy, arrow-shaped leaves, and large, pure white arum flowers with a deep golden-yellow spathe in August through to September. Height and spread 50–100cm (20–40in); depth of water over the soil, 0–25cm (0–10in).

Sparganium erectum, *branched burweed.*

Typha latifolia, *great reed mace.*

Typha minima, *miniature bulrush.*

Veronica beccabunga, *brooklime.*

Zantedeschia aethiopica *'Crowborough', arum lily.*

The line between marginal plants and merely damp-loving plants, and even those that just like the humidity, is obscured in this early nineties Chelsea Flower Show garden by Julian Dowle. That is how it is in nature, and why the garden looks so true to life.

PONDSIDE PLANTS

Your water garden now has its full complement of plants *in* the water, but you can still help it to blend into the environment with the imaginative use of pondside plants. This is how you 'create a sense of place', as some garden designers might say. Perhaps you just want a collection of plants that look good next to water, or you may want to accentuate a style. Alternatively it may be a formal scene, and you want to soften the hard landscaping of bricks and mortar.

If your garden has the traditional 'cottage garden look', then any new additional feature will need careful thought with regard to the planting around it, so that it merges in well. Your water garden may have the rocky look with an alpine feel, perhaps with a lively stream falling in leaps and bounds into what could be a flooded mountain meadow. It could be a Japanese theme, or simply a haven for

wildlife with a 'natural planting'. All these need plants that help lift you, in both eye and mind, up from the marginal areas and into the larger world of your garden.

This would not be necessary where the water has been used for its reflective qualities, or is just a different surface, part of a landscape of textures or shapes. Expressed in formal or informal shapes, these landscapes have emerged at occasional intervals over the centuries in all garden styles, from Le Notre, through Capability Brown to Charles Jenks or Tom Stuart-Smith. These gardens are more to do with philosophy and pure art, than with plants and nature. Capability Brown's water gardens seemed to touch on this, but we think (for he never really expressed a reason) they were designed with nature in mind, but to be viewed from afar. Therefore the division between wet and dry, trees and grass, had to be distinct, with no smudging of the margins.

Reflections in the Tom Stuart-Smith garden at the Chelsea Flower Show 2001.

PLANTS FOR A PARTICULAR ENVIRONMENT

Apart from the snowy wastes of the polar regions, some form of plant life has adapted to exist in virtually every type of environment on earth. Some of these conditions produce very particular characteristics in the plants: in desert conditions leaves have evolved to become spikes and hairs so as not to lose moisture; in humid jungles, plants have large leaves to aid transpiration and catch limited sunlight; and so on. But to the casual observer there is nothing really visually distinctive about the plants that we can grow near to water – that is, unless we observe them more closely.

What we will see very soon is how quickly they all grow. But this is not surprising, for in the wild, many of these plants would grow in the humus and nutrient-rich silt around ponds, lakes, rivers and streams. They need to grow fast because of the intense competition, the short growing season and the tough winter conditions. These plants can tolerate the winter in the wet, and will survive an early spring flooding that provides the nutrient-rich detritus that would suffocate or drown most plants. This is partly because they are dormant when times are really tough, and also because they maintain a root structure near the surface where they can mix air with their superabundance of water. Moreover the perennials, at least, also have a sustaining stored food supply that helps them grow hard and fast through awkward early conditions, such as inches of soggy mud and spells of cold weather.

There are other plants that cling precariously to existence in mountain meadows or in gullies awash with the waters from the melting snows of spring, and yet others that grow in the moist, humid conditions of woodland or woodland edge. They tolerate the heavy drip of moisture from the tree canopy of some types of woodland, and race to achieve maximum growth and to flower earlier on in the year before the trees knit together to create inhibiting shade. Or they produce huge leaves that get the maximum potential from limited light, and shade out the competition, grasping their air supply with the huge surface area of their leaves.

These environments, combined with the ambient conditions of a particular country of origin, have shaped the evolution of certain groups of plants: when used in a garden situation, these plants will immediately remind us of the habitat of their country of origin, and a style that relates to that. For instance, a range of plants that has evolved in the cool, moist, sub-alpine regions of northern Japan would create, to the informed eye, a strong sense of the orient when planted together in a garden. Another group of plants might suggest the mountain brooks and meadows of the Rockies in North America with a backdrop of conifer forests. And if we consider plants indigenous to England, we can find distinct habitats for many of our moisture-loving plants, from the slow-moving canals of the Midlands, through the levels of Somerset, the Fens of East Anglia, the Norfolk Broads and the acid bogs of Dartmoor. These all produce groups of plants that look right together.

There are also plants that inhabit windswept, bleak marshes: these survive the harshest conditions, propagating themselves vegetatively and by seed in an almost ferocious manner; in a domestic environment this aggressive characteristic will completely overwhelm any plant from a milder, less competitive habitat. And amongst the representatives of the moisture-loving trees and shrubs, there are several that have equally anti-social habits, including invasive root runs, rampant growth and sometimes poisonous leaves. On a domestic level, given these sometimes aggressive characteristics, it is therefore essential that the manager of a small water garden chooses his bog plants carefully.

The classic primrose, Primula officianalis.

Primula viallii.

THE BOG GARDEN

The true definition of a bog is an environment of excessive moisture and usually acid conditions, and when selecting plants for a bog garden we will have to make a distinction between those that actually like to sit in water, and those that like very moist conditions, but for the moisture to be draining away. These don't mind the occasional flooding, in fact they appreciate it, but the moisture must be draining away when it arrives. Sitting in stagnant water is as devastating to them as to any other plant, and therefore very particular conditions must be created for them.

There are also plants that will thrive in both environments, which can only be to our advantage if we want to soften the physical boundary between marginal and bog areas; many bog plants are tolerant of quite dry conditions, and can be used to blend the 'watery influence' into the rest of the garden. This is of particular advantage when laying out a 'conservation' or 'natural'-style water garden so that it fits convincingly into the scene. If you have created your water garden correctly, in a well-drained part of the garden, then you will be able to construct the conditions in which these plants will flourish.

A number of species will be happy in this transitional area: starting with the ground-cover plants between the shallows and the bog, our list might include *Lysimachia nummularia* (creeping Jenny), *Veronica beccabunga* (brooklime), *Myosotis palustris* (forget-me-not), *Mimulus* (monkey musk) as an annual left to seed itself, and for small pools and rock edges the little *Sisyrinchium californicum* (yellow), *S. angustifolium* (blue) or *S.* 'E. K. Balls' (mauve).

The slightly taller plants that would tolerate either marsh or bog conditions include sweet flag, *Acorus calamus*, the huge range of many irises, marsh marigolds, and the bog arums.

Plants for the Bog Area

In the proper bog area, where the soil is less deep, the smaller plants that could be suitable would be the primula, from the universally adored primrose, to the *Primula viallii* much later in the summer. They are an essential part of any bog garden.

A mix of foliage and flower from bog plants in July at the Hampton Court Flower Show in 1994. Astilbes to the right, and the big variegated leaf is from Petasites japonicus *'Variegatus'.*

Typical 'mid-range' bog plants would be *Aruncus*, *Astilbes*, *Filipendula*, *Ligularia* and *Rodgersia*. These are great foliage plants, as well as providing huge plumes of flower.

In general leave out the rushes, reeds and grasses, because if they like the conditions they will become invasive, and there will be very little you can do about it; having said that, some *Carex riparia* 'Bowles Golden' brings a bit of bright foliage to duller areas.

For tall, spiky foliage there are the phormiums; they don't spread, but they can grow fairly tall with unlimited supplies of moisture. A better choice might be the irises, which will provide the added bonus of flower: *Iris sibirica* is utterly reliable even if the conditions vary, and its close cousins, *I. laevigata* and *I. kaempferi* (now known as *I. ensata*), provide variation and ornament where the breeders have been at work. Some *Iris ensata* hybrids (Japanese irises) bring a positive atmosphere of the orient – even though they might never be seen in a truly Japanese water garden landscape.

Bamboos leave the onlooker in no doubt as to the style you are trying to emulate. In general they do not need the mollycoddling of a bog, and are best situated in the background in static repose without too much encouragement; they are there just to create the right impression.

Hostas, on the other hand, do need help, specifically protection from slugs: oak-bark mulch or chippings will apparently discourage the latter because of its heavy tannin content – but don't let it get anywhere near the pond water.

A few ferns planted here and there always give a boggy area character, and are particularly good in those areas where the light levels are poor. The male fern *Dryopteris filix-mas* will tolerate wet or dry, and

Hostas are very rewarding if they are in dappled shade and free from slugs.

Osmunda regalis, the royal fern, is the classic specimen for waterside planting, but it must be in acid soil. *Athyrium filix-femina* (the lady fern) will grow in the wet or dry or light or shade, but has a different appearance according to the different conditions.

Plants to Make an Impact

If you want to create an impact, then *Gunnera manicata* will get the neighbours talking. This is a huge umbrella of a plant with bumpy leaves up to 1.5m (5ft) across. It rewards a certain amount of care (particularly in winter) with increasingly enormous leaves. Late frosts in the spring can ruin the grand architectural effect of the emergent leaves in exposed areas.

If you find the size of *Gunnera manicata* rather too intimidating, *Gunnera tinctoria* is only slightly smaller; this variety produces reddish-brown flowers in early summer. *Gunnera magellanica* is much smaller, with shiny leaves and a mat-forming habit. The Rheum (rhubarb family) always makes an impressive backdrop, creating the same 'jungle' atmosphere – but the leaves of *Rheum palmatum* can still be 1m (40in) across, and the flower spike 2–2½m (6–7ft) high. Nevertheless, there are richly crimson and deep mahogany red varieties that are very tempting.

Other plants for impact and foliage would include species of *Petasites* (winter heliotrope) such as *P. japonicus*, *P. frigidus* var. *palmatus* and *Peltiphyllum peltatum* (sometimes referred to as *Darmera*

LEFT: Gunnera manicata *beside a pool at Tatton Park.*

BELOW LEFT: *Ornamental rhubarb*, Rheum palmatum *'Bloodgood', bursting into flower in late spring.*

BELOW: Peltiphyllum peltatum *or* Darmera peltata *in late spring.*

ABOVE AND RIGHT: *The flowers and foliage of* Ligularia dentata *'Desdemona'*.

BOTTOM RIGHT: Astrantia *'George's Form'*.

peltata). These can be very invasive even in their variegated forms, and so may best be avoided for all but the biggest gardens.

My favourites for foliage and late season flower are the *Ligularias*: *Ligularia stenocephala* 'The Rocket', for its huge yellow flower spikes and regularly cut leaves, or *Ligularia dentata* 'Desdemona', for its dark maroon-backed palmate leaves and bright yellow daisy flowers with chocolate centres.

Bog Plants from the Ordinary Garden

Those of you with an established garden of modest size that reflects your likes and dislikes, may already have some suitable plants that might relish a chance to be in the bog, or which would create the right impression by being near it. Examples include *Aconitum* (monkshood), anemones, *Astrantia*, *Chrysanthemum pratense*, *Crocosmia*, *Dicentra*, *Dierama*,

Swedish silver birch, seems to combine all the best qualities of the birches: although not white-stemmed at first, it gradually acquires such a shiny white surface that it tempts you to polish it to a sheen. Its deeply cut foliage hangs with grace without casting too much shade, turning to a golden yellow in autumn.

Birches are often associated with alders, as they are very often found together in the wild. The common black alder is the British native of watersides; although it is unsuitable for the small garden, its propagation must be encouraged since its numbers are seriously under threat from a pernicious disease that is sweeping the country.

Maples

Trees such as the Japanese maples are perfect for the waterside. *Acer palmatum* comes in a particularly finely cut leafed form of 'Dissectum', and the variety *Acer palmatum* 'Dissectum Atropurpureum' has bronze leaves that turn glorious red in autumn; it seems to have a particular love of its own reflection in water. In slightly dappled shade, this small tree makes a wonderful cascade down to the water surface.

For variety of leaf colour and shape, bark, size and shape, there is nothing to beat the *Acer* family: *Acer griseum* for its shiny bronze peeling bark, *A. davidii* and *A. pennsylvanicum* for their 'snake bark', and the variegated *Acer negundo* that brings light to its reflected image in the water. But pride of place must be given to *Acer japonica* and *A. palmatum* for their gloriously strident colouring that lasts the whole year round, and especially in autumn: this makes them indispensable for any ornamental garden, especially the Japanese garden.

The Cornus Family

Still thinking Japanese and trees for small gardens, *Cornus controversa* 'Variegata' is an excellent specimen to have next to the water, its orderly layered branches providing an unimpeachable focal point.

LEFT: *Boardman, Gelly and Co. used silver birch, presumably* Betula utilis *var.* jacquemontii, *to brighten up the interior of their 'Woodland Tranquillity' at the 1999 Hampton Court Flower Show. This would work well.*

BELOW: Acer dissectum *'Atropurpureum' always remains a small tree.*

Similarly *Cornus kousa* is only 3m (10ft) tall, but infallibly catches the eye with its clusters of white bracts. The shrubby *Cornus* provide winter interest. Varieties of *Cornus alba* and *C. stolonifera* 'Flaviramea', if cut back very early in the spring, produce brightly coloured shoots in reds and greens. *C. alba* 'Albo-variegata', *C. alba* 'Elegantissima' and *C.alba* 'Spaetheii' have variegated leaves. These love the waterside, and are extremely tough plants, maintaining a startling appearance even in winter or in the wildest of environments.

Shrubs for the Damp Habitat

Our native damp habitats would look sadly lacking without the hazels. *Corylus maxima* 'Purpurea' is a purple-leaved variety with spectacular autumn red colouring, and a harvest of nuts for you and the local wildlife.

Moving from our native trees and shrubs to the more ornamental varieties, we have *Viburnum opulus* and *V. plicatum* and their particular varieties: perfect anywhere – at home as a native, or grown for its ornamental value – the plants provide flowers, berries and autumn colour.

Other shrubs to consider for a truly damp area are the *Amelanchier*s, *Hydrangea*s and *Spiraea*s; these will tolerate the dry as well.

If the pH of your soil is particularly low, then your choice of plants escalates: azaleas, rhododendrons and *Kalmia latifolia* (calico) love the damp. Sweet gale or bog myrtle (*Myrica gale*) and the sweet pepper bush (*Clethra alnifolia*) are characterized by their sweet scent; *Vaccinium corymbosum* (swamp blueberry) provides berries and autumn colour.

TOP LEFT: Acer japonica, *the essential requirement for any secluded garden.*

TOP RIGHT: Cornus alba *makes an effective winter backdrop to any wildlife water garden, especially if you can get the stems in reflection. Cut them back to the ground in April.*

ABOVE: Viburnum plicatum *'Mariesii' is one of the most spectacular of the flowering viburnums.*

CHAPTER 7

Choosing and Keeping Fish

Many people will build a water garden with the sole motive of creating an environment for fish. Fish-keeping out of doors in ponds is a hobby that has been increasing in popularity since World War II, and nowadays stockists and breeders present us with a bewildering array of species and breeds of fish. However, not all of them are suitable for pond life, nor is it wise to mix some of the species together.

A SUITABLE HABITAT

Before you even think of introducing fish to your pond, you should be quite sure that the habitat is suitable for them. First of all, is the environment stable? Is the pond over 45cm (18in) deep, with over 3sq m (30sq ft) of surface area? This will ensure a fairly steady temperature change as the weather changes.

Late spring is the best time to introduce fish, when they have had time to build themselves up after a long hard winter. Avoid end-of-season 'bargains' at aquatic centres, and if you *are* tempted and buy fish after the beginning of September, quarantine the new arrivals over winter and through the early part of the following spring. This is because winter conditions will affect them before they have had time to recover from the trauma of the move, and any latent sickness or parasites that they may be carrying could flare up and be passed on to the rest of the fish population.

Do not move fish if the water temperature or the temperature outside is very high or very low. A water temperature of 50°F (10°C) is too low, and an outside temperature of 85°F (30°C) is too high. Remember, it is radical change that affects the fish

OPPOSITE: *Koi come in a variety of colours and combinations. Some people mistake them for big goldfish, but the way they hold their fins is a striking giveaway.*

more than anything, be it temperature or water quality (*see* below).

The pH value of the water is particularly important, too, so it would be a good idea to buy a cheap testing kit to test it.

If there has been a lot of building work around the pool, or if there have been considerable amounts of limestone used in the pool construction, lime may be leaching into the pool water. If the water is under pH8, that is generally tolerable; 7–8 is ideal; but if it is getting on for pH9, you have problems. In this case either pump the water out and stabilize the areas leaching lime with Silglaze, or adjust the pH balance with chemical adjusters, keeping a very regular check on it for several days afterwards.

If the water in the pool was mains tap water, you must be sure that it has 'aged' sufficiently: this means leaving it to stand for three days whilst the chlorines, minerals and heavy metals 'drop out'. If it has not, it can be treated with 'pool conditioner', which will achieve the same end after two to three hours. It is advisable to give more than the prescribed dose, just to be on the safe side. Many of these conditioners contain special colloids that help repair any damage to the fish's mucous layer, their only protection from disease and parasites. This can be very easily damaged in transit, or reduced by the stress of the transition.

By the time you introduce fish there should be a complete range of plants growing in the pool. Oxygenating plants are particularly important, and you need to have put in one bunch for every 185sq cm (2sq ft) of surface area.

Some sort of cover is a good idea for shy new arrivals, such as large pipes, slabs raised up off the pool bottom with bricks, and purpose-built 'fish hides'. These are also fairly effective protection against the heron.

GENERAL RULES FOR CHOOSING FISH

1. Whatever the temptation, the one golden rule for a stable healthy environment is to keep the fish population to less than 2in of fish for every square foot of surface area (this translates to 42cm to 1sq m).

Having said that, an amendment to this rule, particularly with regard to koi carp, would be to buy the fish with some regard to their future size. It is true to a certain extent that many species of fish 'grow to the size of the pool', but this brings the whole environment to the threshold of disaster when resources of oxygen and space are limited at certain times of the year.

2. Regulate the number of fish that you introduce to the pool at any one time. Introduce them in ones and twos, and avoid adding more than three or four per season.

3. Buy the fish from a reputable supplier near to home. Fish do not want to be travelling for hours in a car on a hot sultry day.

4. Observe how the fish are dispensed. They should be caught quickly and expertly, and handled as if they were a touch-sensitive bomb. The best ones are probably the liveliest and therefore the hardest to catch, so it is better to get your fish on a quiet day at the retailers, rather than when it is really busy and the fish are being constantly chased around.

5. It is a bad sign if there are any dead fish in the retailer's tank, because you can generally expect that these are not the first dead ones of the day. Usually the retailer's first job of the morning is to 'pick out the deads', and if more fish have died since then, or a dead fish has been left just floating in the tank from the night before, slowly releasing the pathogens that were responsible for its demise, suspect that there may be something potentially wrong with all the fish in the tank. If you were to choose a fish from this tank, take it to a new home and introduce it to a completely different environment, the excessive stress it will suffer will more than likely bring out any latent disorder.

6. Choose a fish with good colour that is lively and active. Small fish are proportionately much cheaper, they generally settle into their new environment very quickly, and they also grow more quickly in a new pond.

If you get a mixture of sizes you will find that the larger fish inhibit the growth of the smaller ones. This happens because there is a definite 'pecking order' for the food supplies, and because hormones are released by the larger fish.

7. The fish you choose should be transported home in a large plastic bag. The depth of water should be enough to comfortably cover the fish when the bag is upright, and the bag should then be pumped up with oxygen and tied off at the top with an elastic band. The bag can then be supported upright in a cardboard box.

FISH TO SUIT THE ENVIRONMENT

Goldfish and their Close Relatives

Goldfish are without doubt the hardiest and most suitable fish for any beginner's pond. They can withstand the rigours of any British winter, they are easy to see, and come in a variety of colours ranging from white or silver through pink and orange, to bright reds with possibilities of blacks or browns. They also come with a variety of lengths of fin and mixes of colours, which means they are given other names such as fantails, sarassas, wakins, calicos, comets and shubunkins (London and Bristol types). However, they are all basically breeds of goldfish (*Carassius auratus*), and as such are perfectly happy in each other's company – although the very fancy 'bubble eyes', black moors, lion

Observe that the fish are caught expertly and quickly, and then whether they are packaged carefully, with not too much water but plenty of oxygen.

Bubble eyes would not be able to compete with other fish in the pool environment, especially in the winter.

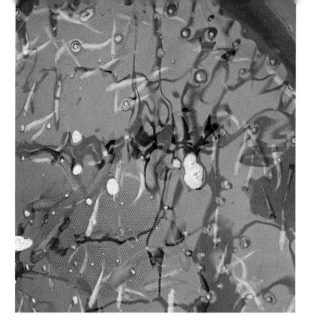

These large goldfish mix quite happily with the smaller golden orfe. The orfe will soon outgrow the goldfish, but the relationship will still remain peaceful.

heads, ryukins and fringetails find it difficult to keep up at feeding time. These are best kept in an indoor tank, especially in the winter.

Being members of the larger carp family (*Cyprinidae*), goldfish are tolerant of most other fish. They are not disruptive, and calmly go about their business. They are the fish we expect to see when we look into an ornamental pool, and so are in keeping with many typical styles, either formal or informal.

The Formidable Koi

One fish that is always easy to see and is definitely prone to upsetting the balance in a pool is the koi carp. Sometimes referred to as 'living jewels', these fish epitomize the brightly coloured elements of some of the Japanese gardening styles. Those of you eager to get into the pastime of keeping koi carp will not need me to extol the beauties of these gems, but it is important to bear in mind the size to which these fish can grow – 75cm (30in) – and to stock the pool accordingly. Allow yourself one koi for every 2sq m (21.5sq ft) of water surface, and expect 15–25cm (6–10in) growth per year.

To make them feel really at home they will need a depth of water of 1–1.5m (3–4ft) minimum, and a filter system processing the total volume of the pool every two hours.

Despite their size, koi are the cuddly big bears of the pond, and are quite happy to share their space with any other ornamental fish as long as it is large enough not to be mistaken for food.

Some people are lucky and find that their koi will exist quite happily with lilies and oxygenators, but most try to keep them out of the planting baskets with heavy pebbles, then wire mesh. However, in the end they nearly always have to admit defeat and take the plants out, and provide a mechanical means of oxygenating the water, and engineering shade with pergolas and netting over the pool. Koi are playful vandals and get bored very easily.

They need to be fed the best quality food available, and food appropriate for that season. This will not only help them, but it will help both the filter and you to keep the water clear.

Golden Orfe

The golden orfe is an essential fish, in my opinion, for the larger pool. They grow to between 45 and 60cm (18–24in) and are active fish, needing at least 15sq m (50sq ft) to move around in. In a group they will always shoal, providing us with a display of constant movement, smooth and elegant, looking like a string of fast-moving, flexible carrots being dragged through the water.

Although very hardy, they are the first to succumb to the effects of pollution, oxygen depletion or rapid temperature change. You will help them through the winter by keeping water movement to a minimum. Also be very careful with fish disease remedies and old-fashioned algicides; read the information on the packaging very carefully, and dose accordingly. These fish will be the first to benefit from the change in EU regulations on algicides.

Apart from this they are as easy to keep as goldfish, and can live for ten to twenty years – the larger the pond, the longer they live. They don't have any bad habits, and they love the company of other species of fish – although they can be harassed to death by some aggressive types.

INTRODUCING FISH TO YOUR POND

Take the fish to the pool as quickly as possible, still in the plastic bag you purchased them in. Float the bag in the water for 15–30 minutes so that the temperature of the water in the bag can adjust to that of the pool; the top of the bag can be opened and rolled down to form a float to keep it upright. Whilst it is floating, slowly introduce several cupfuls of pool water into the bag so the fish can acclimatize to the new water chemistry; this further reduces the possibility of stress. After the prescribed time, gently upend the bag and watch the fish swim away to investigate their new home.

Allow the fish to settle down for a couple of days before you begin to feed them (that is, if you intend to feed them). When you do, start with very small amounts of floating food, and if they are not interested, net it off. Only feed what they will consume in five or ten minutes; if food is allowed to sink to the bottom, it will rot and begin to cause all sorts of problems. The results of overfeeding are the most common causes of death and disease in fish in newly established ponds.

BRITISH NATIVES

As far as native species are concerned, you should never take fish from the wild for an ornamental or garden pond. Similarly, if wild or native species have to be 'rescued' because of building works or housing developments, they should never be introduced into the same environment as ornamental

species: even quite small fish such as sticklebacks and perch can be incredibly aggressive with other species and each other, particularly in a small pond. Also, fish from the wild can carry many sorts of pathogens (killer bugs and parasites) to which they are resistant, but which can become a plague to the ornamental residents of a pond. In certain circumstances the reverse of this can be true, so that either way, mixing them is not a good idea.

Nevertheless, perhaps you have set up a natural or conservation-style pond, and native species are what you feel may be most suitable. If this is the case, you can still get your fish from a reputable dealer. Most species are difficult to see once they are in the water, so get them in groups for their own company, and get species that shoal so that they will be easier to spot. Some species, such as the rudd, will breed so prolifically in ideal conditions that you won't fail to miss them.

Roach, rudd and tench mix well with each other, and will also work well with ornamentals. More ornamental breeds of these species are sometimes available.

Some people consider that buying fish for a pond is just one way of feeding the local heron population; or they would like their pond as a haven for other wildlife and plants, and are not interested in fish. Rest assured that fish are not essential to the well-being of the pond ecology – if anything, they tend to upset the balance, and a fish-free pond is quite a practical ideal.

A GUIDE TO UNSUITABLE POND FISH

Some fish are offered for sale for ponds that are not necessarily suitable, for one reason or another. You should really think twice about considering any of the fish in the following directory, for the reasons given.

Barbel: May be predatory; they also need plenty of oxygen.
Bitterling: Although a member of the carp family, they are only suitable for deep ponds with a low pH of 7 to 7.5. They need the freshwater mussel to breed, as they lay their eggs in the gill cavity of the

mollusc; in turn the mollusc lays its egg in the gill of the fish. This hatches into a weird, shell-less alien creature that is parasitic on the fish until it has grown enough to be self-sufficient as a shellfish.

Bream: These are bottom feeders, and constantly stir up detritus, making the water cloudy.

Carp: Make the water cloudy in small ponds. Keep them separate from bream.

Catfish: Hard as nails. Tolerates pollution, and shrugs off parasites. It grows to an enormous size, and will eat anything, including all other fish. It is the sort of fish that ends up very lonely.

Chub: Very predatory.

Grass carp: Eats everything you don't want them to. They especially do not eat algae or blanket weed, and have a nasty habit of jumping out.

Gudgeon, or stone loach: Need a fine gravel substrata and plenty of oxygen. They bully small fish, especially minnows.

Minnows: Get eaten by virtually everything else that eats live food. They need to shoal for their own protection. They also need plenty of oxygen.

Perch: Carnivorous, aggressive, and very upsetting for other residents. They will soon decimate those minnows.

Pike: May be a way of getting rid of that perch you accidentally introduced.

Sterlet, sometimes referred to as **sturgeon**: Need a clean substrate to sift through on the bottom of the pool. They like a lot of room, also depth and cool water. High-protein sinking food or live food is essential for them.

Sticklebacks: Will harass and damage much larger fish than themselves; they are aggressive to anything red. Prone to whitespot disease. They prefer live food. They are dangerous to other fish if eaten, and the males are dangerous to each other if there are more than two in a pond.

Tench, the doctor fish: They are said to have healing powers for other fish, possibly because they are so slimy; other fish have been seen sidling alongside them, possibly to pick up on this slime, which is really just a thick mucous layer with some to spare. This mucous layer is the only barrier to disease that a fish has, and is easily depleted in stressful conditions.

If the Tench is the green one, take a good look at it before you put it in your pool, because it will be the last time you see it until it's time to clear the pond out. You will know it is there because it lives on the bottom and the mud will always be stirred up as it goes around consuming all the useful caddisfly and bottom-dwelling grubs. It therefore needs to be in a very large pool or a small lake.

Trout: Need masses of oxygen and a gravel bottom. They are visual feeders, so the water needs to be perfectly clear. They need 2m (10ft) depth of water, and should never be mixed with carp.

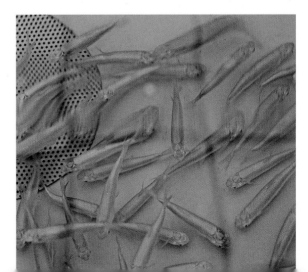

LEFT: *The sterlet eventually gets quite large, so it is therefore unfair to keep it in a small pool.*

BELOW: *Take a good look at the green tench before you put it in the pool, because it will be the last time you see it until you clean the pool out.*

CHAPTER 8

Pond Health

Once your pool is completed it is up to you to maintain it in good heart, and modern technology can help you in this. It may be that sometimes you have had to bend the rules, and as a result your pool water remains green. Perhaps you had to build it too close to some trees and it catches a lot of leaves in autumn; it may be affected by pollutants or sediments from soil run-off; perhaps the plants are being slow to establish themselves – and even if they are established to their full two-thirds complement of pool cover, maybe you just don't want to see so much 'water weed', and would rather see more of your fish. And even if everything seems just right, you might feel happier if you knew there was some way of ensuring the quality of the environment for your cherished fish.

So what does technology provide to help in these situations? And how will you know what is the best way of dealing with a particular problem? The solutions are easy, but the problems are resolved at no little expense.

OBSERVE THE RULES

If your pond has water quality problems, or you think there is the potential for these, get yourself a water-testing kit. This will tell you first and foremost the pH of your water; then next in order of importance, the ammonia content, the nitrite content and the nitrate content; and you can also test for oxygen, although your familiarity with the pond and the pH reading can give you an estimate of this. Get used to using the kit, and try to be familiar with how the readings should be when things seem to be going well.

OPPOSITE: *This concrete koi pool has a small biological filter at the top of the stream.*

So now you are prepared to diagnose any potential problem – although to avoid any in the future, and so you can help solve or abate them, you must be sure to observe the following rules:

1. **Do not overfeed the fish**: only give them as much as they can consume in five minutes, and net off the rest.
2. **The water must be well oxygenated**: nothing is going to help the fish or any of the pond inhabitants unless there is an adequate supply of oxygen. From cloudy polluted water, green water, algae problems, fish gulping at the surface, fish diseases, silting up with organic matter: these are all problems that can be cured with products available from your aquatic store. But none of them will work, be they chemicals, UV sterilizers or filtration units, unless there is enough oxygen in the water to be used in the chemical processes that break down complex chemicals and organic matter to its basic elementary ingredients.

In fact a lot of the problems that inflict pools and ponds can be held at bay with just a good supply of oxygen. This oxygen can come from oxygenating plants under the water, or from the air wafting over the pool surface. But as aquatic retailers will tell you, pump buying starts in earnest with the first hot, still, humid weather, because it is in these conditions that the colonies of oxygenating plants cannot keep up with the supply of oxygen required for all the pond residents. Indeed they use up the depleted stocks come nightfall for their own respiration needs. So here is your first good reason for turning on the fountain or waterfall – and if you haven't got one, then get one. Spreading water out and moving it through the air, creating as much surface as possible to come in contact with air, gives it the opportunity to absorb as much oxygen as possible.

3. This oxygen is required twenty-four hours a day, so **keep your waterfall or fountain running at night**. Apart from the fish needing it to breathe, the aerobic bacteria in the bottom of the pond need it to break down the organic matter that is detritus or fish muck – and they can only exist for two hours or so without oxygen before they die. In order that it gets down there, the whole mass of water needs to be circulating in a gentle cycle: so keep the fountain pump as low as possible in the pond without actually being on the very bottom, and move the waterfall pump well away from the waterfall inlet.

4. **Don't keep adding dead, chlorinated, heavily limed tap water** to the chemical equation, unless there is an emergency; it only provides another problem to work against. However, if an emergency supply of oxygen is required at a moment's notice, or a partial water change is needed without delay, then a hose running into a pond from a height is the only remedy: the splashing of the water beats oxygen into the pool water and dissipates the chlorine content of the tap water by as much as a half.

THE BIOLOGICAL FILTER

If the prospect of emergencies seems daunting and you want to have more positive control, then you can have it at your fingertips with a biological filter. It has a biological effect of making the pool larger, because it allows you to have the maximum amount of fish in a pool with fewer plants, and still be able to see them; not that I would recommend that. The same oxygen-dependent bacteria live in these filters as live in the bottom of a pond. They are fed a constant stream of oxygenated water along with the detritus and chemicals they are meant to digest and break down.

If you saw your problem as green water, in fact it is not: rather, it is a symptom of something wrong. One might easily assume that because the problem seems to be the microscopic free-floating plants that in their millions create the 'pea soup' effect, the best way to get rid of it would be to filter them all out. This is easily done by mechanical filtration; but unless whatever it is that is causing the algae to proliferate is stopped, then they will just keep coming,

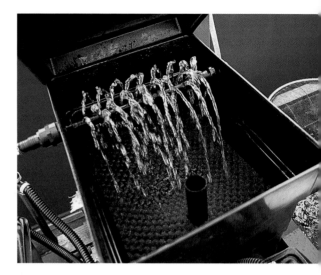

A smaller biological filtration unit in action.

and the filter eventually clogs up and needs to be cleaned out. Those of you who have installed new filters in ponds know that this has to be done on a virtually daily basis in summer.

Bear in mind that even though we can mechanically remove the algae to make the water clear, clear water is not necessarily safe water. If, for instance, you did nothing at all, and the algae were allowed to bloom and bloom in a pool with no other plant life to fill the niches in the ecosystem, the algae would eventually all die once resources were depleted, and sink to the bottom, and the water would be clear for a while. Meanwhile the algae would rot and become the nutrition for the next colony to bloom, and so life would go on. During the rotting phase, the danger of the environment becoming stagnant, devoid of oxygen and unable to sustain life, ever increases, and eventually there could be a build-up in ammonia or nitrites that at certain concentrations would kill fish – but the water at times would still be perfectly clear. If, however, there was oxygen in the water, and then *Nitrobacter* and *Nitrosomonas*, the oxygen-dependent bacteria, were introduced, things would change very rapidly.

The solution is biological filtration: with a biological filter you are not only trapping the algae, the bacteria are digesting them as they decompose whilst treating the chemistry of the water. This is the same breed of aerobic bacteria that would normally be in the bottom of a pond – and what is more, this can happen away from the pool environment. Combine this with the innovation of an ultra-violet clarifier (UVC), and you have a fairly effective solution to your pondwater problems. *But* if you turn it off for more than two hours those friendly bacteria will be starved of oxygen, and the reverse could be true: it could start producing toxins or nutrition for algae straight back into the pond.

Although the aerobic bacteria are capable of turning ammonia into nitrites and nitrites into nitrates, the filtration process may not be considered complete to the extent that nitrates are broken down. This only happens when colonies of *anaerobic* bacteria build up in the slower-moving parts of the filter, and it is these that break nitrates down into the elements of oxygen and nitrogen. Some manufacturers claim they have incorporated de-nitrifying zones in their filters, where the water is processed in a slower, separate filtration area. Other fish-keeping enthusiasts use an amazing volcanic stone called zeolite, which even in very small quantities removes impurities from water; this is also one of the constituent ingredients in water purifiers used by the extremely committed koi keepers. But rest assured, if you plan to take the technological route, there is somewhere, at some level of expenditure, a solution for your problem. Otherwise you can keep to the biological route by depending on the larger plant life of the pond to take up the nitrates as fertilizer before the algae can absorb them.

VEGETABLE FILTERS: POOL REEDBED SYSTEMS

One idea is to establish reedbed systems to do this very thing, where your pondwater filters down through a series of troughs full of gravel planted up with fast-growing plants such as reeds or watercress, which have the ability to break up sewage and pollutants. This is highly effective, and the principle is even used by water authorities in areas of extremely high organic and chemical pollution.

What happens is the microflora around the roots of plants are there to break up organic compounds into the basic chemical constituents that the plant

OUR DEPENDENCE ON PLANTS

The more you learn about pools, ponds and how all aquatic life functions together in its own little world, the more you realize that, in the wider world, our very existence, and that of all animals and fish alike, is totally dependent on the existence of plants. Not only do plants provide us with the oxygen in the air we breathe, but also their roots are host to the microflora and bacteria that are capable of digesting the organic waste we exude, and even a lot of the polluting chemical effluent from our industries.

This is a process that is being harnessed more and more. For landlocked counties, homesteads and even hotels in the back of beyond, there has long been a demand for a system of sewage treatment that is safe and reliable, and is not supported by a crutch of complicated technology. In these days of an ever-increasing consciousness of the environment, many industries are looking for systems for cleaning up their waste in a way that can benefit the environment, without too much maintenance and expense. Plants can help provide that opportunity. They have been doing it in every pond and waterway in the world since the beginning of time, though obviously not in a controlled way, and it is only in recent times that they have been put to the task using a scientifically devised method that is simple and 'sustainable': the reedbed system.

Reedbed system at the organic gardening research centre, HDRA, Ryton. This system copes with the effluent created by the thousands of visitors that come every year and eat at the restaurant. It helps to be running all the time.

can absorb, as it would a fertilizer. These may be nitrogen, oxygen, carbon and other minerals, essential materials for growth – but they can also be chemicals that are poisonous to us; however, once absorbed by the plant, they are trapped there for future disposal. The method relies on just trickling down or forcing up polluted water past the roots of fast-growing water plants. The best plant at doing this is the most innocuous to look at, but it has ingenuity. It is, in fact, one of the most rampant plants on the planet, being indigenous to virtually every country from here to Australia, whichever way you go. It is *Phragmites australis*, the humble Norfolk reed that has been serving man for centuries for thatching and basket making. This plant can pump oxygen down to its roots to feed the aerobic bacteria there, and the bacteria process the pollutants into a form that the plants can absorb – and there they remain.

As you know, this could be going on in the bottom of your pond as a part of the natural process whereby real live plants mop up the nitrates; but for koi keepers a vegetable filter can be a godsend, as many of them have pools completely devoid of plants, mainly because their koi would shred absolutely anything vegetable in their space. A biological filter system can cope with all the fish muck and excess food, converting it to relatively harmless nitrates, but nitrates are good food for algae if there is nothing else to use it up. With a vegetable filter, nitrates are also removed.

Materials Required

The only requirements necessary for fitting a vegetable filter or reedbed system to a pool are a pump, power supply and hose. If you already have a stream or waterfall, this can be planted up to work partly in your favour – though do not plant it with the 'top performer' Norfolk reed: this has to be solidly contained in a robust container. A large system could be created out of concrete blocks, and a smaller system could also be devised from a series of filter boxes or header tanks. There are two models on the market, and I put the Oase Filtofall to the test, fitting it to the top of the stream on the duck pond. The recommended maximum pond size with fish is 2 cu m, and the pump needs to supply 5,000ltr (1,000gal)/hour to the required head; this one coped very well.

DIFFERENT TYPES OF BIOLOGICAL FILTER

Amongst the varieties of biological filter there are 'in-pool' filters and poolside filters, although the biological principles are basically the same. Where you have a filter medium, by its physical make-up it is capable of sieving out the organic matter being sucked through it (in-pool filters), drained down through it, or pushed up through it (poolside filters). The structure of the media needs to be open to allow the free flow of oxygenated water through every part of it, and so it can be colonized by the

The Oase-Filtofall mini reedbed system, planted up and running into the top of the header pool on my stream.

bacteria that help to break down the organic matter passing into the filter with the oxygenated water. In-pool filters tend to be more suitable for smaller pools, although giant 'spider' set-ups, with the filtration occurring across the whole of the bottom of the pond through a thick layer of gravel, have been popular with some enthusiasts. This is the principle that many aquarium systems run on, but just on a larger scale. A central pump that is providing water for a fountain, or even a waterfall, sucks up its water supply into several perforated tubes that spread out in all directions across the bottom of the pond. Water that enters these tubes has to come down through a thick bed of gravel, and within this layer, aerobic bacteria will build up their numbers over time: this is because algae and detritus are trapped in the gravel as they are sucked in with the water, where the bacteria digest them.

Poolside filters need to be fed water by a submersible pump that sits slightly raised from the bottom of the pool on the other side of the pool from the filter. The pump needs to be capable of handling a some solid matter. However, if it has its own foam or gauze pre-filter, it rather defeats the object of the filtration unit. Therefore ask for a pump that has been especially designed for use with a biological filter system. It needs to have a specific output for your system and pool, so go prepared with all the necessary information (*see* Parameters, page 209).

Some filters cleverly use a 'vortex' system, where the water spirals into a chamber and the centrifugal force pushes out any heavy matter into a sump. This helps with aeration as well.

Another way is to spray the water into a chamber of brushes that catch the worst of the sediment. Alternatively the newly arrived water is trickled onto a thin, open-textured sponge surface; this should be cleaned regularly, thankfully an easy task. After that the water rises up through the medium and is then piped back into the pond from the top of the tank; or it drains down through the medium and then flows back into the pond from the bottom of the tank.

The former system prevents fewer 'runways' setting up in the medium. Also in areas where the water hardly moves at all, there is a danger of stagnation, where the wrong sort of bacteria (anaerobic bacteria) might get established and be working contrary to the benefit of the pool inhabitants. Filters that

Vortex-style filtration unit with a variety of chambers containing different media.

A three-chamber filter with an attached UVC unit. The pool water is pumped in through the clarifier and sprays over the brushes, it passes through the open medium on the left, and then rises up through the finer medium and sponges in the middle. It then overflows into the central pipe to be dispensed back into the pool.

empty back into the pool from the top of the main tank are also easier to hide, since because the water emerges at the top of the tank, the system can be set down into the ground just above water level.

This same method of filtration, where the water rises up through the medium, has the added potential facility for instant 'backwashing': with a drain plug situated at the base, when it is removed the effect of the release of the water is to suck out a lot of the undigested detritus caught up in the medium. Once it has been drained out, a quick flush through with rainwater or pool water (not tap water, because the chlorine in the water destroys the valuable bacteria in the medium) is enough to buy you some time before a major cleanout at the end of the season.

The filters need to be hidden behind a group of shrubs – semi-prostrate junipers seem to be the current favourite – and there has to be a fall from the outlet to the pool surface; but there is no reason why the filter should not be right next to the pool itself. One note of caution: if there is a UV clarifier involved it is best to have it situated near an electricity supply. (And remember that all electrics should have residual current circuit-breaking devices on a fused and earth supply, separate from the mains electricity supply. Also, all connections should be weatherproof or waterproof, and must be installed according to the

A biological filter that depends upon the pressure of water from the submersible pump for its efficiency. The cutaway in the side reveals the sponges through which the water is forced after first passing by a central column of UV light. By turning the knob on top you send the water backward through the filter through a waste pipe, thus back-flushing the build-up of muck. To make this even more effective, if you pull the handle on the top, the sponges are compressed, squeezing out the vestiges of the filth.

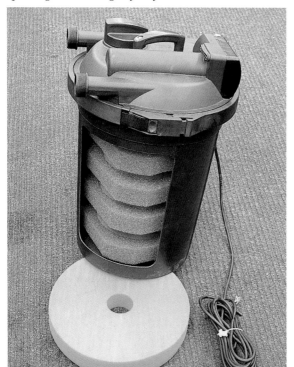

manufacturer's instructions.)

Some people like to have the filter feeding a waterfall or cascade, but it means you can never turn the waterfall off if there are any problems with noise, or if repairs are required to the waterfall.

As the water garden industry evolves, manufacturers now design products for particular purposes in a water garden, rather than 'making do' with items adapted from other markets. Therefore nowadays we find pumps on offer with long guarantees that perform efficiently twenty-four hours a day for years; that are able to cope with water containing solids of organic matter; and that can pump to filters that work under pressure. With the force of water from the pump, smaller filters can process dirtier water through finer mediums at a faster rate. It might have been thought that the filters would merely clog up sooner because they are so efficient, but under this pressure the biological activity is increased, too. Add to this the fact that they are built for instant maintenance, with a backwash facility that is as simple as turning a lever that reverses the flow of water in the filter, and the chore of the six-monthly filter clean-out is merely a matter of rinsing out a sponge in rainwater and changing the lamp every year.

THE FILTER MEDIUM

As far as the filter medium is concerned, I favour a combination of foam and the rocky ceramic material that looks like tufa with the trade name of Alfagrog, or if that is not available or seems too expensive, try Hortag (which is expanded clay granules as used in hydroponics).

Some filters depend upon an open foam filter and a very open medium that seems little more than sections of corrugated plastic pipe or miniature plastic shuttlecocks. The filter foam, although it seems a simple, cheap product, is in fact quite difficult to produce, since the hole in it runs right through from one side to the other, allowing the water and muck through, but slowing it down enough to let the bacteria do their work.

Allow at least one month for the filter system to mature and to start operating on a biological level.

The water first passes by the brushes in the chamber at the back; these strain out the large bits of muck, and then the water passes up through the Hortag filter medium, through the porous sponge, and out through the outlet into the head of the stream.

Closer inspection reveals that the filter medium is seething with life. A food chain has been established! A very biological filter indeed.

PARAMETERS FOR EFFECTIVE FILTRATION

There are certain specific parameters that must be observed in order to achieve effective filtration.

1. The filter must be designed to process the total volume of the pool every two hours for twenty-four hours of the day.
2. The pump to the filter must be capable of delivering the above; for instance, a 5,000ltr (1,100gal) pond must have a filter capable of taking 2,500ltr (550gal) of water through it. The pump for it must be capable of delivering 2,500ltr every hour both the required distance and to the head at which it will be situated.
3. The pump should be situated on the opposite side of the pool from the filter box for the maximum circulation of the water.
4. There used to be a requirement that the filter-bed surface area was one third of the surface area of the pool. With modern filtration mediums this doesn't seem to be such a necessity now, although for those of you embarking on ambitious koi pool projects using gravity-fed filtration systems, you would be best advised to bear this in mind.
5. Don't use any algicides or fungicides (including salt) when they are in operation. Try to avoid cleaning them out with fresh tap water.
6. Don't overfeed the fish. Only give them what they will eat in five minutes, and net off the excess.

Don't overfeed the fish.

It will operate mechanically right from the start, and you will feel as though you are endlessly flushing it out. However, do not clean it out too well, refrain from using tap water, and keep the system running non-stop, and eventually a colony of the right sort of bacteria will become established.

The process can be speeded up if you can borrow a 'starter' of, say, 1kg (2lb) of medium from another healthy functioning filter. Alternatively there are proprietary chemicals available from retailers that encourage the right bacteria in filters; 'Pond Start' is one that comes to mind. Or you can spit in it! Apparently some of the same bacteria that live in the bottom of a pond also live in your mouth – can you live with that? They are beneficial bacteria, after all.

CHEMICALS

Never use any chemicals in the pond either for treating algae or fish diseases whilst the filter is in operation, *except for* pool-conditioning chemicals, which are *essential* if you have to top up the pool with tap water. Any sick fish in the early days of the pond should be treated in a separate tank.

Algae will come under control eventually, but blanket weed or the filamentous algae are by nature tenacious. These often prefer hard-water conditions (water with a high pH), therefore an option for relatively small pools in the early days after construction is to reduce this with proprietary chemicals. Bags of peat pellets floated in the water are a favoured option in Europe, but in the UK the extraction of peat depletes an already severely decimated wetland habitat, so for our purpose, peat is no longer considered an environmentally sound option.

There are 'biological' or 'safe' algicides that gently push the balance in your favour. Some cause free-floating algae to stick together, when they will drop to the bottom of the pond to be sucked up by the filter. At the same time the individual cells of filamentous algae separate, and they, too, get sucked into the filter system. I would nevertheless be wary of using these in the early days of your filter's life.

Chemicals based on the active ingredients of barley straw, and barley straw itself, are also effective – but these are an additive that is just another chemical ingredient to the chemical stew already

Aquatic centres have walls covered in varieties of chemical treatment.

there, which persuades many serious fish keepers, particularly koi keepers, to look for other methods of keeping their water clear. For barley straw to work, the water has to be well oxygenated and the straw removed at the end of the season. And new EU regulations have meant that the barley straw derivatives may be withdrawn.

The favoured approach now is to effectively starve out the algae. This is really what the higher plants could do for you, but there are clever compounds and additives that absorb nitrates and phosphates, the main source of nutrition for algae, and the latter particularly for blanket weed. These are effective but not cheap and usually only work at a low pH.

OTHER GIZMOS

Ultra-violet clarifiers, magnets and bubblers are all subsidiaries to a good filtration set-up. They all help it run more efficiently to varying degrees, and with relevance to certain conditions.

Ultra-Violet Clarifiers (UVCs)

These are the most effective accessories to a biological filter, and are now incorporated as part of the many proprietary systems. They used to be called sterilizers before they were properly adapted for treating pond water, because in the medical world and the water industry they were used for sterilizing water. It had been found that passing water around a lamp that gave off ultra-violet light would destroy virtually every living thing in that water. However, when it was decided to use them to treat pond water, it was quickly realized that this was not beneficial to the pool environment, especially the fish. Algae and microbes are essential to the welfare of the pool inhabitants, and many fish gain huge benefits in coloration, scale condition and disease resistance from the vitamins and nutritional elements in algae. So now, just a mild dose of ultra-violet light is given, which has the effect not of killing the algae outright, but of causing a large proportion of them to clump together and to sink to the bottom of the pool, or be taken up into the filter.

Ultra-violet clarifiers sit on the pipeline before the inlet to the filter. The water from the pond passes into the chamber of the ultra-violet clarifier, within which a lamp beams out rays of ultra-violet light, before passing on to the filter. There are several different sizes of lamp: 4-watt, 7-watt, 8-watt, 11-watt, 15-watt, and 30-watt.

An 8-watt lamp will be suitable for ponds for up to 2,300ltr (500gal), and will need a pump and filter to suit; 11 watts treats about 3,000ltr (650gal), and is a relatively new size in a new design of longer-life bulbs; 15 watts will treat 4,550ltr (1,000gal) with a suitable filter, and 2,300ltr (500gal) per hour pump. Manufacturers' claims for the performance of these items vary in the extreme.

Ultra-violet bulbs need to be changed every six months to maintain efficiency if they are of the straight tube, neon light style of design. As these units get older they can become extremely fragile, and it is during these routine maintenance episodes that the costs of having clear pool water soar as you break yet another bulb, or the quartz sleeve (the tube that houses the lamp). However, newer designs from moulded materials have been specifically developed for efficiency and the purpose to which they are put, and are also designed for ease of maintenance. Also the 'life expectancy' of a bulb has been extended to one year.

If you have just introduced a filter system with an UV lamp incorporated, or have just added one to your already existing system, consider running the UV only part of the time, especially at first, and then perhaps more in sunny weather.

Magnets

The manufacturers claim that suspended particles are polarized as they pass through a magnet before the UVC on the way to the filter. The result is a reduction of lime scale on the quartz sleeve in the clarifier, thus maintaining efficiency. It is also claimed that they break up blanket weed over time. Electronic versions employing the same principles claim increased efficiency.

Bubblers or Venturi

These accessories are really for the fish-keeping enthusiast. They need a pump to supply water that is forced into a narrow jet, passing at speed into a larger tube; the effect is that air is dragged into the tube through a vent that mixes with the water and bubbles into the pool just below the water surface. The same effect can be achieved with some fountain jets – the gushing style. But the advantage of venturi is that you can use a relatively small size of pump and not only get your water oxygenated, but the action of the water coming sideways into the pool encourages a very effective circulation.

THE NATURAL WAY

Those of you contemplating conservation-style ponds, natural ponds or ponds with just no fish, must be wondering what all the fuss is about. Indeed, there is a lot to be said for letting nature take its course and just keeping a warden's eye on things. It's simple, cheaper and interesting to watch a sort of evolutionary trail of events. Eventually though, even as wardens, we have to intervene because the natural development of a pond is eventually to silt right up and become just a boggy place. But that is another story.

Appendices and Formulae

Calculating your liner size:

Liner length m/ft = Maximum pool length m/ft + (2 × maximum pool depth m/ft) + 0.3m (1ft) overlap
Liner width m/ft = Maximum pool width m/ft + (2 × maximum pool depth m/ft) + 0.3m (1ft) overlap
Before buying a submersible pump for your pool for a fountain, waterfall, filter or a combination of any of these, you must know the volume of your pool.

Volume of your pool in litres:

Average length in metres × average width in metres × average depth in metres × 1,000
A metric cubic metre of water weighs 1 tonne.
To convert to US gallons, multiply by 0.26.
To convert to Imperial gallons, multiply by 0.22.

Volume of your pond in gallons:

Average length in feet × average width in feet × average depth in feet × 6.25

Volume of a circular pool:

(½ the diameter in feet × ½ the diameter in feet × depth in feet × π) = Volume of a circular pool in cu ft
Volume of a circular pool in cu ft × 6.25 = Gallonage of a circular pool

Estimating stream liner length:

Length on the horizontal × (2 × head). The width is governed by the standard widths of liner. A 5ft-wide liner, for instance, would produce a stream with 2ft 6in header pools, with 9–12in outlets. A 10ft-wide liner gives you 4–6ft headers, with possible 2ft-wide waterfalls.

OPPOSITE: *Andy Sturgeon's 'Circ Contemporary Man's Garden' at the Chelsea Flower Show in 2001 used a clean-moulded concrete edging to create this modern look.*

Estimating the size of pump required for streams or waterfalls:

Estimate roughly for 60gal (300ltr) per hour per inch of sill or waterfall width (just over 100ltr per hour per cm) that can be delivered to the height you require.

Estimating the number of skips required for the removal of spoil from the pool:

((Volume of the pool in feet) × 2) ÷ 27 = Volume of spoil to be disposed of
Volume of spoil ÷ 6 = Number of large skips to be filled

Estimating the number of blocks for pools with liners in the ground:

(2 × length in feet) + (2 × width in feet) ÷ ⅔
or take the measurement from your draped tape measurement around the circumference in feet, and multiply by ⅔ for the approximate number of blocks required for the pool.

If you are building-in support for the marginal shelf, measure this in feet and add two thirds of the number to the total.

Estimating the number of blocks for raised pools:

(Height above footing in inches ÷ 9) × number of blocks for perimeter (*see* above) for number of blocks required for the perimeter. Allow extra blocks for the creation of the marginal shelf areas and pools set in unstable ground.

Estimating the number of blocks for waterfalls and streams (approximate rule of thumb):

'Head' of the stream, i.e. its starting height above the pool surface level (in feet) added on to its length and then doubled.

SUMMARY OF THE IDEAL SITE

- It will be in full sun. Nearly all plants associated with water need some direct sunlight to flower, especially lilies.
- Away from trees, but not too exposed to cold or prevailing winds.
- Can be seen from the house.
- Where electricity and water supplies are accessible.
- Not on low-lying, boggy land.

Size and shape:
Keep it simple, and more than 3.3sq m (30sq ft), and 50cm (20in) deep, with a shelf for plant support 23cm (9in) down below the proposed water level.

Further points to remember using flexible liner materials:
Economically it is best to design the pool in one dimension to fit in with the standard widths of liner sizes.
Avoid dramatic indentations in pool shapes and streams; measure around the longest contour to take in the extra liner that is required to accommodate this shape.

Estimating quantities of sand for lining pools and streams:
A metric tonne (1,000kg/2,200lb) will cover (very) approximately 10sq m (108sq ft) at 5cm (2in) in depth.

Underlay (cheap material for laying under the liner):
Take pool liner sizes, and add on 10 per cent.

Estimating rockery stone:
Height × width in feet = 1 cwt or 50kg.
This is the same for estimating the rockery surround or rock edging and the stream face.

Estimating footing materials for blockwork and walling:
Gravel chips of varying sizes down to dust: cement for concrete in a 6:1 ratio,
or 15 to 25mm gravel chippings, sand, cement in 4:2:1 ratio.

The foundation depth should be between a quarter and a third of the wall height, and twice the wall width. Estimate 2 tonnes to the cubic metre.

Sand for building:
Allow 100kg (220lb) for each 4sq m (40sq ft) faced walling and one 25kg (55lb) of cement, but more if there is a lot of backfilling.

Estimating paving:
Most paving is priced by the square yard or metre, apart from crazy paving.
Estimate that 1 ton will cover 11sq yd (9sq m).

Estimating plants:
1 bunch of oxygenators for every 0.2sq m (2sq ft) of surface area.
1 lily or deep water aquatic for every 2.3sq m (25sq ft) of pool surface area.
1 floating plant for every 0.9sq m (10sq ft).
1 marginal for every 0.5sq m (5sq ft).

Estimating pump capacity:
For those of you with ambitious designs for waterfalls with regard to height and volume, you will find that pumps of a certain size need special 'starter switches' that accumulate enough current in capacitors to thump the pump into action, for instance a 'starter' for a 1.5hp pump needs to be 300amps. Certain pumps that can really pump large volumes to great height will be drawing so much current that you will need 'three-phase electricity', the sort of power normally demanded by a small industrial unit. Here are some formulae that might help you with your calculations. They come from the old-fashioned world of Imperial measurements, but that doesn't detract from their usefulness.

$$\frac{\text{Gallons per hour} \times \text{head in feet}}{33,000} = \text{horse power (hp)}$$

You can multiply hp by 7 to get a rough idea of the amps you will require.

760 Watts produces 1 hp
Watts = Volts × Amps

Glossary

Algae Although considered by the pond keeper in the singular, there are over 4,000 common species to be found in and around the UK. Many of them are free-floating and single-celled basic forms of plant life, as essential in the fabric of life within the water garden as any other living thing. However, when an excess of nutrients and an imbalance of plant and animal life causes a population explosion, the observable result for the pond keeper is that he has **green water**. Other forms grow in long strands of cells linked together, giving rise to another collection of algae referred to as **blanket weed**.

Aquatic plants Plants that will thrive when growing in or under water.

Bog plants Definitively these are acid-loving plants (plants that can only tolerate a low pH in the soil) that will thrive in wet spongy ground rich in organic matter. For the purposes of this book they can be lime-tolerant plants, preferring moist, humus-rich conditions in which there is a certain amount of drainage – the moisture is retrained but not restrained.

Bottom-draining filtration A system of filtration that is much vaunted by specialist koi carp keepers. It involves a large biological filtration system at water level, generally consisting of at least three chambers containing filtration media of progressively increasing density. This is **gravity fed** from a free-flowing drain in the bottom of the pool by a large pipe that rises up in the filter just a little below the mean water level. After passing through large filter brushes, the water moves from chamber to chamber as it attempts to maintain the same water level in the filter as in the pool. The process is continuous because a pump at the far end is pumping the filtered water back into the pool. The advantages are that water and detritus are taken from the very bottom of the pool without having to go through the grill of a pump, and the pump can operate at a maximum potential with very little wear because it is pumping clean water. The disadvantage is that it is not a 'nature-friendly' system. Plants are to be discouraged. It needs to be planned in detail in advance. It needs to be approximately 2m (7ft) deep, and it is very expensive even if you do it yourself.

Chippings to dust An expression for a form of limestone aggregate from the South West of England that comes with a maximum size chipping of stone mixed with all the smaller sizes right down to the dust of the stone. The ready-made mixture makes rock-hard concrete with the addition of cement powder, without the need for any extra sand.

Deep-water plants Plants that grow from the bottom of a pool or pond, sending their leaves to the surface for gaseous exchange and light. Water lilies are the most important and typical example.

Floating plants Plants that float on the surface of a pool or pond with their roots dangling freely underneath.

Footings Another term for foundations, but in particular reference to walls and blockwork. They can consist of a trench filled with compressed mixed stone chippings and sand, but usually they are trenches filled with a 'lean mix' (6 aggregate to 1 cement) of concrete at a depth of roughly one third to a quarter the height of the wall, and two or three times the wall width.

Gate valves or flow valves Two different methods of adjusting the flow of water in a pipe. One is based on the old plumbing fitting that has a tap that you screw down to close off the **flow** of water. The other, by a quick twist, blocks the pipe quickly and efficiently. Both types come with 'male' or 'female' threads.

Geomembrane Any material used to retain soil or stone. Sometimes it is used to retain banks whilst plants get their roots established, or it is often used under paths or mulches to suppress weeds and prevent the aggregate or mulch from mixing with the underlying soil or mud. Some are biodegradable materials such as jute or hessian, and others are ceramic, plastic or nylon based. There is a soft, felt-like material that is used under pool liners to protect them against penetration from sharp stones, and in the text I refer to this as **underlay**.

Head (in reference to pumps and their **flow rate**) This is the height above the surface level of the pool that a water pump will deliver water to. Since it can be seen in respect to a column of water, it can be expressed in terms of pressure, e.g. 1 bar = 10m column. The **flow rate** is usually in gallons per hour (gph), litres per hour (lph) or litres per minute (lpm).

Header pool The small pool at the top of a waterfall or beginning of a stream, into which the water from the submersible pump in the pool emerges before it begins to flow back to the main pool. This small reservoir evens out the inconsistencies of supply from the pump, and enables the pool constructor to engineer the width and dynamics of the flow.

Hosetail An aquatic store expression for the plastic hose connectors that screw into pumps, UVCs and filters, and also into '**hex sockets**' or '**hex nipples**' for joining or reducing hose diameter. The screw ends can come in 'male' or 'female' forms. On the 'male', the screw thread sticks out in order to screw into a 'female'.

Marginal plants Plants that not only enjoy the water's edge, but actually grow in the shallow water. For the purposes of this book and the techniques employed within these pages, they are all quite happy

with the water just over the level of the soil. There are some often referred to as deep-water marginals that are tolerant of greater depths, such as *Typha* spp., *Calla* spp. and *Menyanthes trifoliata*, but they can find this depth for themselves from the shallows.

Oxygenating plants Plants that grow underwater, and have underwater foliage that exchanges gases and absorbs nutrients directly from the water. They release oxygen into the water during the daylight hours

RCD, RCCB, RCB or ELCB Devices for breaking the circuit to an electrically powered device, as soon as there is a difference in the current flowing in the neutral and live wires supplying the power, on the basis that it may be leaking to earth, through a human body or some other object. This difference should be set at 30ma (milli-amps) or less at the time of writing. The specifications for the way they operate, and the specifications on their sensitivity, are constantly being reviewed, so if you have an old 'trip' switch for your outdoor power supply, get it checked out by an electrician before you run a submersible pump off it. One of these devices should be fitted to your exterior power supply, to isolate it from your interior power supply.

'T' Piece A hose fitting that allows you to join two bits of pipe to one. These come in threaded forms – 'Threaded T', both 'male' and 'female' for attachment to other fittings (useful if there are different size hose pipes to step up or down to) or in a hosetail form (*see* above) for direct attachment to your hoses.

Ultra-violet clarifiers (UVCs) An ultra-violet lamp, waterproof and contained within a waterproof container, through which pool water travels. When the lamp is switch on, the resultant 'dose' of UV light from the lamp causes free-floating algae in the water – which are responsible for its greenish hue – to clump together and be taken out by the biological filter, or to sink to the bottom of the pool and become digested by bacteria.

Waterfall Stones
Base stone: The support for the 'facing stone' in a waterfall and also the stone onto which the water

falls. It helps prevent erosion and undermining of the waterfall face.

Facing stone: The stone behind the falling water in front of the stream liner, which can be one stone or a number of stones made up to give the appearance of a rock face. The resulting fascia will be backfilled with cement mortar.

Flanking stones: These sit at the top of, and either side of the waterfall, and retain the water in front of the fall face. They are cemented into place and can be made up of several stones in order to suit the purpose.

Sill stone: In a waterfall, this is the stone over which the water flows before tumbling to the next level. It needs a slight fall in the direction of the water flow, and sometimes it is useful if it is slightly higher at the edges than in the middle. It needs a sharp front or bottom edge in order to 'shed' the water as it flows over. If it is a slab of stone in a formal or modern 'mirror-style' waterfall, a groove should be cut along the underneath to prevent water travelling back to the wall face.

A wild, natural look to Peter Tinsley's rock and water garden at the 1999 Chelsea Flower Show.

Suppliers

Liner materials in large quantities:

Manufacturers and installers of Butyl, EPDM
rubber, PVC and other liners:
Butyl Products Ltd
11 Radford Crescent
Billericay
Essex CM12 0DW
Tel: 01277 653281
web site: www.butylproducts.co.uk.

Gordon Low Products Ltd
Rookery Road
Wyboston
Bedford
Bedfordshire MK44 3UG
Tel: 01480 405433
web site: www.gordonlowproducts.co.uk.

Stephens (Plastics)
Hawthorn Works
Corsham
Wiltshire SN13 9RD
Tel: 01225 810324
web site: www.stephens-plastics.co.uk.

*Manufacturers of prehydrated sodium bentonite
waterproof sheeting:*

Rawell Environmental Ltd
Carr Lane
Hoylake
Wirral
Merseyside CH47 4AZ
Tel: 0151 632 5771
web site: www.rawell.com.

*Manufacturers and suppliers of pumps, filters,
fountains and a complete range of aquatic products for
domestic supply:*

Blagdon, the Pond Masters
Vincent Lane
Dorking
Surrey RH4 3YX
Tel: 01306 881033
web site: www.blagdonthepondmasters.co.uk

Hozelock Ltd
Midpoint Park
Birmingham B76 1AB
Tel: 0121 313 1122
web site: www.hozelock.com.

Oase (UK) Ltd
3, Telford Gate
Andover
Hampshire SP10 3SF
Tel: 01246 333225
web site: www.oase-livingwater.com

OPPOSITE: *The simple solution by Ebb and Flow in 'The
Solar Garden' at the Hampton Court Flower Show 2001.
Note the solar-driven water feature.*

Further Reading

Allison, James *The Encyclopedia of Water in the Garden* (Interpet, 1999).

Chatto, Beth *The Damp Garden* (Weidenfeld & Nicholson, 1986).

May, Peter *The Perfect Pond Recipe Book* (Peter J. May Publications, 2004; also Kingdom Books, 1996).

Perry, Frances *Water Gardening* (the author's copy is the 1947 edition published by Country Life Ltd).

Slocum, Perry D., Robinson, Peter, and Perry, Frances *Water Gardening, Water Lilies and Lotuses* (Timber Press, 1996).

David Robinson at the 2001 Malvern Spring Flower Show took the concept of 'the outdoor room' to comic extremes. Complete with floating flora carpets and furniture, the focal point was naturally the mantelpiece and its 'steaming' water feature. Unfortunately the recent floods around the country subdued many people's appreciation of the joke.

Index